THE
HAPHAZARD ORIGINS
of the
BRITISH PUBLIC
ART GALLERY

Isabel Wilkinson

First Edition, 2021

Acknowledgments

M Y MAJOR DEBT is to the late Giles Waterfield, a former Director of the Dulwich Picture Gallery, a fount of knowledge about British art galleries whose expertise has not been fully recognised (perhaps because he produced wonderfully informative catalogues rather than academic papers). The art historian Francis Haskell's last book *The Ephemeral Museum* provided me with an invaluable insight into the links between the development of art exhibitions and the development of art galleries. *Towards a Modern Art World* (edited by Brian Allen) gave me very useful background information on the social context from which public art galleries emerged. The Open University publication *Academies, Museums and Canons of Art* (edited by Gill Perry) also gave me invaluable historical context. James Hamilton's *A Strange Business: Making Art and Money in Nineteenth-Century Britain* was an enthralling and highly informative look at a somewhat neglected topic.

During my research, I was rather surprised to discover the scholarly American interest in this topic (I probably shouldn't have been). *Transformative Beauty: Art Museums in Industrial Britain* by Amy Woodson-Boulton gives a lively in-depth account of public art gallery development in Liverpool, Manchester and Birmingham, while Carol Duncan's *Civilising Rituals: Inside Public Art Museums* provides an equally lively critique of the cultural assumptions behind art galleries (not all of which I agree with, but that's all to the good).

The academic papers of Jonathan Conlin, Ann Bermingham, Charlotte Kronk, Suzanne MacLeod, Tim Barringer, Bruce Robertson, Rob Breton, James R Moore, Lily Crowther, Lucinda Matthews-Jones and Michael Harrison were also very fruitful in widening my knowledge and outlook, and are acknowledged in the text where appropriate.

I was fortunate that these days it is possible to do a great deal of research online. Naturally, gallery websites were very useful, as were online resources like the 'Oxford Dictionary of National Biography'. Without these sources, this book would have taken much longer to produce than it did.

Isabel Wilkinson 2021

Contents

Acknowledgments i
Introduction 1
1. Encouraging the Polite Arts 5
2. A First in the Suburbs 23
3. Art for All 33
4. Improving Industrial Design 45
5. Portraying the Nation 57
6. Beyond the Metropolis 65
7. Intellectual Underpinnings 73
8. Art and the New Industry 85
9. Art and Civic Pride 101
10. Bringing Art to the Masses 115
11. A Home for British Modernity 125
12. In Memoriam 133
13. First World War to the Aftermath of the Second 145
14. Just One More Thing… 157
15. Reassessment 169
References 174
Bibliography 177
Index 179
About the Author 186

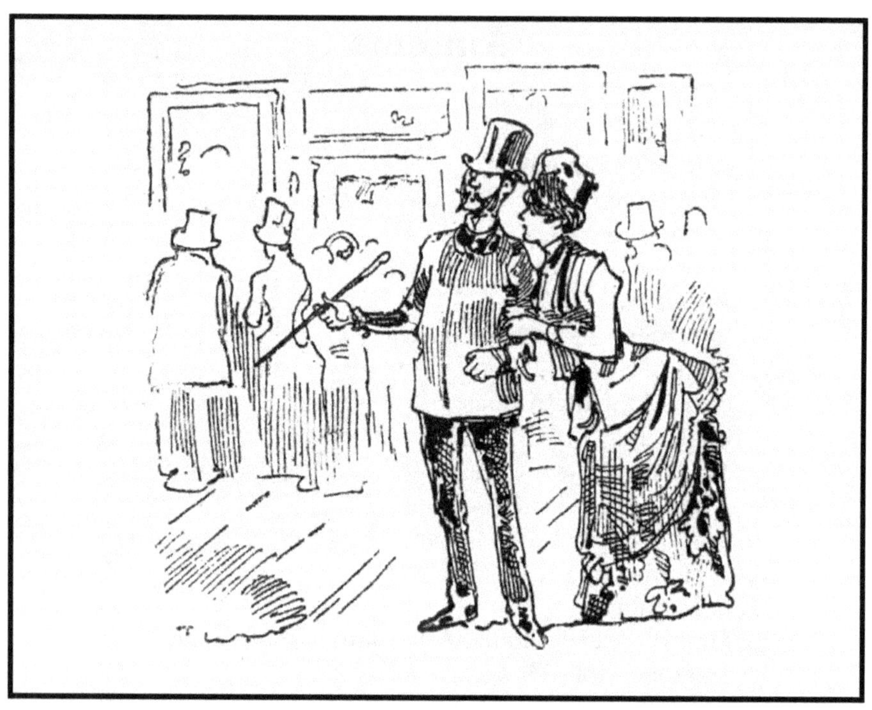

iStock image

Introduction

THIS BOOK IS not about art. There are plenty of books about art, and I own quite a few of them myself. But I am also interested in the phenomenon of art galleries, and in particular how and why public art galleries came into existence in Britain during the nineteenth century (one is much older, as you will see). So this book is about the people who founded those galleries – often after a long and hard campaign – what motivated them, and what happened afterwards.

Britain went from being a laggard in setting up a National Gallery of fine art in its capital city, to having an excellent network of public art galleries covering cities in all its regions, many with collections of national and international significance. This was achieved by a motley selection of mostly men (but the first had significant input from a woman), who were mostly middle class (but one was a cork cutter and two were illegitimate sons of aristocrats). Some were set up with funds extracted (sometimes with great difficulty) from national or local government. A few were founded by universities. But the first impetus was often a donation from a prominent individual, with a variety of motives. Most are publicly owned, but some are private charitable organisations, which may explicitly be intended to commemorate their founders.

The story did not end with a gallery's foundation, of course. Equally important was the cohort of directors and curators, who built collections, oversaw expansions, and generally made sure the gallery was solidly established and attracted visitors. They were a resourceful and hardworking bunch (one of whom is credited with inventing the Christmas card). Also significant were sometimes magnificent bequests to established galleries. These range from prominent businessmen and industrialists to a pair of Welsh sisters and a successful Irish art dealer.

All this was assisted by the activities of dealers and auction houses, which encouraged an interest in art and art collection, and the growth of mass media, especially specialist art magazines, which reviewed exhibitions and informed the public. In the later nineteenth century, the media helped to maintain visitor numbers, and on at least one occasion acted as the forum for a national public debate on proposals for a new national museum.

And it is also necessary to bear in mind the new legal framework which made nineteenth-century regional public art galleries possible, and the rich Victorian intellectual world which informed both those who ran the galleries and their visitors, as well as many donors and collectors.

The growth of public art galleries has had its ups and downs. The major development in the later nineteenth century was interrupted by the First World War and impeded by the Depression. The Second World War not only put a stop to all new development but caused serious damage to some galleries which took some time to repair. Post-war, there was a new spurt of growth and expansion in the second half of the twentieth century, which slowed almost to a halt after the crash of the financial system at the beginning of the twenty-first century.

In recent decades, diversity and inclusion within the public art gallery world has become a prominent topic. In the nineteenth century there were often successful efforts to attract working class visitors. Today the emphasis is of diversity of gender and race, not just of visitors, but of the artists displayed and of gallery staff.

So yes, the story is haphazard, without the central direction of most Continental countries, or the prominent role of privately funded galleries seen in the United States. But this, I think, is a strength, not a weakness. The British way, largely fortuitously, involved a greater number of ordinary citizens and a greater degree of national and local debate. This meant that, with any luck, these galleries could be rooted in their locality and be seen as a valued local asset by a fair proportion of residents.

But I hope you will agree with me that it is also a fascinating story of fascinating people which deserves to be better known.

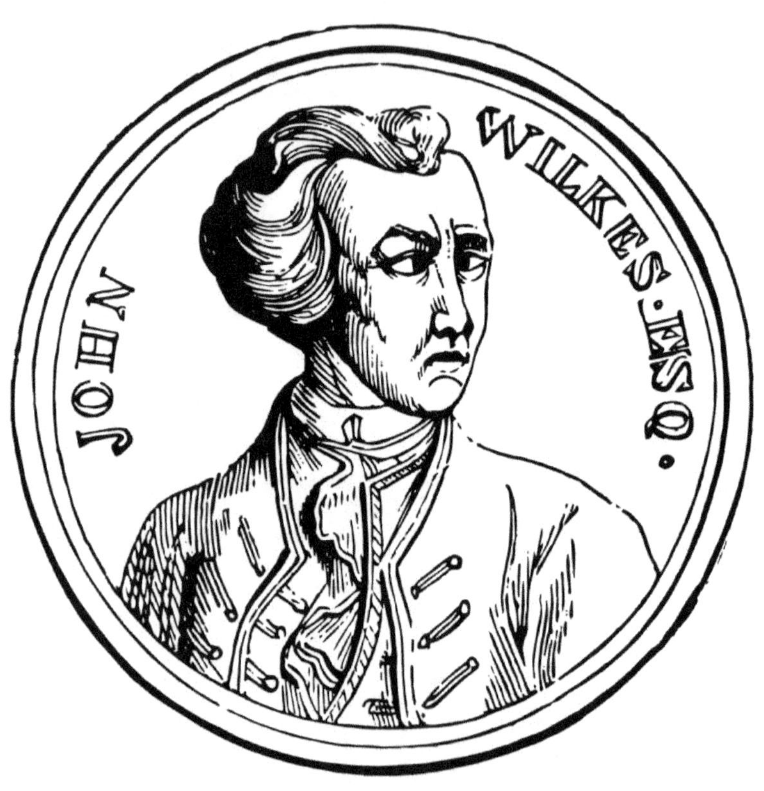

John Wilkes: Agitator, MP, Champion of Liberty
– and of a national art collection

1. Encouraging the Polite Arts

WHEN JOHN WILKES rose to his feet in the House of Commons in April 1777, his listeners may have been surprised at the subject of his speech. Wilkes was known as a political firebrand, a radical demagogue, and a champion of liberty. But on this occasion his concerns were cultural rather than political. He proposed that the House should agree to buy the magnificent art collection of Sir Horace Walpole.[1]

Sir Horace was the grandson of Sir Robert Walpole, the first Prime Minister, who had been a keen and discerning art collector. On his death, Sir Robert's unrivalled collection of Old Masters, portraits and antiquities duly passed to his heirs, but his grandson proved to be such a profligate wastrel that he was forced to sell much of his inheritance. The art collection thus came up for auction.

Wilkes now boldly proposed that the nation should buy these artworks and entrust them to the British Museum, founded only a few decades before. The Museum's holdings (based on the Soane, Cotton and Harley collections and the Royal Libraries) mainly consisted of natural and manmade objects, books and manuscripts. It held very few works of art. Incorporating the paintings to be auctioned – which included works by Rembrandt, Poussin and Claude – would give it a collection which could compare favourably with any publicly accessible art on the Continent. And it would help Britain to become, as Wilkes put it, "a favourite abode of the polite arts".

This was the first time Parliament had been asked to set up an art collection to be owned by the people. As entry to the British Museum was free, it was also the first time it had been asked to arrange public access to major works of art without charge. Wilkes expected (almost certainly forlornly) that private individuals would follow Parliament's lead and choose to donate works of art to the nation.

In his speech Wilkes pointed out that the public at large now had even less access to important artworks than they used to, as the royal collection, once open to public view at Hampton Court, was now hidden away in Buckingham Palace. Truth to tell, even the British Museum was notoriously inaccessible to the public, as tickets had to be purchased weeks in advance and it could only be visited as part of a guided tour.

Unfortunately for British art lovers, on this occasion the response to Wilkes' famous oratory skills was resoundingly negative – the first of very many setbacks on a very rocky road to a national art collection. Now that almost everyone has relatively easy access to a public art gallery, it is difficult to appreciate there was a time when most people never laid eyes on an oil painting in their entire lives. So the lost opportunity was more disastrous than it might appear at first sight.

Wilkes is far better known for his political campaigns than his support for "the polite arts", but it was his radicalism which indirectly led to his interest in art. He had used his newspaper *The North Briton* to attack King George III and his government, which led to a prosecution for seditious libel in 1763. A dramatic legal duel ensued. The Lord Chief Justice ruled that, as Wilkes was a Member of Parliament, he was protected from prosecution. Wilkes was hailed as the champion of liberty. But the following year Parliament retaliated by voting that parliamentary privilege did not extend to the writing and publishing of seditious libels. Having lost the battle and facing prosecution, Wilkes was forced to flee to the Continent.

His exile in the 1760s gave him the opportunity to catch up with the latest cultural ideas in France and Italy. Wilkes had celebrity status on the Continent and his sharp mind more than held its own in Paris society. He became close to Denis Diderot, a leading intellectual and art critic, best known as the editor of the *Encyclopdie* which had been published in sections from the 1750s. This was not the first encyclopedia, but it was the first to include contributions from many writers and to cover practical matters like mechanical and production processes. It was also a vociferous advocate of secularism.

As an art critic, Diderot had written about the potential dangers of a decadent art corrupting public morality. (He was thinking of the erotic nudes of Boucher.) This prompted Wilkes to consider that art could have a positive as well as a negative effect. Perhaps more pertinently, given that Wilkes regarded a belief in liberty as a characteristic English trait, Wilkes also took on board Diderot's opinion that liberty was necessary for artistic creativity to flourish.

Wilkes left Paris to travel on to Rome. He took the opportunity to view several state art collections on the way, noting with dismay the absence of such a collection back home. In Rome, he became friendly with Johann Winckelmann, who had published his *History of Ancient Art* the previous year, in 1764. This ground-breaking work is seen as the beginning of the modern academic discipline of art history. His advocacy of an "ideal" version of art, which creates beauty by combining the most perfect aspects of nature to create an idealised whole, became hugely influential. A major element of Winckelmann's book was that the art of a civilisation is an expression of its political, social and intellectual conditions - not an encouraging thought in an English context. Wilkes must have been equally chagrined to learn that the Prussian state, Winckelmann's homeland, gave extensive support to the arts in a way completely unknown in Britain.

Winckelmann was sufficiently impressed by Wilkes to overcome his usual disdain for English tourists and became his guide to Rome's classical remains. Wilkes thus had the benefit of the expertise of Europe's leading classicist during his exploration of the ruins of ancient Rome. Like every other tourist, he also viewed the Capitoline gallery of classical statuary, part of the Vatican collection open to the Roman public since 1734. Wilkes was witnessing yet another example of great art being made available freely to the local population. Why was England so far behind?

When Wilkes finally returned to England in 1768, he brought home not only the latest thinking on art, but ideas about how the state could encourage the polite arts to the general benefit of the population. He had also developed a strong desire to put these ideas into practice.

Not that he gave up his increasingly eventful political career. He was elected as Member of Parliament for Middlesex, but was arrested and imprisoned. Around 15 000 people promptly gathered outside the prison, chanting "Wilkes and Liberty". Troops opened fire and killed seven people, leading to rioting all over London. Wilkes was found guilty of libel and sentenced to 22 months' imprisonment. For good measure, he was fined £1,000 and expelled from the House of Commons. (This did not prevent him being re-elected three times, each time the result being overturned by Parliament. In response, his supporters formed the Bill of Rights Society, which eventually adopted a radical programme of parliamentary reform.)

Prison did not dampen his political energies. On his release, Wilkes joined a campaign for the freedom of the press. In 1771, the House of Commons had tried to prevent several London newspapers from publishing reports of its debates. Wilkes published a challenge to this decision, and two of his printers were arrested on government orders. A large crowd soon surrounded the House of Commons, persuading the government to order the release of the two men and abandon its attempt to prevent the publication of reports of its deliberations.

This was an important milestone for the freedom of the press and, ultimately, for the expansion of the art world. The new freedom led to a spectacular growth in the number of newspapers and periodicals during the following century. As a result, art criticism and reviews of art exhibitions became widely distributed, which in turn was a significant factor in increasing the popularity of art.

Wilkes' political career peaked in 1774 when he was elected Lord Mayor of London and finally succeeded in representing Middlesex in the House of Commons. He continued his political activism, campaigning unsuccessfully for the repeal of 17th century legislation discriminating against Roman Catholics and Dissenters. (All those who were not members of the established Church of England were barred from public office, becoming army officers or attending Oxford and Cambridge Universities – the only English universities at the time.)

In 1776 he put a motion to the House of Commons to extend the vote to sections of the new and growing middle class. He also proposed that fast growing newly industrial towns like Manchester, Birmingham, Leeds and Sheffield should be represented in Parliament. This had a direct, if unintended, relevance to the development of public art galleries. When these towns eventually succeeded in becoming self-governing, it opened the door for municipal funding of art galleries. And the (by then) newly enfranchised middle classes were major players in the development of these regional art galleries. But Wilkes' motion was ahead of its time and failed, just like his call for a national art collection. Neither parliamentary reform nor a national art collection came to pass until well into the nineteenth century, but in both cases Wilkes performed an essential role as a pioneer.

Why did a political activist like Wilkes want the public to have the right to view art of the highest quality? It was largely because he thought it would encourage the development of native fine art, in the face of an aristocratic preference for foreign Old Masters and fashionable contemporary works from the Continent. The art collections of stately homes might well include paintings from the Italian Renaissance, or seventeenth century works from the Dutch Golden Age, plus perhaps a Canaletto as a souvenir of Venice. But they rarely bought work from contemporary British artists. Not only did the aristocracy see British artists as generally inferior to Continental artists, but British artists had to go abroad to be trained to the highest level (usually in Rome). So many were not even able to study the kind of art admired by the elite, adding insult to injury.

(As a point of clarity, the term "British" did not come into use until the Union of the English and Scottish Parliaments in 1707. Wilkes' notion of "liberty" was based on England's Magna Carta of 1215. Scotland's contribution to "liberty" was its call for national self-determination in the face of the depredations of the English, expressed in the Declaration of

Arbroath of 1320.)

Wilkes did not just want Parliament to follow the example of the governments of France and some German states by opening royal and aristocratic collections to the public. He wanted it to follow their policies of applying fine art principles to native manufacturing. Support for the fine arts would thus have multiple benefits: it would increase Britain's cultural standing, it would encourage the development of a native school of painting, and the production of higher quality goods would help the expanding manufacturing sector to equal (and possibly surpass) the luxury trades of France.

Since the British Museum, the King, and the aristocracy had woefully failed to act, Wilkes insisted, only Parliament was left to advance the cause of fine art and its accessibility to the people. In the event, Parliament failed too, and most of the Walpole collection was snapped up by Catherine the Great of Russia, to grace the walls of the Hermitage in St Petersburg. Carried away by enthusiasm, perhaps Wilkes had failed to remember that the British Museum itself had been funded by the proceeds of a lottery, not by the state.

What made matters worse was that this was the second time that parliament had failed to secure a major art collection for the nation. In the seventeenth-century Cromwell's Commonwealth had disposed of Charles I's equally magnificent collection. The beheaded king had been an obsessive art collector, and his collection was one of the greatest ever known. Rather than take it over for the state, Parliament decided to sell off the collection to pay some of the king's enormous debts (partly caused by his art collecting) and to cover military expenses.

Keen interest from abroad meant many of the works ended up as the backbone of major Continental collections. (Fortunately for the current Royal collection, the king's son Charles II was able to buy back many of the works on his restoration to the throne.) There was one positive outcome, as the display of the works before the auction gave many ordinary people the chance to see and even to buy art for the first time. A seed was sown.

Not all was lost however. Wilkes had some success with his second aim, the advancement of art by living British artists, via a rather surprising route. Since the dissolution of the monasteries by Henry VIII in the sixteenth century, the role of the church in relieving poverty and supporting the arts had drastically declined. Charitable organisations dependent on private donations had developed to fill the gap. Wilkes was a Governor of one of them, the Foundling Hospital, which from 1745 had occupied a building in Bloomsbury, central London. The charity had been set up in 1739 by a retired sea captain, Thomas Coram, to care for

London's many abandoned children.

Visiting the Hospital became popular with the aristocracy and the gentry as an opportunity to display their sympathy for the poor. They could also view paintings donated by leading artists such as Hogarth to decorate the Hospital's walls. The artists were not being entirely altruistic. Their generosity not only attracted the eye of potential patrons, but associated the artists with gentlemanly charity. The latter was important to a group which was anxious to improve its social status. Thus the first public exhibitions of contemporary art in England took place in an orphanage.

Wilkes was also involved in a spin off from these exhibitions. The artists who exhibited at the Foundling Hospital went on to set up the Society of Artists of Great Britain in 1759. Wilkes, then the young MP for Aylesbury, was the President of the meeting which planned its formation. The Society's first exhibition was held the following year in the rooms of the Royal Society for the Encouragement of Arts, Manufactures and Commerce, set up in 1754 to encourage innovation and excellence. This exhibition marked the beginning of regular art exhibitions in London, which soon became an exciting new way for the public to see and talk about the latest British art.

Some Society members wanted to add an academy of painting to the exhibiting facilities. This was vehemently opposed by Hogarth, who felt such an academy would impose what he saw as the stifling creative hierarchy rampant in France. But Joshua Reynolds (born a gentleman, unlike Hogarth) and other defectors from the Society used their court contacts to set up the Royal Academy in 1768 with funding from George III. (Wilkes was not in favour of the Academy either. He wrote from jail on his return to England that he thought no good would come of this royal patronage.)

By the time of Wilkes' Parliamentary speech, Reynolds had become the first President of the Royal Academy and had already called for the establishment of a national gallery. This plea was to be echoed in vain by the second and third Presidents, Benjamin West and Thomas Lawrence. Yet the National Gallery which now sits in Trafalgar Square was not founded until 1824. (Lawrence was at least still alive to witness it.) This made Britain one of the last major countries in Europe to establish a public national art collection.

This foot dragging was in spite of the fact that an event which hugely influenced British attitudes to art had taken place all of 30 years before. What was undoubtedly by far the most important landmark in the development of public art galleries took place in Paris in August 1793.[2]

After the French Revolution and the beheading of the French King, the royal palace of the Louvre was taken over by the state for the display of the Royal collection. Admission was free and open to anyone, although the public was only admitted at weekends as artists were given priority at other times. Its first exhibition was of 400 artworks from the Royal collection (mainly Italian, Flemish and French drawings). Rather to everyone's surprise, it proved to be enormously popular with the common people. A catalogue was hastily produced, incomplete and with errors, but nevertheless a major scholarly event and a significant achievement.

In 1798 there was a display of a selection of 86 works seized by Napoleon in Italy (thankfully, most were subsequently returned) and 56 from Versailles (including the Mona Lisa, which attracted little or no attention). An excellent catalogue aimed at the "less fortunate" was produced. Three further exhibitions took place in 1798, 1802 and 1814.

These displays were originally intended to be permanent, but the unprecedented rapidity of Napoleon's military success meant more and more booty was sent to the Louvre, which displaced works already on the walls. The effect was a series of temporary exhibitions, accustoming the public to such events.

British visitors were able to visit the 1802 and 1814 shows, during the lull in Napoleonic exploits, and were mightily impressed. They noted that there was nothing similar at home, although there was much work of high quality in private hands, not least as a result of the ruination of many French aristocrats by the Revolution. In fact, by far the most sensational art sale in eighteenth-century London was the disposal in 1798 of the collection of one of these impoverished aristocrats, the Duke of Orleans, whose collection had been one of the glories of Europe.

The collection was considered so important that a plan was concocted to acquire 150 paintings from the sale for the nation, a plan which was supported by both the King and the Prime Minister, Pitt the Younger. It will come as no great surprise that this came to nothing. Nevertheless, the sale was a huge development for the British art world. As with the sale of Charles I's collection, the exhibition and sale of the collection gave British aristocrats, bankers, and merchants the opportunity to view and acquire works of the highest quality. The result was that private collections in England now rivalled those in Paris, Madrid and St Petersburg.

It is pleasing to record that 25 paintings from the Orleans sale did eventually find their way to the National Gallery in London, once it finally came into existence. In fact, what was considered the showpiece of the Gallery when the new building at Trafalgar Square opened to the public in 1824, *The Raising of Lazarus* by Sabastiano del Piombo, was bought at this sale by the Duke of Bridgewater.

Bridgewater had made a fortune from canal development and was no art lover, but his artistically inclined nephew, Lord Gower, succeeded in persuading him that art could be a good investment. In partnership with the Earl of Carlisle they bought all the French and Italian pictures at the Orleans sale. They kept the best for themselves, and sold off the rest through highly innovative selling exhibitions.

The general public reacted enthusiastically to this further chance to view large numbers of high-quality Old Masters. The result was a greatly intensified public interest in such works, and a desire to keep these pictures in England, both of which helped to develop support for a National Gallery.

Ironically, all this meant that the reluctance of the powers that be to fund a national art gallery took place at a time when London was the largest art market in Europe. There was by now a huge appetite for art in England. Up to the seventeenth century, it had been quite common for wealthy aristocrats and newly rich businessmen to build up major private art collections, but upper class collecting really took off in the eighteenth century with the advent of the Grand Tour. Young aristocrats brought back Old Masters from their European travels, perhaps along with a Canaletto or two, or a portrait by Pompeo Batoni. Cash-strapped Roman aristocrats proved to be a good source of high-quality art at reasonable prices. Art, of course, always follows the money, and by this time it was the English upper class which had it.

It became a sign of gentlemanly status to build an art collection, usually made up of sixteenth and seventeenth century paintings by Italian, French, Flemish and Dutch masters. Roman sculpture was also highly prized, as archaeology developed and excavated antiquities came onto the market. This kind of art collecting became an important element in the formation of an upper-class identity, an expression of shared tastes, interests and a classical education.

To give an idea of the enormous scale of the English art market at the time, it has been calculated that in the eighteenth century 50,000 paintings, 500,000 etchings and engravings, and large numbers of classical antiquities entered Britain from France, Italy and Holland. Around 100 000 paintings passed through the auction houses.[3]

It was a matter of considerable annoyance to artists and others that this wealth of high-quality art in upper class collections was only occasionally available to view by outsiders. Some English collectors, such as Thomas Hope, the Marquis of Stafford, and Lord Grosvenor, began to admit the public to their galleries, but under fairly restrictive conditions which were not conducive to careful study. This mattered, because most artists could not afford to visit the Continent to view the famous artworks in public galleries and churches.

And there was no guarantee that a particular artist would be admitted to an aristocratic home. Visitors were expected to be well-born, educated, and possessed of a gentlemanly "taste" – meaning a knowledge and understanding of the work of those artists then deemed of the highest quality. The viewer had to be capable of identifying and interpreting individual paintings with few clues (often deriving from classical Greece and Rome), which meant that an ability to do so was a demonstration of social status. Access to an aristocratic art collection was a social test as much as an aesthetic experience.

The only bright lights in this darkness shone in the university sector – in the two English universities and in one of the four universities in Scotland. Since all three institutions still flourish, a historical digression is necessary for the sake of completeness.

The Ashmolean Museum opened in 1683 as part of Oxford University, the first university museum in the world. It was freely open to the public and contained some artworks among its very varied collections. Unfortunately, its name betrays the story of its rather dubious origins.

The Museum is named after Elias Ashmole. He was an occultist and astrologer – which was not incompatible with science at the time – who helped to found the Royal Society and became one of its first Fellows. He was an active royalist supporter of Charles I during the Civil War, and later become a favourite of his son, Charles II. He was a lawyer but his second marriage to a wealthy widow allowed him to pursue his interests unencumbered by the need to make a living. He became an antiquarian and a collector of manuscripts and curiosities. In other words, he was canny enough to strike it lucky socially, scientifically and financially.

He was also a neighbour of the Tradescant family. John Tradescant was a gardener and botanist who travelled the Continent, partly in search of botanical specimens. His son, John junior, was also a gardener and botanist who visited Virginia several times. Both collected plant, animal and mineral specimens, as well as "artificialls" – household objects, arms, pictures, footwear, and clothing. They allowed the public to view their collections for a fee.

Ashmole befriended the Tradescants and helped them to catalogue their collections. John junior deeded the collection to him after his death, but when he died this was challenged by his widow, who claimed he had been duped while drunk. She brought a lawsuit, but lost and was later mysteriously found drowned in a pond. Critics said Ashmole had in effect stolen the Tradescent collection, taking another man's glory because "acquisitiveness was his master passion". Maybe, maybe not, but the scandal came to nothing. Perhaps his royal connections helped to smooth things over.

Be that as it may, Ashmole offered to leave both his own collections and the Tradescant collections to Oxford University if they could be suitably housed. A building was duly put up which had a laboratory in the basement and displays above. In the event, a great deal of Ashmole's own collection was destroyed in a fire, so the Tradescant part of his bequest ended up being a much larger proportion than originally intended.

Ashmole's library went to the Bodleian Library, one of the oldest libraries in Europe with roots in the fourteenth century. After a decline it was revived by Thomas Bodley and reopened as the Bodleian Library in 1602. It was also the home of Oxford University's own small art collection, which was joined by a coin collection later in the century. The general public were admitted to both the library and the museum. There then followed a great deal of to-ing and fro-ing of the collections between the two institutions.

The Bodleian Library's curiosities went to the Ashmolean Museum when it opened, and the art was brought together in the Bodleian, which became the museum of art. During the eighteenth century it grew to contain portraits, eighteenth century landscapes, historical paintings, genre works, and Old Masters. There was a small admission fee and a catalogue produced by the janitor. Greek and Roman statuary was added in 1755, joining a group of inscribed marbles given in 1667. As these were too heavy for the upstairs gallery, they were put on the ground floor.

There were further developments in the nineteenth and twentieth centuries, which will be dealt with in a later chapter, but the upshot was that in the end it was the Ashmolean Museum which became an internationally important museum of art and archaeology, named after a man who quite possibly did not deserve it.

Glasgow University also had a museum at an early stage, and one which was very strong on art from the beginning. The Hunterian Museum opened in 1807 as a result of the bequest of Dr William Hunter. It can be seen as an early indication of that city's exceptional importance to art collecting and art galleries.

Hunter was born in East Kilbride, Lanarkshire, and studied divinity at Glasgow University. He then studied medicine in London where he became a very successful obstetrician, surgeon, and anatomist. He acquired a nationally significant collection of paintings, including works by Rembrandt, Chardin and Stubbs, as well as buying engravings from Hogarth and building up an important collection of coins. He is one of Britain' most significant collectors, as he also acquired an extensive collection of medical, scientific and pathological specimens, and an important collection of books.

Although he rose to become both Professor of Anatomy at the Royal Academy and a Fellow of the Royal Society of Antiquaries, he, like Ashmole, had his detractors. London gossip accused him of acquiring corpses for dissection by dubious means and using his society connections to avoid the consequences. In both cases, no definitive proof one way or the other is likely to be discovered at this late stage.

The purpose of Hunter's bequest was explicitly educational: it was intended to be a resource for teaching and research in the arts, humanities and sciences. These things ran in the family - his brother also founded a museum, at the Royal College of Surgeons in London, also known as the Hunterian Museum.

The original purpose-built building housing the collections was in the classical style and adjoined the original University campus. It is the oldest museum in Scotland and the first museum in Britain to have a gallery of paintings. It was open to the public from noon to 2pm every day except Sunday. Further developments in the nineteenth and twentieth centuries will be dealt with later.

A third university also managed to acquire a museum and art gallery before the National Gallery – but only just, as it opened in 1816. Cambridge University founded the Fitzwilliam Museum as the result of a bequest from the Irish Viscount Richard Fitzwilliam (1745-1816). He was a Fellow of the Royal Society, an MP, and the developer of part of southeast Dublin. He left his Irish estates to his first cousin's son, and his art collection and library to Cambridge University "to increase the learning and other great objects of that Noble Foundation", plus £100,000 to house them.

Fitzwilliam was born in Richmond near London, but spent much of his time in France, where he had three children by his French mistress. He was a strong supporter of the French monarchy and the Catholic Church. When travel to France became too risky because of the French Revolution, and his Irish estates were also considered unsafe, he increasingly stayed in Richmond.

Fitzwilliam had collected paintings during his Grand Tour and acquired Old Masters from the Orleans sale. But the bequest of 144 paintings also included Dutch works inherited from his mother's father, a former Chairman of the Dutch East India Company. There was also a huge collection of prints, including a series of Rembrandt's etchings, and autographed music by Handel and Purcell among others.

His bequest was an attempt to establish public art galleries in England, as his Continental travels had shown him how far behind it was.

The Fitzwilliam collection was originally housed in a school building and did not find a permanent home for some decades. Again, this will be dealt with in a later chapter.

The aristocratic collections and the university museums provided opportunities to view Old Masters and contemporary works, but mainly outside London. The London public were able to view Old Masters and contemporary works when they were displayed by auction houses before sales. Many artists and connoisseurs eagerly took advantage of this. From the later eighteenth century, contemporary paintings could be viewed at the annual Royal Academy shows, which became major society events. All this widened access to paintings for a section of society, mainly the upper middle class, but for most people the main access to art was via prints.

The sale of engravings of paintings by well-known artists grew enormously in the eighteenth century, and even if an individual could not afford to buy they could be viewed when hung up in print shop windows. Prints became the main medium through which artists were known to the general public. Hogarth knew this very well; his main income was from engravings made of his paintings.

As Hogarth also well knew (with considerable annoyance), it was not just Old Masters which were imported from abroad. Contemporary art, and artists, were imported too. Artists from Italy, Holland, Sweden, Germany and France flocked to Britain to obtain aristocratic commissions. Hogarth may well have been right when he complained that upper class interest in "foreign" art and artists stifled the development of native skills. However, by the end of the century the status and success of British artists had grown considerably. Reynolds, and Hogarth himself, had European reputations. The fees Reynolds could charge matched the prices paid for Old Masters. By then, England was a net exporter of prints to Europe. These changes were underpinned by widespread amateur art practice, which created both an interest in and knowledge of art and artistic techniques, and created a large market for art supplies which benefitted professional artists too.[4]

This was part of a general expansion in all the arts. Music and concert halls flourished, and the theatre revived, with new theatres in London and the provinces by mid-century. The lapse of the Licensing Act 1695 led to a boom in printing during the eighteenth-century. Newspapers, pamphlets, books and periodicals flowed from the presses in such numbers that it became possible to make a living as a writer.

The "art critic" began to appear in publications which linked the different arts together, presenting "polite culture" as a single entity aimed at a new growing audience for cultural activities. There were new places where this audience could pursue their cultural interests - assembly rooms, coffee houses, concert halls, auction houses. Significantly, this new cultural infrastructure was commercially based, not dependent on upper class patrons.

Not that this new, predominantly middle class, polite culture went unchallenged. It was buffeted by traditional aristocratic culture from above and by far less genteel popular culture from below. But middle-class culture did all it could to stake out its (new) territory. For example, the Society of Artists charged admission to their 1762 exhibition so only "suitable" people would be admitted.

Middle class entry to the art scene was accompanied by commercial considerations which began to affect demand for art. Grand "history" painting – large scale works usually depicting high minded subjects from the classical world or the Bible – had long held the highest status aesthetically, but this was beginning to fade. They were mainly an aristocratic taste, but there were few aristocratic commissions and such work was marginal commercially. It could only be made to pay if an engraving deal was attached. Royal Academy shows were dominated by the portraits and landscapes which had a ready market.

Commerce further asserted itself with the activities of entrepreneurs in middlemen roles, some of whom achieved considerable success in their own right. These middlemen dealers and publishers enabled artists to make a living from their art, but at the same time they allowed artists to distance themselves from direct commercial activity. Artists could maintain a genteel outward appearance of being uninterested in money, useful for a group which aspired to be gentlemen (or, in a few cases, ladies).

All this meant that by the end of the eighteenth century one of Wilkes' aims, the support of living British artists, had achieved some success. The interest in the "polite arts" by the rising middle class helped to raise the status of the arts generally.

Wilkes had also wanted to combine the polite arts with the improvement of manufacturing. Adam Smith, the Scottish moral philosopher and founder of the discipline of economics, provided another motive in his *The Wealth of Nations* of 1776. He thought the state should provide 'diversions', particularly for poor mechanics, because through "publick works and publick institutions" the poor could be kept orderly, respectable and "less liable…to the delusions of enthusiasm and superstition." The support of art for reasons of morality became a major factor in the first half of the Victorian era. But Wilkes' aim of state support for the application of the fine arts to industry would have to wait until the 1850s.

In the meantime, valiant efforts to found a national art gallery continued. Two collectors, the Scottish dealer William Buchanan and Joseph, Count Truchsess, both collected with the express intention of providing the basis for a future national collection, but their respective offers – both made in 1803 – were yet again rebuffed.

In the face of all this negativity, a group of mainly aristocratic connoisseurs and collectors founded the British Institution in 1805. It was set up in Pall Mall for the purpose of promoting the Fine Arts in the United Kingdom. It gave artists access to Old Master paintings by holding annual exhibitions of such paintings lent by Members, and an art school was held in the summer. The Old Master shows were for artists only (with restrictions to prevent forgery), but the Institution also ran annual exhibitions of contemporary art for the general public. The Institution's efforts were not without critics. The paintings were not always of the highest quality, and some artists resented the Institution's dominance by the aristocracy (unlike the artist-run Royal Academy).

Nevertheless, in 1813 it broke new ground by holding an exhibition devoted to Sir Joshua Reynolds, the first celebration anywhere of the achievements of a past master. Perhaps for the first time, it was possible to follow the development of an artist's whole career. The exhibition was a big success, with up to 800 visitors a day. This was followed up in 1814 with an exhibition covering other British artists – Hogarth, Gainsborough, Richard Wilson and Zoffany. The show greatly increased Hogarth's reputation as a painter, but although attendance was good the response was muted and a disappointment to the Institution.

The Institution's reaction to this relative failure was another breakthrough. It was decided to show Dutch and Flemish masters the following year, thus introducing to the world the Old Master exhibition, whose popularity has increased unabated ever since.

The Louvre had already pioneered the holding of exhibitions showcasing a living artist (Vernet), and shows devoted to a school of art (French, of course). Now that London had pioneered the retrospective celebration of a recent past master (Reynolds) and the Old Master show, not only was the art exhibition itself firmly established, but so was the format of most such subsequent events.

The scene was set for the eventual emergence of the blockbuster exhibition, whose combined possibilities for fundraising, aesthetic education and the pursuit of scholarship have been of inestimable benefit to public art galleries. The Reynolds show was also a first demonstration of British patriotism in the field of art, a factor in the establishment of at least two British nineteenth-century public art galleries (and an idea later imitated on the Continent with the growth of European nationalism).

But in spite of these ground-breaking achievements, it would be nearly another half century before Britain established a national gallery of fine art. By that time, national art collections had already been set up in many parts of the continental mainland, as royal or princely collections were given over to the public. Even before the Louvre and the French royal collection were taken over by the state in 1793, the Bavarian royal collection had opened to the public in 1779, and the last heir of the Medici had donated his peerless family collection to Florence, as the Uffizi Gallery, in 1743. And long before this, Rome's Capitoline museum and art gallery had been founded by Pope Sixtus IV in 1471 (although it did not become a public art gallery until 1734) and the Vatican opened its sculpture gallery to the public in 1506. The Belvedere Palace in Vienna was opened to the public in 1781 for the display of the Hapsburg collection. Spain's Prado Museum, again housing a royal collection, just pipped Britain by opening in 1819.

Some public galleries on the Continent originated from princely collections in countries occupied by Napoleon. Following the example of the Louvre, he had opened them to the public, and after Napoleon's defeat the duly reinstated princes donated their collections to their subjects (it being politically unwise to overturn Napoleon's largesse with other people's property). This in itself indicates why Britain did not follow a similar path.

By far the best royal art collection, that of Charles I, had been dispersed by Cromwell, and thus was not available for takeover. More pertinently, the model of an absolutist ruler who could magnanimously donate his collection to the nation no longer existed in Britain, as it had been explicitly rejected by the 1688 settlement which established the current constitutional monarchy. The British Royal Collection remains firmly in the sovereign's possession to this day.

As for John Wilkes, like many radicals he became increasingly conservative with age. When the Gordon riots erupted in response to the removal of some of the legal discriminations against Roman Catholics, troops under his orders fired into a crowd attacking the Bank of England. He lost a great deal of support as a result, and subsequently withdrew from politics.

But he never gave up his insistence that parliament should create an infrastructure which would give the wider public access to great works of art. In the event, it was only when an entirely fortuitous combination of circumstances came about that Parliament finally bowed to decades of pressure in 1823, and agreed to the formation of a National Gallery. And it was not until 1857 that a German Prince spearheaded the foundation of an institution which was explicitly intended to improve the design of commercially produced goods.

At the turn of the nineteenth century, yet another opportunity was turned down by the state, but this time there was ultimately a successful outcome. In 1799 the Swiss art dealer Noel Joseph Desenfans offered to bequeath to the British state a collection of Old Master and Dutch genre paintings. It had been put together for the King of Poland, but he was forced to abdicate when Poland was partitioned between Russia, Prussia and Austria. It was then offered to Britain on condition that a building be provided to house it. True to form, the offer was not accepted.

Desenfans' collection was eventually bequeathed by his heir, the artist and Royal Academy member Sir Francis Bourgois, to his old school, the charitable Dulwich College on the outskirts of London. A gallery was built to house the collection, designed by a fellow member of the Royal Academy, Sir John Soane. The building opened to the public in 1817. Thus the first purpose built public art gallery in Britain which showed a permanent exhibition was a charitable rather than a state project. Wilkes would probably have been unsurprised.

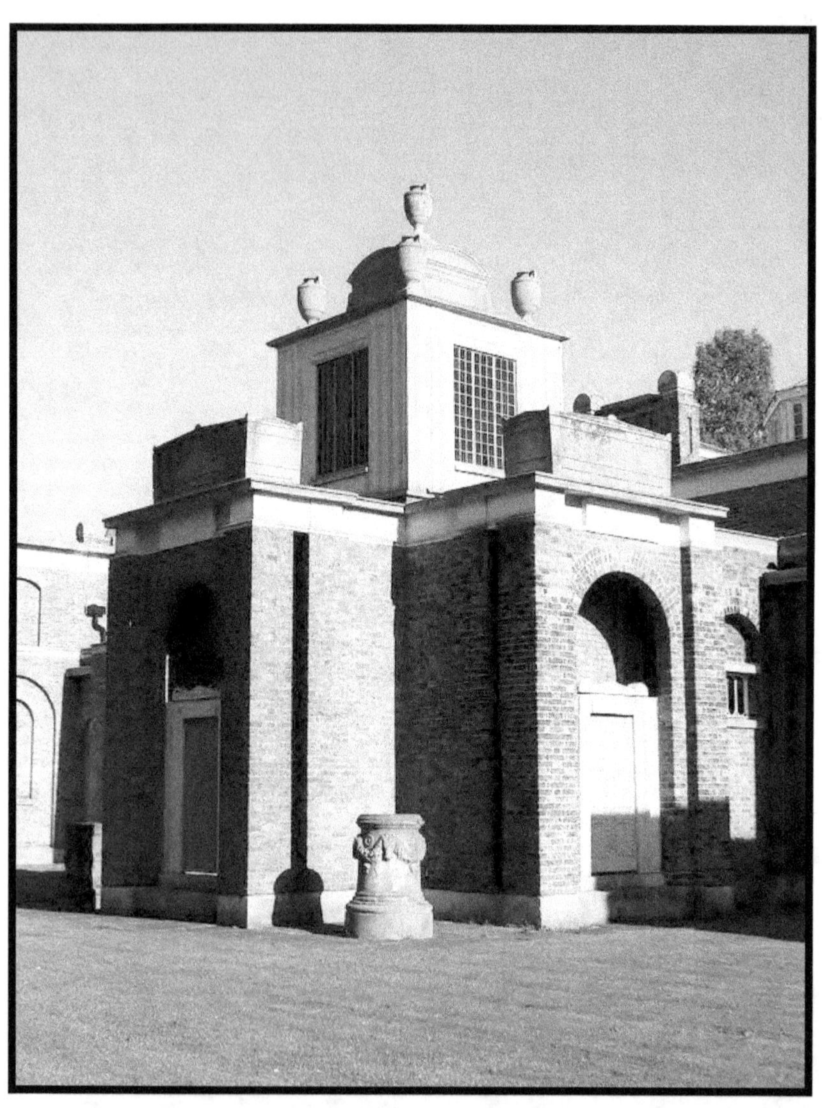

The first gallery with a public permanent collection: the urns on the roof of Dulwich Picture Gallery are above the mausoleum of the Gallery's three founders

2. A First in the Suburbs

WHILE CALLS FOR Parliament to found a national art collection continued to fall on deaf ears, the first purpose built standalone public art gallery in England quietly came into existence in 1814, not in central London but in the suburban village of Dulwich.

As already noted, its origin was a collection of paintings the Swiss born art dealer Noel Desenfans had assembled on behalf of the King of Poland. When, tragically, Poland was partitioned for the third time in 1795 and ceased to exist as an independent country, the unfortunate King was forced to abdicate and move to Russia. Desenfans was left with the pictures on his hands, unsold. The collection was offered to the British government, but the offer was, yet again, declined (probably to no one's great surprise).

The situation was eventually resolved, largely thanks to Desenfans' unusual domestic arrangements. His dealing activities were mainly financed by his older wife Margaret, a wealthy heiress. Margaret shared her husband's passionately held view that the collection should somehow be made available to the public, as did his partner, Sir Francis Bourgois. Bourgois was a painter and, like Desenfans, a member of the Royal Academy. Desenfans had taken him into his household as an orphaned teenager, and he, his wife and Bourgois shared the same house thereafter. (There was much excited gossip about the precise nature of this arrangement, but nothing was ever substantiated.) This meant there was a trio of enthusiasts for the project – two to provide the professional vision, backed by the loyalty and financial resources of the third.

When Desenfans died, Bourgois inherited the collection. When Bourgois himself died in 1811, he left the pictures to his old school, Dulwich College, with £10,000 to build a gallery to house it. Margaret, who outlived Bourgois by two years, then stepped in to provide necessary additional funds from her own fortune to make sure the project finally came to fruition. She also provided the gallery with furniture and tableware from her own household and initiated the custom of an annual dinner for members of the Royal Academy. This was an important link with the art establishment which lasted well into the nineteenth century.

Bourgois had commissioned another Royal Academy colleague, the eminent architect Sir John Soane, to design the gallery. Soane worked wonders with his limited budget, carrying out the work without a fee. His design for the building was quite simple: a line of connected rooms, based on the cube or double cube, top lit with skylights, which provided a pleasing vista of arches. The founding trio became a quartet.

Soane was an architectural genius, but little of his work has survived. Dulwich Picture Gallery not only survived, it had a profound effect on the design of subsequent art galleries right into the twentieth-century, both in Britain and abroad.

Soane's gallery was built in the style of ancient Greece. This was typical of cultural buildings at the time, as it neatly symbolised the classics-based liberal education of the middle and upper classes. References to ancient Greece both flattered their knowledge and clearly marked their social status. As Soane was in fact an almost obsessive advocate of the architecture of classical Greece and Rome, there was actually little chance that he would have chosen any other style. But this was not a slavish copy of the past; it was a personal interpretation of classicism which incorporated dramatic lighting effects influenced by the Romantic movement of his own era.

The gallery had a noticeably church-like feel. This was partly because the gallery contained – uniquely – a mausoleum to its founders, Desenfans, his wife Margaret, and Bourgois. But it is also because Soane wanted to evoke the semi-religious contemplative response to art then considered appropriate in gentlemanly circles (to which Soane did not belong by birth – he was from very humble origins). The top lights used coloured glass, so the lighting alternated a cathedral-like gloom with vividly bright highlights. (Not surprisingly, the dim lighting was heavily criticised and was subsequently modified – Soane was not the first or last architect to let his enthusiasms run away with him.)

In 1817, four years after Margaret's death, Dulwich Picture Gallery was ready to open its doors to the public. The Bourgois collection was joined by pictures already owned by Dulwich College (mainly portraits). The paintings were displayed in the still fashionable eighteenth-century manner. Pictures were hung in a decorative or "picturesque" style: a symmetrical pattern with a large picture in the centre and pairs of smaller pictures on either side. There was often a theme to the pictures in the arrangement, to create an attractive unified ensemble.

During the eighteenth century, paintings from the same geographical area of Europe began to be classified as belonging to a particular national school. By the end of the eighteenth century, it had become the norm in England to hang paintings from the same school in the same room. Dulwich followed this convention, so the Dutch, Italian, Flemish and English paintings could be viewed together. This, then, was the arrangement that met the eyes of the earliest visitors, and the permanent collection is still largely displayed in this way.

While Soane's building was widely admired, the Gallery's management was not. Dulwich Picture Gallery might be public, but this did not mean that access was free or convenient. Until 1857, tickets could only be obtained from four printing shops in central London, and children under twelve were banned. The gallery was closed on Fridays and Sundays. As Sundays were the only day off for the growing urban working class, they were effectively excluded. In fact, the opening hours of 10am to 5pm from April to October, and 10am to 3pm for the rest of the year, made it difficult for *any* kind of employee to visit. The gallery was "public" only to those who did not need to work.

But even if the Gallery's hours and location made a visit impossible, there was some consolation in that many of the paintings were available by way of reproductions. An enterprising publisher produced aquatints of 50 of the Gallery's "most celebrated pictures" between 1816 and 1820 (mostly by Dutch painters, reflecting English taste at the time). For those who could afford it, this was certainly better than nothing.

Under these circumstances, it is not surprising that visitors were rather sparse. An anonymous writer of 1824 remarked that if plans then being debated to place the national art collection in the British Museum (again!) came to fruition, "the pictures, if buried there, will be rather more visited than Sir Francis Bourgois' at Dulwich, but not much".[5]

But while general visitors may have been fairly thin on the ground, the gallery maintained strong links with the contemporary art establishment. Desenfans, Bourgois and Soane had all been prominent (if rather dissident) members of the Royal Academy, and the regular dinners or breakfasts put on for Royal Academy guests included leading art figures like Turner. The link was further strengthened when the Gallery started lending its paintings to the Academy to be studied and copied by its students. This innovation meant that Dulwich Picture Gallery was responsible for introducing painting classes to the Academy Schools, which up to that point had only taught drawing.

The Gallery also lent pictures to the exhibitions organised by the British Institution, which had been set up in 1805 by a group of aristocratic collectors to make their Old Master paintings available to a wider public. Evidently this activity was seen as of some importance – when Dulwich refused to lend to the Institution's 1818 show, it was attacked for a lack for public spirit.[6]

But for the general public, there were even more barriers than potential access problems. Just like visitors to collections in aristocratic houses, those who managed to reach the gallery were not given much information about the paintings. For the first 60 years the only published catalogue was a list of paintings with the artists' names, available for one shilling.

The attributions on this list came in for heavy criticism from one exceptionally knowledgeable visitor. The German scholar Dr Gustav von Waagen – pioneer art historian and first Director of the Royal Picture Collection in Berlin – had unrivalled knowledge of the paintings in England's stately homes because he had visited England many times from 1835 to 1862, cataloguing them on behalf of their aristocratic owners. Regrettably, not only did he complain that many paintings were misattributed; he thought the Dulwich collection as a whole was overrated. It is true that the paintings were of mixed quality, and sometimes they were indeed attributed to the wrong artist. Nevertheless, Dulwich also displayed many acknowledged masterpieces, and was particularly strong in seventeenth century Dutch works – the Dutch Golden Age.

It is also true that the paintings were originally so densely hung, covering the whole wall, that the mediocre paintings tended to overshadow the masterpieces. It is just as well then that in 1824 a commercial publisher came to the aid of the non-expert by producing *The Beauties of Dulwich Gallery*. This summarised the highlights of the collection for the casual visitor, who could thus better appreciate "the burning glow of beauty…which greets him on his first entrance to this exquisite Gallery", especially the "delicious work of the Flemish landscape-painters". The book could be bought where tickets were purchased, and was widely used as a guidebook.

But whatever the ordinary visitor made of the Gallery, it was highly popular with the cultural establishment. Up to the 1860s the gallery was visited by many well-known artists, including Canova, David Wilkie, Turner (who copied a Ruisdael), Constable, William Etty and Holman Hunt. Admittedly, Dulwich lost some of its appeal for artists once the National Gallery opened in central London, as it could not compete for accessibility and the quality of its collection. Still, the Royal Academy connection was maintained and it remained popular with writers throughout the century. Dickens, Thackeray, Browning, George Eliot and Carlyle all registered their approval of the gallery, pleasantly situated as it was amid suburban greenery. And it maintained its attraction for at least one foreign artist, Vincent van Gogh, who visited in 1873. Later in the century, Camille Pissarro briefly lived nearby, and it seems unlikely that he would have failed to pay a visit, although there is no record.

The gallery also played an important part in the career of the famous art critic, John Ruskin. He was brought up locally, visited many times, and made watercolour copies of some of its paintings in 1844. The gallery proved useful to him in his early career when he was producing Volume One of *Modern Painters*, the book which made his name. The paintings referred to in that book were solely from the National Gallery and Dulwich Picture Gallery - although the references to Dulwich were far from flattering. Ruskin used the seventeenth-century landscapes in Dulwich to vent his distaste at their failure to be true to nature, according to his view of the matter. Cuyp came in for a particularly severe drubbing. This was contrasted with the exquisite naturalism of his protégé, Turner, whose reputation soared as a result. It will therefore come as no surprise that Ruskin made a diary entry for 30 January 1844 which reads: "Walked down to Dulwich Gallery, and thought the pictures worse than ever; came away encouragingly disgusted."[7]

That was not the only heavyweight criticism. Henry Cole, later the first director of the South Kensington Museum (the Victoria and Albert Museum from 1897), made a number of negative points in a handbook on the Dulwich Picture Gallery which he wrote under an alias in 1844. He recommended extended opening hours for "the clerk employed all day", the abolition of tickets, and the lifting of the ban on children. He supported von Waagen on the inaccuracies of the catalogue, and he too considered the collection overrated.[8] (The views of von Waagen, Ruskin and Cole on the quality of the pictures may be rather harsh, but it is worth repeating that the collection has always contained many undoubted masterpieces.)

Many of Cole's criticisms were dealt with in 1857, when a new constitution and governing body was introduced. It was no longer necessary to buy tickets in central London, and the hours were extended to 10am to 4pm in winter and 10am to 5pm in summer. This almost certainly expanded the social function of visits to the gallery. This can be glimpsed from Dulwich Picture Gallery's visitors' books. The earliest which is still available dates from 1869.

An analysis by this writer of the 1869 book shows the gallery was a popular venue with local suburbanites, unlikely to have been the case when a journey into central London was required. Over half of the roughly nine and a half thousand visitors that year were from Dulwich and the surrounding suburbs. A fifth of the signatories were female, presumably women who attended without a male "protector", showing that visiting the gallery was seen as a safe and respectable undertaking for a middle-class woman. Many of the visitors were in parties of families or friends, indicating the popularity of a visit for social as well as cultural reasons. These numbers create a mental image of the gallery being seen by local residents as a focal point for a walk, a place to take visitors, and a place to meet friends, not just as a cultural event.

It is also clear that the gallery was valued for its educational effect, as several visits from educational establishments are recorded. These include pupils or staff from three local charitable schools, a school in Surrey, as well as the elite public schools Eton and Lancing Colleges, and Dulwich College itself. There were also visits from unnamed schools led by a female teacher, probably small schools for young ladies.

A number of visitors had aristocratic titles, but (judging by their addresses) the vast majority were middle class. Some indicate a predominantly middle-class occupation, such as lawyer, doctor or minister. The handwriting is mostly a (sometimes illegible) scrawl, but a significant minority have a neat "clerical" hand, which may indicate a lower middle-class background, while a few have an unformed hand which could indicate a child or a working-class visitor.

Some visitors give Oxbridge colleges as an address, and two German professors are recorded. There are visitors from the National Gallery, the South Kensington Museum and the British Museum – all presumably with a professional interest. One of the German professors, Dr Julius Lessing, may be the art historian of the same name who was the first director of the Berlin Museum of Decorative Arts.

All this adds up to a visitor profile which looks pretty similar to what one would find today: a minority of serious, informed art lovers, a larger proportion of those with mixed cultural and social motives, and some, no doubt, with purely social reasons for the visit. Even the school visit turns out to be not as modern a phenomenon as one might suppose.

What might seem surprising is the presence of the long-distance cultural tourist at this early stage. In 1869, most gallery visitors were from other parts of London, mainly from the City and West End and from other London suburbs, and a few from the East End. There were visitors from major English cities like Manchester, Liverpool, and Bristol, and from places in Scotland, Ireland and Wales.

But some came from much further afield. Throughout 1869, Dulwich had several visitors a month from abroad, from all over the world. Some visitors are clearly empire builders on home leave, such as the officers in the Indian army. But those from France, German speaking areas, Russia, the United States, Canada and Australia would probably have been permanent residents of those areas. It is easy to see how the gallery's influence spread internationally.

This art tourism was not all one way of course. English travellers visited foreign galleries and were often envious of the larger continental art galleries even after the National Gallery was founded. (Nevertheless, the opinions of nineteenth-century English visitors could have an effect on foreign galleries. For example, their views affected the attitude of the Prado in Madrid to its collection and how it was displayed.)[9]

Dulwich catered to art students as well as visitors who simply came to view the pictures, as students could apply for permission to copy paintings in the collection. This was more significant than it looks today, as the copying of works by masters was an important part of art training at that time. However, as a former Director of the Gallery, Giles Waterfield, noted, many of these students seem to have been local middle-class women, rather than would-be professional artists.[10] This is not really a surprise, though, as by this time copying and drawing had become an important element of female accomplishment for well brought up girls, and a widely practised pastime for middle class women.[11]

The Dulwich Picture Gallery remained a one off. It can be seen as being run partly as a middle-class offshoot of the artistic and literary establishment. Its original collection was based on eighteenth century aristocratic tastes, now being made available to a wider, mainly middle class, audience. It certainly remains the only gallery which contains a mausoleum. It served as an important model, nevertheless, both regarding gallery building (usually positively) and administration (usually negatively). When Ruskin and Cole were directly involved with their own museum projects they ran them in a very different way, but the role of Dulwich as a catalyst was undoubtedly ground-breaking.

The founders themselves probably had mixed motives. A significant reason for founding Dulwich Picture Gallery would have been its usefulness as professional education for dealers and artists like Desenfans and Bourgois. Socially, it provided a link with the collections and social status of their aristocratic clients. Soane's biographer Gillian Darley points out that a gallery in memory of Bourgois was a "suitably defiant gesture towards the artistic establishment from two of the Royal Academy's least compliant members".[12] Desenfans was a self-made foreigner, while Soane was a prickly self-educated man from very humble origins. The founders of Dulwich Picture Gallery probably had a range of reasons for their pioneering efforts, and they probably expected a range of responses. The responses they actually got were more than likely even better than they anticipated.

Be that as it may, a mere seven years after Dulwich Picture Gallery opened to the public, its founders' original intentions for a national art collection were finally fulfilled when the National Gallery was founded in 1824. Desenfens, Bourgois and his wife would undoubtedly have approved, though probably disappointed that government funding for the National Gallery was less than generous, and space was inadequate right up to the First World War. Their own claim to fame, however, remains significant to the present day.

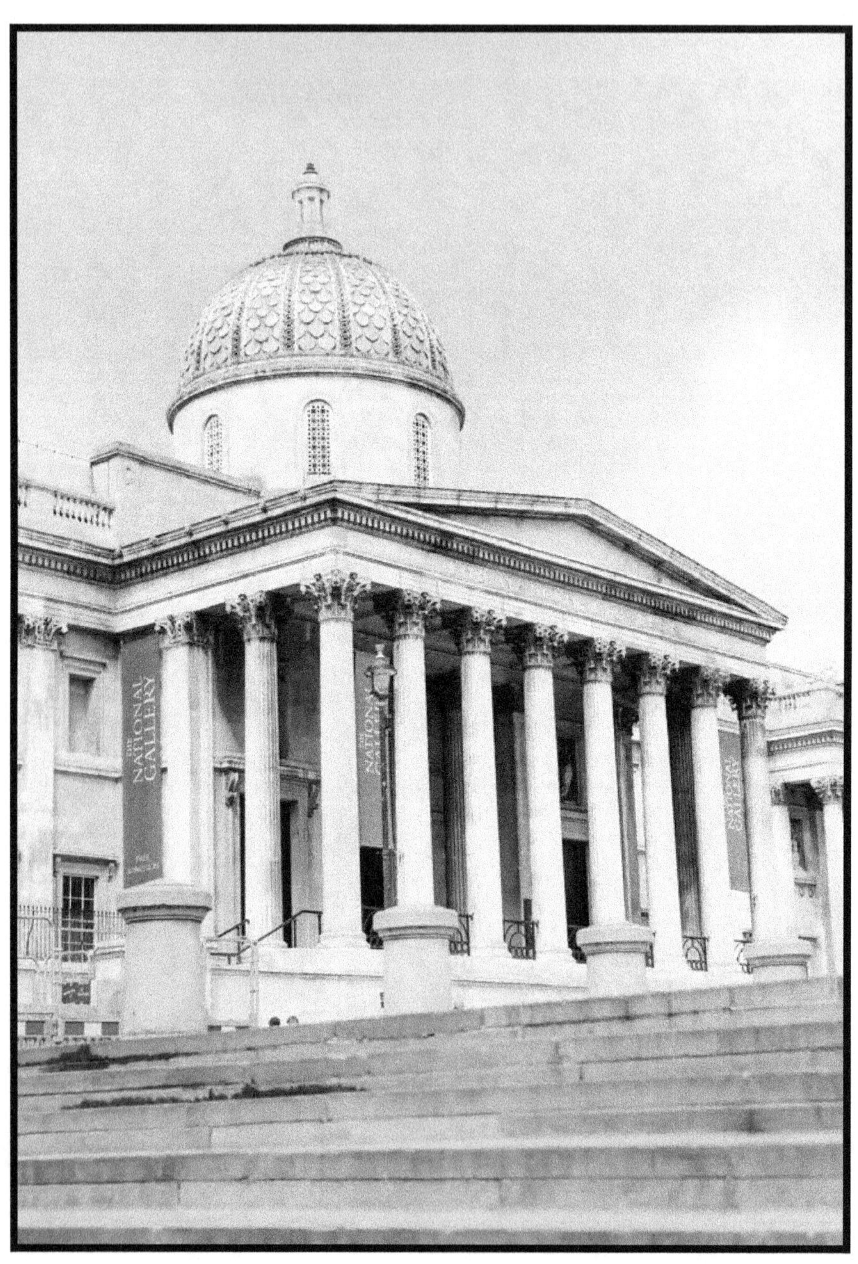

National Gallery, Trafalgar Square, London (Pexel: Yelena Odintsova)

3. Art for All

IT TOOK 46 years after John Wilkes' speech before another MP raised the matter of a national art collection. In 1823 the Whig MP George Agar Ellis proposed to Parliament that the government should buy 38 paintings from the collection of the recently deceased City businessman, John Julius Angerstein. Angerstein had been a wealthy City businessman, an immigrant from Russia whose obscure origins were the subject of much speculation. The most sensational gossip claimed that his mother was a member of the Russian royal family (several were mentioned as possible candidates), but it has to be admitted that it is highly unlikely that he really had Romanov blood.

Most probably his mother was Eva Angerstein, the wife of a St Petersburg merchant, and his father was another St Petersburg merchant, an Englishman called Andrew Thompson. In any event, it was Thompson who brought the young John Julius to England in 1749, where he thrived and became hugely successful. His early fortune was made out of investment in West Indian slave plantations, then he played a major part in developing Lloyds insurance brokers into the international institution that it became. Of course, Lloyds was also involved in the slave trade, as the insurer of slaving ships. West Indian profits funded many enterprises and affluent lifestyles at that time. Inevitably, they would permeate British cultural life too.

His social circle came to include most of the prominent men of the day. Like many members of the *nouveau riche*, he also became a very active philanthropist. But as a former slave-owner, one cause he supported might seem surprising, even bizarre.

The Committee for the Relief of the Black Poor raised funds to assist destitute West Indian and African residents of London, many of them former slaves. The Committee included both slave owners and abolitionists, the latter including the prominent Quaker banker Samuel Hoare. Many committee members were solely concerned with alleviating the distress of its clientele, mostly unemployed West African seamen and former American slaves freed for fighting for the British in the American

War of Independence. Others may have had more interest in a project to relocate as many as possible of these black Londoners to Nova Scotia and Sierra Leone, where their descendants remain to this day.

Angerstein's wealth allowed him to indulge his passion for art collecting from the 1790s onwards. This is a common interest of the newly rich, then and now, and is sometimes associated with social climbing. But Angerstein pointedly differentiated himself from the aristocracy by making his collection freely available to writers and artists. His main interest was in Old Masters, both figurative works and landscapes (he was especially fond of Claude). But he also liked eighteenth century British artists like Hogarth and Fuseli. He proudly displayed his collection at his leased private house in Pall Mall, where the paintings completely covered the walls of two rooms.

After his death, one of his influential friends, the prominent portrait painter Sir Thomas Lawrence, proposed that Parliament should buy the best of his collection at below market value. "The best" included paintings by Raphael and Hogarth's *Marriage A-la-Mode* series.

The proposal gained the support of the successful landscape painter Sir George Beaumont, one of the founders of the British Institution. Beaumont offered to add 16 paintings from his own collection, on condition that the government bought the Angerstein paintings, and provided a suitable building for their display. His hope was that a national art collection and gallery would improve public taste.

Beaumont's support was highly significant, because he was a pivotal figure in the art world of the day. Not only was he a highly regarded artist who exhibited at the Royal Academy for over 30 years, he also presented the Academy with its most prized possession, Michelangelo's bas relief the *Taddeo Tondo*. His own collection consisted of Old Masters, but he supported living artists like David Wilkie, and allowed Constable to study his collection.

Purely by coincidence, just as these proposals were being put forward, public funds became available because of the unexpected repayment of an Austrian war debt. This fortuitous combination of events persuaded Parliament to end its resistance to funding a national gallery at long last, and the paintings were purchased in 1824, along with the lease of Angerstein's house in Pall Mall to display them.

This was a good start, but the Pall Mall house was not really big enough to display the pictures properly. Because of this, and because the lease on Angerstein's house was running out, there was agreement all round that a new purpose-built building was needed. A site on Trafalgar Square was chosen, on the former location of the King's Mews. This was an excellent choice, as it was at the heart of London's new commercial, governmental and residential quarters, but also within reach of the poor in the East End.

The new National Gallery eventually opened in 1837 and was immediately a huge hit with the public. Around 400 000 visitors a year entered its doors in its first few decades, rising to around 900 000 a year from the 1870s to the end of the century.

What this enthusiastic public saw as it approached the Gallery was a façade based on a Greek temple. By this time the classical style was not just a reference to upper class education and culture, as at Dulwich. It also referenced Britain's growing imperial power - Britain as the new Rome, the Thames as the new Tiber. The National Gallery evoked the military success of Rome as much as the cultural success of Greece.

Unfortunately, in spite of the grandiloquent associations of its architecture, the new building by no means solved the space problem, especially as it was originally shared with the Royal Academy. It has been pointed out that behind the imposing frontage "the only space appropriate to a grand civic building was the Great Hall".[13] All in all, the relatively small size of the National Gallery collection at its foundation, and Parliament's initially penny-pinching attitude towards the Gallery's funding, added up to a rather half-hearted cultural effort from what was, after all, the richest and most powerful nation in the world at the time.

Nevertheless, the new gallery did represent a significant increase in public space. It was an important part of the nineteenth-century growth in public cultural facilities which helped to develop a wider a sense of citizenship – not just art galleries, but libraries, museums and parks too.

In spite of the huge visitor numbers, the initial staffing levels were minimal. The Keeper had to do most of the work, under the direction of the Trustees, who did not meet often. But the Gallery was always available to students to copy paintings, then regarded as an important part of art training.

The National Gallery's popularity was at least in part because it was deliberately different in scope and intention from Dulwich Picture Gallery. In the words of its parliamentary sponsor George Ellis: "there must be no sending for tickets – no asking permission – no shutting it up half the days in the week; its doors must always be open, without fee or reward; accessible, and conveniently accessible, to all ranks and degrees of men, to the indolent as well as the busy – to the idle as well as the industrious."

This ambition was much more daring than it sounds today. Because of the French Revolution and numerous instances of social unrest at home - two serious London riots in the eighteenth century, and naval mutinies and arson attacks more recently - the middle classes often saw the masses as unruly and destructive. The Tory MP Robert Inglis, for example, was convinced a National Gallery would not work because the people would destroy what they could not understand. In practice, the early visitors to the National Gallery were perfectly respectful of the paintings.[14]

The National Gallery was a public enterprise which belatedly followed a continental model. But its foundation followed a very different trajectory from the foundation of continental national galleries. The Louvre was a royal collection in a royal palace, made public by a revolutionary act. Like many continental galleries, it appropriated ceremonial space associated with wealth and privilege for the benefit of a wider society.[15] The space originally used for the National Gallery, however, was hardly "ceremonial" in the public sense; it had been the leased home of a wealthy middle-class businessman, not a site of demonstrations of aristocratic power. The permanent home of the collection was specially built, not the takeover of a palace, and was originally the cramped location for fewer than 40 pictures.

But to most of its advocates the National Gallery was not intended to be a grand national statement. It was seen as an improving space, where the working man could take his leisure with his family, alongside his betters.[16] The Radical MP Joseph Hume enthused that easier access to works of art "would still further change the public character, and tend to produce a higher taste for art, and introduce a purer class of enjoyments".

The National Gallery was seen as one element in the fight against drinking, cruel sports, and political extremism. Not that many concessions were made to the limited prior knowledge of the working class – labels were not introduced to the gallery until after 1856. Fortunately, Joseph Hume himself recognised this and produced cheap visitor guides which were invaluable to the less educated.

Labels or no labels, visitor numbers continued to be very high. Over a million were recorded in 1851, 1877 and 1880. (Though by 1898 numbers had fallen to under half a million, and they did not reach the levels of the 1880s again until after the Second World War).[17]

Gallery Keeper Thomas Unwins gave evidence to Parliament in 1853 which demonstrated the mass appeal of the Gallery, even if visitor behaviour was not always deemed appropriate: "I saw some people, who seemed to be country people, who had a basket of provisions, and who drew their chairs round and sat down, and seemed to make themselves very comfortable; they had meat and drink; and when I suggested to them the impropriety of such a proceeding in such a place, they were very good-humoured, and a lady offered me a glass of gin, and wished me to partake of what they had provided."

This popularity was not without its problems. Middle class people like the German pioneer art historian Gustav von Waagen, who visited in 1853, were sometimes so repelled by the odour of the working class visitors that they cut their visit short.[18] In the same year, the painter William Dyce stated that although he supported general access to works of art, he felt this was taken to extremes in Britain, as compared to continental galleries where the "common people" were admitted less frequently.[19]

On the other hand, Charles Kingsley, the popular writer of the children's book *The Water Babies*, saw the gallery as an escape from the reality of metropolitan life. He wrote lyrically in 1848 that:

> "…picture galleries should be the townsman's paradise of refreshment…in the space of a single room, the townsman may take a country walk…beyond the grim city world…into the world of beautiful things".

The essayist William Hazlett also compared a gallery visit to a journey, enthusing in 1824 (when the gallery was still in Pall Mall) that a visit to this "sanctuary", this "holy of holies" was "like going on a pilgrimage – it is an Act of devotion performed at the shrine of Art!"[20]

The way the pictures were displayed was very cluttered by modern standards. In the National Gallery's original home, two rooms in Angerstein's former home, the walls had been crowded with "picturesque" symmetrical displays. Typically this involved large paintings placed in the middle of a group, usually flanked by two full length portraits, with the remainder of the wall space filled with smaller landscapes and genre works. When the Gallery moved to Trafalgar Square, the displays were initially just as crowded.

There was nothing unusual in this kind of display. Royal Academy exhibitions also followed this pattern, even after the Academy moved out of the Trafalgar Square building to Somerset House in 1868 (subsequently moving again to its current location in Piccadilly).

This arrangement meant that paintings were not shown isolated as individual objects, as they usually are today, nor was there a fixed viewing position. Some felt this did not do the pictures justice: in 1847 the art critic John Ruskin (newly famous for *Modern Painters*) called for all pictures to be at eye level. Galleries, he said, should be long enough to hang the paintings in one line, and wide enough to see the largest pictures at the proper distance. However desirable, it was many decades before this became common practice.

As for the walls on which the pictures were hung, originally they were olive. A greenish grey was typical at the time, both green and grey being seen as neutral, although the stronger effect of red was becoming popular and was used in Dulwich Picture Gallery and the new London commercial galleries.

Initially, there was no acquisitions policy. Paintings were bought at the whim of the Trustees, who met infrequently. As more paintings were acquired, the original overcrowding of the National Gallery became so severe that the 1847 Vernon bequest of British paintings failed to find a home in the building. They had to be displayed first in Vernon's house, and then at the government-owned Marlborough House. When Marlborough House was allocated to the Prince of Wales in 1859, the paintings were moved again to the South Kensington Museum (as the Victoria and Albert Museum was then known). They are no doubt thankful that they have been allowed to repose there peacefully ever since.

Things began to change when Charles Eastlake became Keeper in 1843. Two years later, he boldly stated his belief that: "Every specimen of art in a national collection should, perhaps, be assumed to be fit to challenge inspection, and to be worthy of being well displayed." In other words, whim should give way to foresight and agreed standards. Eastlake gave much thought to the best methods of lighting and the way the pictures were hung. Influenced by contemporary scientific investigation of human perception, he was also much exercised by the best colour for the walls of the Gallery. But little changed – for example, Eastlake did not manage to persuade the Trustees to change the colour scheme until 1853 (with a redecoration in deep red flock paper).

Eastlake's background as a successful practising artist, his many roles within the art establishment, and his influential writing about art made him eminently suitable for his position at the National Gallery. However, he decided to resign to concentrate on his writing. He married Elizabeth, a formidable art historian in her own right, their successful marriage creating a strong working partnership.

Eastlake nevertheless returned in triumph as the National Gallery's first Director in 1855. By then, the National Gallery had 265 paintings, a big increase in 30 years, but only a fifth of the number in the Louvre. The paintings reflected the hierarchy of art which had been laid down by Joshua Reynolds in his *Discourses on Art*, a collection of lectures he gave to the Royal Academy from 1768 to 1790. Italian art of the fifteenth and sixteenth centuries was held in the highest esteem, because it reflected an idealised view of nature, an art which required intellect as well as technical skill. Dutch landscape and still life art was popular, but its exact representation of nature was regarded as straightforward copying, requiring great technical skill but allegedly little intellect (later generations were to dispute that assessment). Furthermore, it usually dealt in the everyday, rather than the grand themes of much Italian art. Portraiture was also tainted by its association with mere "copying", although Reynolds himself did much to raise its status.

During his ten years as Director, Eastlake both drastically modified that view of art and introduced a series of technical innovations. He ensured pictures were labelled with the title of the work and the artist. He commissioned scholarly catalogues. More fundamentally, he adopted the principles of German art history. This was under the influence of his friend Gustav von Waagen, who had reported to a Parliamentary Select Committee as far back as 1836 that "An historical arrangement, following the spirit of the times and the genius of artists, would produce a harmonious influence upon the mind of the spectator." Art should no longer be judged by a universal standard but in the context of its time and place.

Inspired by this viewpoint, Eastlake wanted to form a representative collection of the history of western European paintings, and was particularly keen to fill the gaps. These were mainly in Northern European works, but also in Italian works of the early Renaissance and eighteenth-century paintings. He was able to persuade the Treasury to give him the princely sum of £10,000 a year for acquisitions. Now that he had the wherewithal to put his ideas into practice, he travelled widely on the continent in search of suitable works and bought over 150. The scope of the collection widened considerably, one result being that the Italian collection could now hold its own with the best in the world.

German thought was also highly influential in the other major change in attitudes to art. The Romantic Movement, which originated in Germany, saw art as a vehicle for the artist's unique individuality. As the historian and philosopher Thomas Carlyle, a famous admirer of the Germans, taught: "Let each one become all that he was created capable of being." From the mid-nineteenth century, works of art became thought of as the unique creations of a unique personality. The best art could reach each individual viewer directly on a deep spiritual level.

In spite of the unique individuality of art, art historians like von Waagen thought that art history could develop ways of systematically studying and mapping art practice. There was a new appreciation of the diversity of styles, and differing developments though time and place. Art was no longer judged by comparison with a fixed ideal. All these ideas permeated the more cultivated parts of the general public, which encouraged acceptance of Eastlake's approach.

Lighting was an area where Eastlake did not fully agree with von Waagen. Top lighting was usual for art galleries, but Waagen recommended lighting from the left, as this was thought to be usual in artists' studios. Eastlake himself thought different paintings required different lighting, particularly as the various schools of art tended to have their own preferences for the size of paintings, but this was not practical.

Wall colour came up again in 1861, when there was a scheme to redecorate rooms in different colours to reflect the qualities of different schools, but this was not implemented. The walls remained a deep red. The crowding also remained until 1887 when a new wing was opened which provided seven additional rooms. Finally, it was now possible to arrange a single row display.

In 1856, however, the overcrowding remained, and it affected the astonishingly convoluted way the National Gallery dealt with the 1,000 oil paintings, watercolours and drawings it received from the Turner bequest. Turner had wanted the finished paintings in his bequest to be displayed in their own room at the National Gallery, except two which were to be displayed next to a pair of Claude paintings to demonstrate that he was of the same standing. Turner's relatives disputed the will but those two paintings went to the National Gallery and were displayed as he wished (and still are). The will was resolved in 1856, when all the art works were given to the nation and the relatives were awarded the rest of the estate. Lack of space meant the other Turner works were displayed at Marlborough House in Pall Mall. When this building was given to the Prince of Wales, they were moved to the South Kensington Museum to join the Vernon collection.

The question of the Turner bequest had not been resolved by the time Eastlake died on one of his Italian buying trips, on Christmas Eve 1865. He bequeathed 26 of his own paintings to the National Gallery. Eventually, a decade after Eastlake's death, the completion of an extension to the National Gallery building in 1876 meant Turner's finished paintings could be displayed as a separate collection. Finally, Turner had his wish.

But by then the idea had been planted that Old Master and British works were to be displayed separately. When lack of space continued to be a problem as the collection grew, it therefore seemed natural that the bulk of the Turner bequest should move again when the Tate Gallery of British art came into existence (though some works remained in Trafalgar Square). It is difficult to imagine the French being quite so cavalier with the works of one of their most highly esteemed artists. (In fact, it is difficult to think of any other nationality behaving like this – maybe it was one of Wilkes' English "characteristics".)

Though they did not match the significance of the Turner bequest, the National Gallery hugely benefitted from other outstanding donations up to the First World War. One was from the Royal family: Prince Albert had acquired 100 German, Italian and Netherlandish works as a result of a loan default. On his death Queen Victoria offered the collection to the nation, and 25 of the works went to the National Gallery. Another was a lot of 77 mainly Dutch and Flemish works which were donated in 1871, from the collection of the late Prime Minister, Sir Robert Peel. A third was from the Reverend William Hollwell Car, a lifelong collector lucky enough to marry an heiress (and vicar of a parish in Cornwall which he never visited), who bequeathed 35 works.

It was fortunate that in 1907 five new galleries were created, when the barracks at the rear of the gallery were demolished. Otherwise, how would the two major donations made in 1909 have been housed? The industrial chemist Sir Ludwig Mond, founder of Imperial Chemical Industries (ICI), bequeathed 42 works. Art collector George Salting may have been less well known, but he bequeathed 192 paintings, 31 of which were subsequently given to the Tate Gallery. (He also bequeathed artefacts to the British Museum and the Victoria and Albert Museum.)

By the time of the eve of the First World War, the future of the National Gallery was thus on a reasonably sound footing, but its elite position in Britain's male-dominated cultural life made it a target for suffragette militancy.[21] The attack by the Canadian suffragette Mary Richardson on the Gallery's Velasquez painting known as the "Rokeby Venus" in March 1914 is by far the most famous. Contemporary reports say that she produced what was described as a "chopper", and attacked the painting by breaking the glass and repeatedly slashing the painting until she was restrained and arrested. It was a protest against the imprisonment of prominent suffragette Emmeline Pankhurst, on hunger strike in Holloway at the time.

The painting had a high profile because it had been saved for the nation by the National Art Collections Fund (now the Art Fund). The Fund had been set up in 1903 in response to growing concern at the number of paintings being sold abroad by members of the aristocracy, in financial difficulties because of falling agricultural prices. The Fund raised £46,000 by public subscription, bought the painting, and presented it to the Gallery in 1906.

The painting's iconic status ensured huge publicity for Richardson's act, but also meant she gained little sympathy for her protest. *The Times* reported that Richardson set the value of the painting against the value of a life by saying "You can get another picture, but you cannot get another life, you are killing Mrs Pankhurst." No doubt an additional motive was that the Venus represented a typically patriarchal view of femininity – a beautiful, passive young woman. Richardson said much later "I didn't like the way men gaped at it all day."

The National Gallery, the National Portrait Gallery, the Wallace Collection, the Guildhall Art Gallery in the City, Hampton Court and Windsor Castle all closed temporarily in response to the attack.

Later in the same year there was another attack at the National Gallery, on five paintings by Giovanni and Gentile Bellini. Again, the National Gallery was closed, and it only reopened at the declaration of war when the movement's leader Mrs Pankhurst declared that suffragette militancy was over.

The National Gallery was not the first gallery to be the target of suffragette protest. There had been a (rather tremulous) cry of protest at the opening of an extension of Leicester Art Gallery in 1912. In 1913 the glass of thirteen of the most famous paintings in Manchester Art Gallery was smashed, damaging four of the paintings beneath. In the same year, Millais' portrait of Carlyle in the National Portrait Gallery was attacked. Paintings were also attacked at the 1914 Royal Academy exhibition.

In a startlingly gender-specific response, many galleries were closed to women, while others closed completely just before the First World War. Another attack led Birmingham Art Gallery to introduce a "no muffs, wrist-bags or sticks" rule, and other galleries brought in similar restrictions. As a precaution, photographs of well-known suffragettes were circulated to gallery staff throughout the country. In Hull Art Gallery, a painting by the anti-suffrage Lord Leighton was taken down, though there seems to have been no specific threat.

Militant suffragettes also carried out a number of arson attacks, but art galleries were a particular target because violence against the paintings could lead to the closure of galleries and affect income from tourism. It also helped that most suffragettes were middle class ladies whose presence in an art gallery would not, initially, attract suspicion. Although the militancy was effective in publicising the suffragist cause, it was counter-productive in terms of public opinion and the movement ceased art gallery attacks completely after 1914, no doubt to the acute relief of all staff and visitors.

Were Wilkes in a position to take stock in 1914, he would surely have felt that the first part of his vision – the state encouragement of the polite arts – had come into being, if not with full-throated enthusiasm on the state's part. Even better, the second part of his vision – art as inspiration for the better design of manufactured goods – had also come to pass, not only with equal success but to keen international interest. But it was a development so fragmented it made the National Gallery's stuttering progress seem like a model of forward planning. The next chapter tells the story.

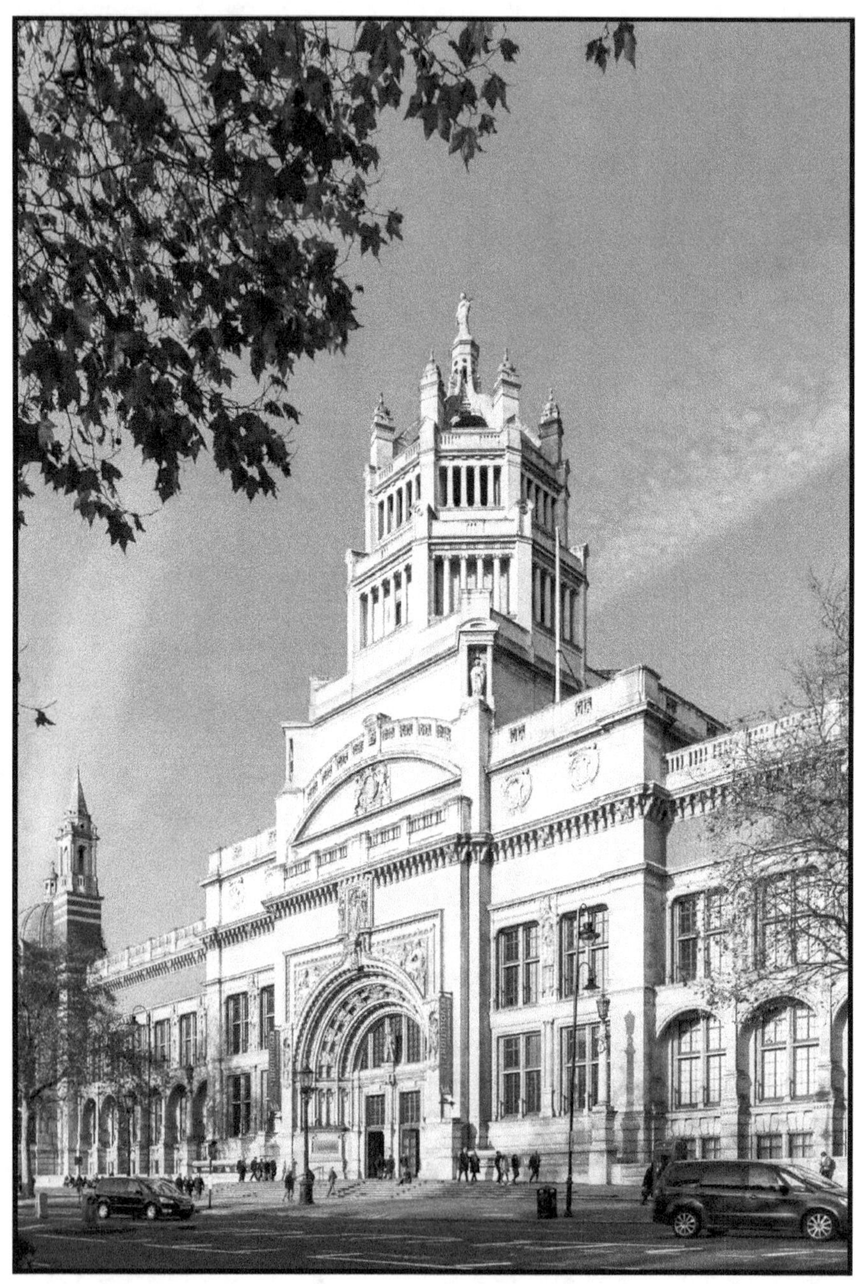

The façade of the Victoria & Albert Museum is designed to impress

4. Improving Industrial Design

WHAT (EVENTUALLY) ENDED up as the world's largest museum of the decorative arts came about through a combination of the profits made by the 1851 Great Exhibition and the energy of one of the most successful bureaucrats England ever produced. But it was not a smooth process. The late Giles Waterfield, historian of public art galleries and former Director of Dulwich Picture Gallery, described it in pretty trenchant terms:

> "In architecture terms, the vast building demonstrates to an almost ludicrous degree the refusal of British officialdom to conceive of the grand or comprehensive approach in dealing with building projects."[22]

And, on the whole, he had a point.

The energetic bureaucrat who got what was originally known as the South Kensington Museum off the ground was Henry Cole. He had a varied and distinguished career before his involvement with what was later renamed the Victoria and Albert Museum. He rose from humble clerk in the Record Commission to the Assistant Keeper of the new Public Records Office. He had an important role in the development of the Penny Post as assistant to Rowland Hill from 1847 to 1850. Under the pseudonym of Felix Summerly, he was a prize-winning designer and a successful children's writer.

Perhaps his most intriguing connection is with the introduction of the Christmas card. In fact he sent the very first Christmas card in 1843. The reformation of the British postal system and introduction of a uniform Penny Post service led to many people sending seasonal greetings through the post on decorated letterheads and visiting cards. The Victoria and Albert Museum website relates how the Cole household was inundated with unanswered mail at Christmas, so Cole came up with a timesaving solution.

He got his friend, artist John Callcott Horsley, to illustrate a design for a printed card. Horsley's illustration showed the extended Cole family raising a toast, surrounded by decorative trelliswork and scenes of charitable giving. A thousand cards were printed and posted, signed individually. The cards were also offered for sale, but they were quite expensive and did not sell particularly well. However, attitudes changed, the commercialisation of Christmas took off, and Cole's innovation ended up spreading over most of the globe.

But his greatest legacy arose out of his passion to improve the quality of mass-produced items for the rapidly expanding consumer market.

Cole obtained the backing of Queen Victoria's consort, Prince Albert, to set up the Royal Society for the Encouragement of the Arts, Manufactures and Commerce (RSA). With Albert as patron, he set up an Exhibition of Arts and Manufactures in 1847, with follow up exhibitions in 1848 and 1849. His keen eye noticed that the highly successful Paris Exhibition of 1849 did not have international exhibits, a gap which he was determined the RSA should fill. With Queen Victoria's support, he established a Commission to set up an international exhibition, with Albert as President. The resultant Great Exhibition of the Works of Industry of All Nations, held in Hyde Park in 1851, was an enormous international success, and made an equally enormous profit of £186,000.

In the meantime, Prince Albert had his own ambitions. Even while the Great Exhibition was still open, he had dreamed of "A College of Arts and Manufacturers". This would be a group of institutions which covered a wide range of educational objectives linked to the improvement of industrial design. Albert wanted to introduce Britain to the idea of learning through objects; now he had the means to put his idea into practice.

The Royal Commission which oversaw the Great Exhibition was made permanent, "to increase the means of industrial education and expand the influence of science and art upon productive industry". Prince Albert was at the head of the project, supported by Henry Cole and the painter William Dyce. Cole's objective was "to assemble a splendid collection of objects representing the application of fine arts to manufacture".[23]

The project bore fruit only a year after the Exhibition closed, at Marlborough House on Pall Mall. Built for the Duke of Marlborough and designed by Christopher Wren, Marlborough House had been taken over by the Crown in 1817. In 1852 two bodies concerned with industrial design were established in the building: the Museum of Manufactures (renamed the Museum of Ornamental Arts the following year), and the National Art Training School.

When the building was assigned to the Prince of Wales four years later, both institutions moved to a site in South Kensington which had already been bought by the Commissioners of the Great Exhibition. Thus began the South Kensington Museum, and, after 75 years, the fulfilment of John Wilkes' dream of an institution devoted to improving the artistic quality of manufactured goods. Cole became its first Director in 1857, serving until his retirement in 1873.

It has to be borne in mind that in the nineteenth century English education was run by a bewildering range of local and national bodies, a situation which was not tidied up until the Board of Education was formed in 1899. At the time, it was not assumed (as it probably would nowadays) that higher education had to take place in a university. Running an avowedly educational programme through a collection of objects in a museum fitted into this organisational kaleidoscope more easily than it might today.

South Kensington had already been seen as a suitable locale for a major cultural institution. There had been calls to move the National Gallery to South Kensington, as some saw the Trafalgar Square location as being too attractive to casual visitors who were not really interested in art. Others claimed the "miasma" from working class crowds damaged the pictures. South Kensington was far enough from the East End to filter out the "less desirable" elements.[24] That proposal came to nothing, but now an institution which would come to rival the National Gallery's prestige did arrive well to the west of central London. In 1897 its name was changed to the Victoria and Albert Museum, in honour of Queen Victoria's Golden Jubilee.

The subsequent history of the South Kensington Museum is highly complicated and fraught with bureaucratic red tape, inadequate funding and overcrowding. In the end, all this was more or less successfully disguised behind a façade which made it look as if it had always been intended to turn out as a fine example of solid impressiveness. But there was a long and rocky road before that happy conclusion.

Perhaps, then, it is not entirely inappropriate that the first step was relatively unsuccessful. Prince Albert personally designed the first structure of the new Museum, a huge cast iron building which housed two two-story galleries. Unfortunately, it turned out that although Albert had many excellent qualities building development was not one of them. The roof leaked, there was poor drainage and insulation – and the galleries soon acquired the derogatory nickname of the "Brompton Boilers" because of their industrial look.

A temporary building was then put up for the School of Ornamental Art. This time it was designed by a professional architect, overseen by Captain Francis Fowke of the Royal Engineers. Captain Fowke's contribution to the development of the South Kensington Museum is probably second only to Henry Cole. His concern for forward planning and what would nowadays be called customer service was invaluable in building public support for the new venture.

Great strides were made between 1856 and 1861. Fowke was responsible for the Sheepshanks Gallery, built to house the Sheepshanks Collection of British art, the first bequest to the Museum. Sheepshanks was a wealthy cloth manufacturer who passionately believed that art and beauty improved the people, spiritually and mentally. He left 233 paintings and 259 drawings to the nation, which included works by Blake, Landseer, Millais and Turner.

The exterior of the two-storey building had decorative brickwork and depictions of famous artists and architects. The lower storey contained objects from the existing collections while Sheepshanks' paintings were on the upper floor. The top lighting and coving were designed to illuminate the walls while avoiding glare, and gas lighting was installed. This latter was highly significant, as it meant the gallery could open in the evenings, allowing the "working man" access after work. Unlike the Brompton Boilers, this innovation received much praise in the press. The interior was deliberately non-palatial, with plain sage green walls and sturdy red tile floors.

According to Cole, Sheepshanks had "an abhorrence of trustees; he dislikes the noise and crowd and clatter...of Trafalgar Square". He thought the National Gallery did not do justice to British painting, and wanted his collection to be shown in a decent building near the parks. Later donors to the South Kensington Museum had similar motives.

Fowke added refreshment rooms, making the Museum the first to offer this service on site. They were promptly called "hideously ugly" (unfortunate for a body dedicated to good design) but no doubt its patrons were more than willing to put up with that for the sake of a rest and a cup of tea.

With these buildings in place, the Museum officially opened in 1857 as the South Kensington Museum. Fowke went on to design a gallery to house the Vernon and Turner bequests, and another gallery to house paintings the National Gallery was unable to accommodate. With the Sheepshanks gallery, these three buildings formed three sides of a square, the square being completed in 1861 by a building housing the Museum's own art collection (a welcome escape from the Brompton Boilers). This arrangement meant that as the Museum's collections expanded Fowke was able to roof over the square to make additional galleries.

The Vernon bequest was a collection of paintings Robert Vernon had bequeathed to the nation in 1847, with the intention of establishing a national collection of British art. (This did not actually happen until the establishment of the Tate Gallery 50 years later.) Vernon's paintings were originally consigned to the basement of the National Gallery. They were then moved to Marlborough House, but lost that home on the reassignment of the building in 1856. So they finally ended up in the South Kensington Museum.

The Vernon bequest shared a gallery with the Turner bequest, which was also in need of a new home. On his death Turner left all finished and unfinished work still in his possession to the nation, with the proviso that two of his works be shown next to paintings by Claude Lorraine in the National Gallery. This was duly carried out (the four paintings are still displayed together), but lack of space meant the rest of the bequest was originally kept with the National Gallery's British collection at Marlborough House. Following a ruling upholding Turner's wish that his completed works be shown together at the National Gallery, his finished paintings moved again to the National Gallery at Trafalgar Square, but the rest of his bequest was allocated to the South Kensington Museum.

Accordingly, in 1858 work started on a new temporary gallery for the Vernon and Turner bequests next to the Sheepshanks Gallery, and like that gallery it was built by the Royal Engineers. Both the exterior and the interior were purely practical, the interior being similar to the Sheepshanks gallery. An unforeseen complication arose because the paintings from these two collections actually belonged to the National Gallery. Initially, the National Gallery insisted the communicating door between the new gallery and the Sheepshanks Gallery be kept locked so that their pictures would be approached by a separate entrance. It took considerable pressure to make it relinquish this ludicrous position. In the end, this "temporary" gallery became permanent and is still there, though the paintings no longer remain.

For ten years from 1863, Fowke was able to implement his master plan, a rare luxury in British gallery history. This included on site staff accommodation and new art schools on the top floors. A lecture theatre was completed in 1869 and became the southern entrance. Unlike other parts of the complex, the lecture theatre was a showpiece of elaborate design. It contained a staircase designed by Frank Moody, Master of the School of Design, and his students, which was decorated with intricate ceramic paintings. The Museum economised on its mosaic floor by having its mosaic pieces cut by women in Woking Jail – a rather backhanded tribute to female craftsmanship. The final touch must have been especially satisfying - the completed lecture theatre turned out to have almost perfect acoustics.

Another Refreshment Room was built, notable for being the first major commission for William Morris' company. It is still in use, and is the practical embodiment of Morris' Arts and Crafts movement. Its striking stained-glass windows are by Edward Burne-Jones and Phillip Webb. The tiles were painted by ladies at the School of Design – this was ground-breaking, as it was highly unusual for women to get that kind of training at all, never mind being given a public commission. Fowke even made sure that visitors could have breakfast when the Museum opened at 9am. But it has to be admitted that although there were first- and second-class menus, the food was not cheap.

In the 1860s the unloved Brompton Boilers were moved to Bethnal Green Museum, the Museum's offshoot in the East End. Part of the vacated site was used for an Architectural Court, which included casts of huge monumental pieces like Trajan's Column in Rome. The leading Victorian painter Millais was of the opinion that these rooms should "be made not to assert themselves" as he felt the works spoke for themselves. His view was ignored, however, as the Court was highly decorated. In 1873 Science Schools were built, in a similar showpiece style to the lecture theatre.

This is only some of the piecemeal building work that went on. So what were the buildings intended to exhibit? It is important to note that art was only one aspect of the Museum's educational functions in its early days. Prince Albert's vision had encompassed all sorts of scientific and artistic interests. The final format of "Albertopolis" (as it came to be known) followed this vision closely and included many different institutions.

These days, it is difficult to appreciate just how many scientific institutions were originally included in the South Kensington Museum. This is partly because some of them, such as the School of Naval Architecture, moved to other sites. But also because many of these scientific and technical bodies are nowadays within Imperial College, and the Science Museum contains within itself a number of bodies like the Patent Museum.

But although the art collection was only part of a much larger educational enterprise, it was always an important part of the museum's activities. It even housed the National Portrait Gallery from 1865 to 1885, one of the many stops on that institution's journey to its final resting place at Trafalgar Square.

The most distinctive part of the South London Museum's art collection, however, was not so much its paintings but its sculpture. The Museum "benefitted" from the fact that the National Gallery did not include sculpture. Not only did the South Kensington Museum acquire sculpture from 1844, it became the place to house donated sculpture, just as it did for donated British art. It also actively sought out sculpture. The Museum purchased the Gherandini collection of sculptors' models in 1854, sculpture from the Soulage collection in 1856, and the Gigli-Campana collection of Italian sculpture in 1861. The efforts of curator J C Robinson in the latter half of the nineteenth century eventually created a collection of Italian sculpture unrivalled outside Italy.

Other kinds of sculpture were also strongly represented. A large collection of medieval ivories was built up by the 1860s, bought through London dealer John Webb. J H Fitzhenry gifted Romanesque and Gothic sculpture between 1906 and 1910. The Salting Bequest of 1910 added important bronzes and ivories. Rodin's gift of eighteen of his sculptures in 1914 was housed in the Museum, establishing it as an important site for the study of his work.

From the beginning, the Museum had plaster casts of well-known sculptures, as drawing from casts was then an important part of art training. Casts had been collected by the government's School of Design since 1841, and 1,551 examples were taken over by the Museum when it opened in Marlborough House. The Museum also took over on loan the cast collection of the Architectural Museum. (The collection was sent to the Architectural Museum building in 1869, but came back to South Kensington in 1916.) In 1861 3,000 casts of Gothic architecture, produced as models for carvers of the Houses of Parliament in the1830s, were given to the Museum.

The Museum itself created casts, when J C Robinson arranged for a programme of cast reproductions of famous sculpture on the Continent, covering the Italian Renaissance, medieval German sculpture, and Spanish works.

It had always been difficult to display these casts effectively, so a special building to house them was built, consisting of two large rooms called the Cast Court, which opened in 1873. Because of changes in art training methods, plaster casts went out of fashion after the First World War, but interest has revived, especially as some casts now preserve the image of works which have been destroyed, or damaged irreparably by pollution.

Nevertheless, highly significant as these collections were, the science exhibits were just as important in the early days, and the South Kensington Museum was not an art gallery in the modern sense. In fact, until the end of the century it was not even a museum as understood today, that is, an institution whose first priority is to acquire, safeguard and use a permanent collection. Its Annual Report of 1877 (four years after Cole retired) lists its priorities as: (i) instruction in science and industry; (ii) instruction in drawing and fine art applied to industry; (iii) running the museum complex, including the Bethnal Green offshoot; (iv) the Geological Survey; (v) supporting learned societies. It was not run by Trustees like the National Gallery but was a department of government which grew out of the School of Design, which had been established in 1836. Henry Cole had been appointed to reform the School, and it became part of the new Department of Practical Art in 1852 under the Board of Trade.

Another departure from modern sensibilities is that some collections, like fish hatcheries (visitors could watch salmon and trout hatching), seem wildly inappropriate in a design museum, but in those days all kinds of things came and went constantly. The history of the South Kensington Museum is not so much a steady progress toward a museum of art and design, but more like a bazaar or emporium, with new products arriving and departing all the time. It was more akin to the fluidity of a school's academic curriculum over time as needs change and develop than an activity aimed at building a coherent permanent collection. The eventual siting of the arts museum on one side of the Exhibition Road, near the Royal College of Art, and the science museums on the west side, near Imperial College, is a clear sign of the strongly educational purpose of this project, under the control of a branch of the civil service and guided by government policy of the day.

The government link had a big effect on the Museum's priorities. It was committed to purposeful activities consciously directed at its intended audience. Prince Albert founded the leading programme for advanced training in chemistry within the Museum. In 1879 the India Office collection was turned over to the Museum (as noted later, this has now become problematic). Cole boasted that "There is no university in the world where one can learn so much about India." (Cole himself never attended a university.) Rooms were made available to learned societies in the evenings. The Art School "had a collection to which the public was also admitted". South Kensington Museum was full of thousands of students, including the areas open to the public. Originally, Cole was only in charge of the arts side, but eventually he was head of both art and science activities. The art schools, the science schools and the collections were not disentangled until 1899.

The museum's explicitly educational purpose was to improve the design of goods produced by skilled artisans and smaller manufacturers (in effect, the upper working class and lower middle class). As such, it was run very differently from the National Gallery. A report of 1858, referring to the highly successful experiment of opening the museum in the evenings, commented that this had been done in order "to ascertain practically what hours are most convenient to the working classes." The report made the important point that "It would appear to be less for the rich that the State should provide public galleries of painting and objects of art and science, than for those classes who would be absolutely destitute of the enjoyment of them unless they were provided by the State". It turned out that evening visitors had exceeded daytime ones by a margin of five to one; a survey revealed only a relatively small proportion had visited the National Gallery.

As the displays were intended to be studied as a means to improve industrial design, rather than having a direct moral effect on individual behaviour, this museum can be seen as more explicitly secular than the National Gallery. It was certainly an effective expression both of the Utilitarian question "What use is it?" and of the industrial spirit of the age.

"Old King" Cole (as he was popularly known) was a committed Utilitarian and a close friend of John Stewart Mill. It was Cole's vision of the museum as an educational force that worked through the study of material objects that was so attractive in the United States and throughout the British Empire. What was admired and copied by museums like the Metropolitan in New York was not South Kensington's collecting ethos, but its usefulness, its educational vision. Cole was intent on providing a practical learning tool, an offer which was enthusiastically taken up by a significant section of the lower classes.

Meanwhile, the collections grew continuously through purchases and gifts. One of the most notable later donors was Constantine Ionides (born in 1833). He was the son of Alexander Ionides, a successful businessman who was an art patron and friend of leading artists like Whistler and Rossetti. He had a long connection to the leading Victorian painter G F Watts, who painted five generations of the family. Both father and son were keen art collectors. Constantine was also a successful businessman, and like his father he maintained links with the art world at his Holland Park residence.

Constantine's wide-ranging art collection covered Old Masters, seventeenth-century works, nineteenth-century French works, and contemporary British art. He bequeathed all his pictures (except family portraits), etchings, drawings and engravings to the South Kensington Museum. He stipulated that the bequest was to be kept as a separate collection. The works were not to be lent and were to be framed and glazed at the Museum's expense "so that students there can easily see them". In 1901 the Museum received 1,138 pictures, drawings and prints, with a further 20 added on the death of his widow in 1920.

Although the audience for the scientific exhibits grew from 150,000 in

1884 to 260,000 in 1888, in the end the arts side triumphed on the original (and current) site on Exhibition Road. The National Art Training School and the separate Female School of Art (often referred to as the South Kensington Schools) were primarily teacher training colleges. Students included the artist Luke Fildes and the landscape gardener Gertrude Jekyll. When they separated from the Museum in 1896 to become the Royal College of Art, the emphasis changed to the practice of art and design. The science also moved out, across the road to the science museums.

The indefatigable Cole continued to play a role in the establishment of South Kensington institutions, notably Imperial College and the Royal College of Music. His efforts on behalf of British cultural and scientific life were fittingly rewarded with a knighthood in 1875.

Unfortunately, the knighthood came at a time when the Museum's funding became seriously inadequate. In 1870 all public buildings came under the control of the government's Office of Works and very little money was allocated to maintain existing buildings or add new ones, in spite of the fact that the Museum's collections were still growing. The Treasury finally gave way to Museum pressure in 1890 and announced a competition for a new design. This presented quite a challenge because by then the Museum consisted of a jumble of buildings with gaps between. The winner was Aston Webb (who later designed the façade of Buckingham Palace), but his design became a political football for a decade because official priorities shifted to the sciences. He managed to revive his plan (which he had continued to work on) when the Museum's science activities moved across the road, a design which is much the same as the Museum's present form.

Queen Victoria laid the foundation stone for the new building in 1899, when the Museum was also renamed the Victoria and Albert Museum. (She had wanted it to be named only after her beloved consort, but was persuaded to add her name too.) It took a full ten years for the work to be finished.

When completed, it became obvious that the new scheme was on a huge scale – the Cromwell Road frontage is 219 metres long. The inscription round what was now the main entrance reaffirmed the original purpose of the Museum, which had become somewhat blurred over the years: "The excellence of every art must consist in the complete accomplishment of its purpose."

The finished work had some faults in its layout (because of an inadequate briefing to the architect, according to *The Times*), and some said it was too plain. Claude Phillips, art critic of the *Daily Telegraph* (and Keeper of the rival Wallace Collection), complained that:

"The general impression…is that of some immense, finely-appointed modern hospital for the analysis and dissection of applied art, rather than that of a temple of the higher delight."

Be that as it may, overall, the redevelopment was seen as a great success.

The state opening of Webb's scheme in 1909 marks the end of the first phase of the Victoria and Albert Museum and the beginning of the institution as we know it today. But it continued to develop and even to expand onto other sites, as will be seen in a later chapter.

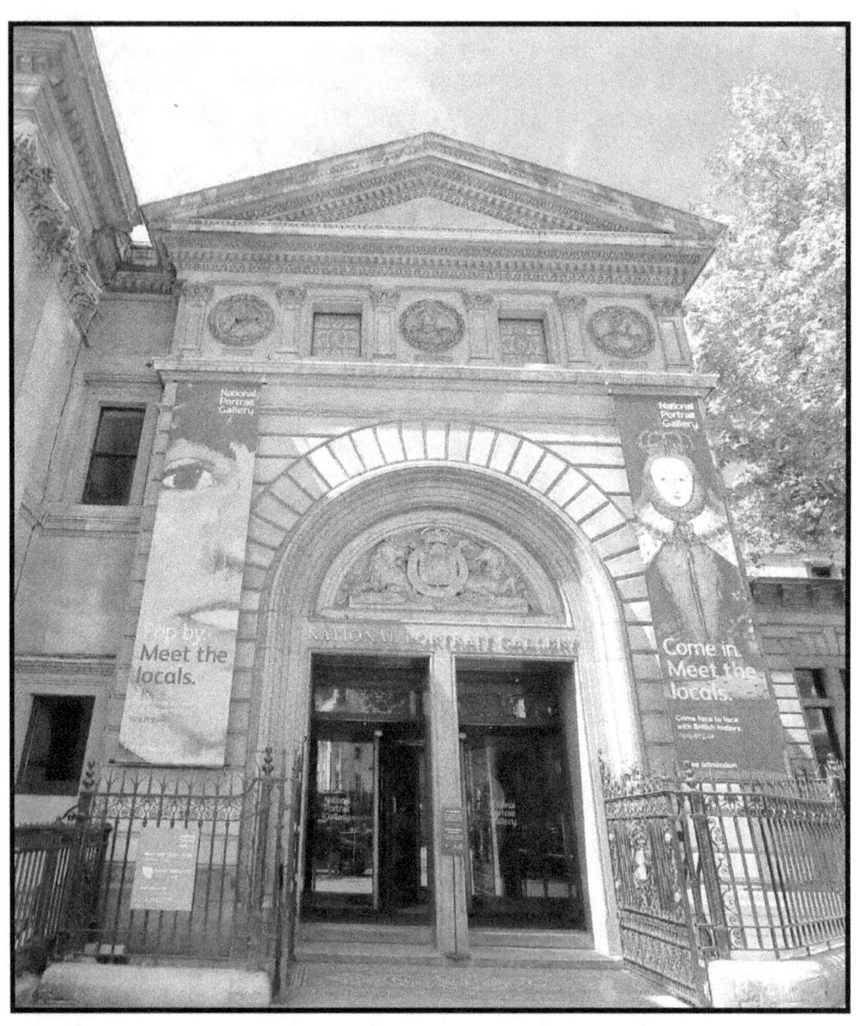

Entrance to the National Portrait Gallery, situated next to the National Gallery

5. Portraying the Nation

THE NATIONAL PORTRAIT Gallery stands out among Victorian art galleries, and not just because of its unusually broad popularity since it opened in London in 1856. For one thing, it is the only gallery where the subject of the painting is of far more significance than who painted it. For another, it was not inspired by the aesthetic or moral ideas behind most other nineteenth-century galleries. It owes its existence to the work of a dour Scottish historian, philosopher and social commentator whose political views were those of a reactionary Tory, and who thought Parliamentary eloquence led to "nothing but sheer Anarchy" (according to an 1855 letter). Thomas Carlyle had little in common with John Wilkes it would appear.

In spite of his great influence in the nineteenth century, Carlyle is little read now. In fact his reputation took a nose dive in his own lifetime, when he wrote an article which combined his idealisation of the medieval social order with his pronounced racism. *Occasional Discourse on the Negro Question* (1849) referred to the fact that although slavery was abolished in the British Empire in 1834, it still existed in the USA, Brazil and Cuba. Carlyle proposed that the solution to the "slavery problem" was not to free slaves into a world he considered they would be unable to negotiate, but to set up a modern version of feudal serfdom which would ensure they would be looked after into old age. This bizarre idea was strongly criticised, even by his closest friends, and led to a fierce response from John Stuart Mill, but Carlyle never recanted and his reputation never really recovered.

Nevertheless, Carlyle was one of the major figures of nineteenth-century intellectual life. His most famous work in his lifetime was *On Heroes, Hero-Worship and The Heroic in History*, published in 1841. The book examined the role of the hero in a variety of contexts. In the beginning, the hero was worshipped as a god. Then, as a prophet, he provided inspiration for his people. He could also be a poet, giving nations an articulate voice. Or a priest, trying to create God's kingdom on earth. As a man of letters, he can show the reality behind appearances.

Finally, as a king, he provides order and stability. This is the all-male line up of role models in human societies who, to Carlyle, are the people who bring about progress and change.

Some other strands of Carlyle's thought are discussed in Chapter 7, but it is his thoughts on "Great Men" which inspired the National Portrait Gallery.

Carlyle thought that "The history of the world is but the biography of great men" who shape history through their intellect, their leadership, their artistic vision, and, most importantly, their divine inspiration. (A contemporary Londoner had a very different take on the agents of change – but who had heard of Karl Marx and his modes of production in those days?) This view of history became known as the "Great Man Theory".

It is not difficult to see why this theory was highly attractive to Victorian Britain, with its abundance of "Great Men" in all sorts of guises. Founding a gallery to commemorate prominent British notables by displaying their likenesses could be portrayed as a patriotic duty, a celebration of the offspring of a country then at the height of its power and influence. A campaign was started to achieve just such an institution.

It turned out that Parliament must have been insufficiently patriotic, because it took ten years to get it to agree to the idea. Earl Stanhope spent a decade of his life pursuing the cause. He first proposed the gallery in 1846 when he was a Member of Parliament in the House of Commons, and by the time he succeeded in 1856 – at his third attempt – he had to make his plea to the House of Lords, as by then he had been elevated to the peerage. The statement that turned the tide and favourably impressed the Lords called for the establishment of a National Portrait Gallery that would contain:

> "...a gallery of original portraits, such portraits to consist as far as possible of those persons who are most honourably commemorated in British history as warriors or as statesmen, or in arts, in literature or in science".

After that, things moved relatively quickly. Three months later, and with Queen Victoria's approval, the House of Commons agreed to vote a sum of £2,000 towards the establishment of a "British Historical Portrait Gallery". Although collections of portraits of famous people had been brought together in Europe since the sixteenth century, this was the first time such a collection was proposed solely on nationality. The founder Trustees included Earl Stanhope, the historian Thomas Babington Macaulay, Thomas Carlyle (of course), and the future Prime Minister Benjamin Disraeli. Lord Ellesmere donated the gallery's first acquisition, the so-called "Chandos" portrait of Shakespeare.

The Gallery opened in 1859 in a Georgian house in Westminster, occupying "two apartments of very moderate size, a very small back room on the same floor and the walls of the staircase" according to its 1862 Annual Report. George Scharf, an illustrator and recently the Director of the wildly successful Manchester Art Treasures Exhibition, had been appointed as the first Secretary in 1857. There he continued his sterling service to the British art world, remaining in office for almost 40 years, and seeing the Gallery through its migrations in search of a permanent home.

Scharf was the son of a Bavarian painter and had studied at the Royal Academy Schools. He had a varied career, successful in numerous fields. His travels in Asia Minor (now Turkey) produced drawings of views and classical antiquities which are now in the British Museum. He also exhibited paintings of classical tombs at the Royal Academy, and illustrated scholarly books on art and antiquity. But he was mainly engaged in lecturing and teaching before he joined the Gallery. Unsurprisingly, he took the opportunity to become an unrivalled expert on historic portraiture, writing extensively on the subject.

In the early years he ran the Gallery almost single-handedly, from authenticating portraits and writing notes on the acquisitions, to acting as guide and keeping the accounts. He used his artistic skills to record the portraits offered to the Gallery as annotated sketches in pocket books (which are still a valuable source of information).

The portraits of historically important British people covered paintings, drawings, sculpture, caricatures and photographs, a much wider range of media than in other public galleries at the time (with the possible exception of the South Kensington Gallery). Portraits of living people were restricted to the monarch and his or her spouse, as the original Trustees had ruled that "No portrait of any person still living, or deceased less than 10 years, shall be admitted by purchase, donation, or bequest, except only in the case of the reigning Sovereign, and of his or her Consort". (The living have been included since 1969.)

During the thirteen years the Gallery was in Westminster, the collection increased in size from 57 to 288 items, and the number of visitors from 5,300 in its first year to 34,500 in 1869. However, the lighting, the display of the portraits, and the circulation arrangements were all inadequate, and there was an increasing lack of space as the collection grew. Embarrassingly, there was even insufficient space to display the government's gift of George Hayter's painting *The Reformed House of Commons*. To make the best use of the space available the collection had to be arranged primarily by size rather than by any more logical scheme.

In 1869, the collection made its first move, to join the South Kensington Museum in Exhibition Road. It was housed in buildings managed by the Royal Horticultural Society, where it was allocated two rooms and a long gallery. There was now much more space and the display methodology was improved, with the portraits arranged, as far as possible, by the death date of the subject. Visitor numbers continued to increase, with 59,000 in the first year of the new location, rising to 80,000 in 1877. By the 1880s, explanatory labels were provided for each object, said to be "more than very acceptable to the class of people who attended the Gallery" on public holidays (in other words, the less affluent).[25]

But the display arrangements were still not wholly suitable. Following a fire in the same buildings, which was fortunately controlled before it reached the Gallery, and a damning report on the site's fire risks, the collection was moved to the other end of London, Bethnal Green Museum in the East End, in 1885.

The Bethnal Green Museum had opened in 1872 as an offshoot of the South Kensington Museum, to provide scientific and artistic exhibitions for the people of the East End of London. Unfortunately, it was no better a location for the National Portrait Gallery than the Kensington site. It was inconvenient for Gallery visitors from central London, and, worse, the building was not a suitable environment for paintings. It gave little protection from heat and cold, was not waterproof and suffered from condensation, with the result that many pictures were damaged. It was just as well that the collection was considered to be so important to national esteem that 350 public figures signed a petition to the Prime Minister to find a more suitable permanent home for the Gallery.

Finally, the philanthropist William Henry Alexander donated £60,000, followed by another £20,000, for a purpose-built building. The government provided the new site, next to the National Gallery (the location of a former workhouse), and £16,000. The building's neo-classical façade was clad in Portland Stone and the interior featured intricate mosaic floors. The gallery opened at its permanent new location on 4 April 1896, and 4,200 people flocked in on its first day.

Having seen the Gallery through its first 40 years with great success in the face of innumerable difficulties, it is a great pity that its first Secretary George Scharf, now retired, did not witness this event as he died shortly before the opening. Lionel Cust of the Department of Prints and Drawings at the British Museum had taken over in 1895, and it was he who oversaw the move. Nearly 169,000 visitors attended in the first six months, better than the best yearly figure at South Kensington, in spite of an entrance fee of sixpence on two days a week. Its combination of art and history has always been popular with the general public.

The new site did not solve all the problems, as by the time the new

Gallery opened it was already too small to display the Gallery's still growing collection. Almost immediately, the Trustees put forward proposals for expansion on the site of St George's Barracks. Further appeals were made in 1902 and 1906. Plans were actually made to divide the site between the National Portrait Gallery and the National Gallery, but they came to nothing because of the First World War. Expansion had to wait until 1933, with a further expansion in 2000.

By all accounts, before the First World War the Gallery was a quiet, scholarly place in its final location, but the peace was broken by an astonishing event which took place in 1909. According to an account by employee James Milner (who rose to be Director), an elderly man shot his wife and himself in the East Wing. The man died instantly, the woman died later. It turned out the 70-year-old assailant was paranoid and delusional, and had left a letter saying he could not go on and wanted to kill his wife and himself. Why he chose the National Portrait Gallery to commit the deed is not known. (It is rather disconcerting that Milner's account seems more concerned with seeing to the removal of the bloodstains than with the victims, though this may have been for the benefit of the Trustees.)[26]

The following year another violent event took place at the Gallery. Suffragette Annie Hunt "attacked Millais's unfinished portrait of Carlyle with a butcher's cleaver which she carried concealed beneath her blouse, and before she could be restrained made three large cuts on the face and head of the portrait". She does not seem to have been targeting Carlyle specifically, but was merely acting as part of a wider campaign to damage paintings in galleries, the most famous being the attack on the "Rokeby Venus" at the National Gallery next door.[27]

Suffragette militancy ended with the outbreak of the First World War. Given the nature of the gallery, it seems only fitting that major players in the war effort were commemorated in the Gallery. The financier Sir Abraham Bailey commissioned three large portraits of those politicians, Admirals and army Generals who were seen as the main actors in bringing the war to an end, and gave all three works to the National Portrait Gallery.

After the First World War, the Gallery returned to its peaceful existence, which was severely jolted by the outbreak of the Second World War. After that War, it received another jolt from a young, innovative and publicity-conscious Director. But that story is for a later chapter.

Scotland has its own National Portrait Gallery, which opened in 1889. Unlike the Trafalgar Square enterprise, the Scottish Portrait Gallery has always been in the same place, an imposing red Sandstone building on a prime Edinburgh site, thanks to a donation by John Findlay, owner of *The*

Scotsman newspaper. Scotland of course has many world-famous people to commemorate, including notables of the Scottish Enlightenment and famous writers, scientists and engineers, so the project was entirely fitting.

The building was designed in the Victorian Gothic style by Robert Anderson, who trained with George Gilbert Scott, architect of the Houses of Parliament. The building was originally shared with the Society of Antiquaries of Scotland, but the Society moved out in 1985. From 1895 sculptures of famous Scots like Adam Smith and David Hume were added to the exterior, and a large processional frieze of notable Scots was added to the entrance hall.

It is worth bearing in mind that although Carlyle's Great Man Theory has gone out of fashion (not least because of highly destructive "Great Men" of the twentieth century like Stalin and Hitler), the idea is still around. Nowadays economic, social and political factors are usually considered more important in shaping history than the activities of one individual. But the image of the heroic figure is far from dead and it still strikes a chord in the world of art and the art gallery.

Art is still primarily seen as a matter of the genius of the great artist, who is often regarded as someone who changed the course of art development (for the better, of course). It is behind the fact that the attribution of the name of a Master to a painting can increase its price tenfold, that blockbuster exhibitions usually feature the work of one "name" artist, and that books on art are most typically monographs on famous artists. And what would art galleries be without the big names to draw in the visitors, whether in the permanent display or for a temporary exhibition?

It is unlikely that most visitors to the National Portrait Gallery thought of Carlyle, nor did they necessarily see all those portrayed as "great". But equally it is unlikely that they found the idea of the heroic individual uncongenial. And surely it also resonated in the municipalities which started their own galleries in the later nineteenth century – for often the only paintings in the founding collections were portraits of local worthies. In these cases, civic pride took precedence over national pride, and proved to be just as powerful, as will be seen in the next chapter.

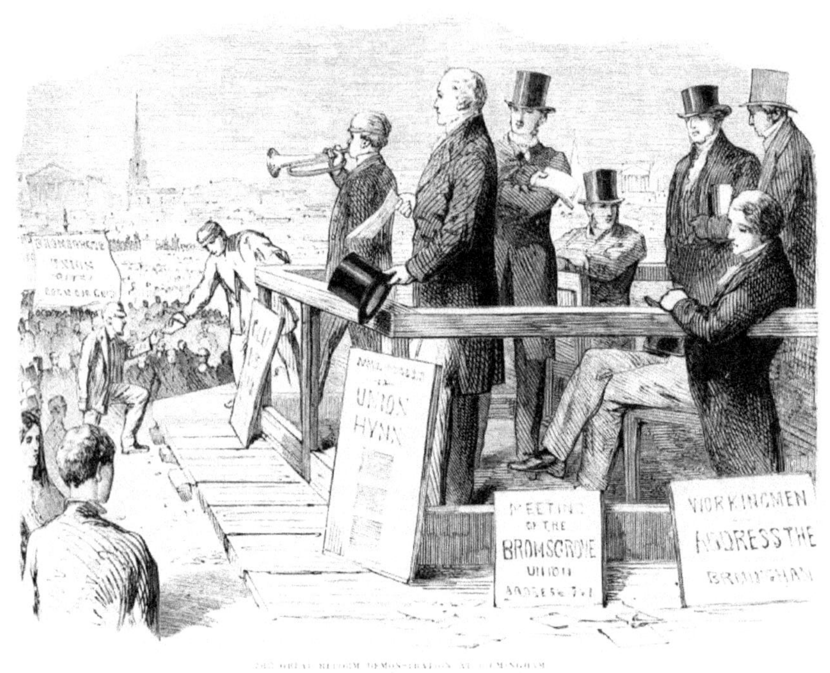

*Speakers address a demonstration demanding reform of the voting law,
Birmingham, 1840s*

6. Beyond the Metropolis

IT IS MORE than likely that John Wilkes would have heartily approved of the public art galleries which were established in London up to the 1850s, if only because most of them were rooted in attitudes derived from the previous century. Initially at least, Dulwich Picture Gallery and the National Gallery reflected his own eighteenth-century ideas about art, still current in the early nineteenth century. The South Kensington Museum aimed to add to Britain's growing industrial importance, which also began in the eighteenth-century. Wilkes had campaigned for just such institutions. The National Portrait Gallery was more firmly nineteenth-century, inspired by one of the leading Victorian thinkers, and by Victorian confidence that Britain could supply a steady stream of "Great Men". But Wilkes, as an English patriot, would have had no difficulty with such an idea.

Nor is it likely that Wilkes, the life-long Londoner, would have had any quarrel with the fact that all these institutions were in the metropolis, the cultural, political and financial centre of the country. Furthermore, the processes by which they were established would have been perfectly familiar to him. The National Gallery, the South Kensington Museum and the National Portrait Gallery came into existence by Parliamentary decree, Dulwich through the charitable actions of private individuals.

But at this point John Wilkes' world begins to become an irrelevance, and even a hindrance. Further expansion would require a radical approach of a different kind. It needed a new legal framework for towns outside London, a new intellectual climate to inspire activists, and a new kind of charitable activity. Once these were in place, the way was clear for almost every town of any size to acquire an art gallery. Even more radically, the new reformist spirit resulted in a fair number of highly successful projects which took art right into working class areas.

Nowadays, it is hard to appreciate how difficult it was to view paintings or sculpture outside London in the 1850s. True, the university museum collections – the Ashmolean in Oxford, the Fitzwilliam in Cambridge, and the Hunterian in Glasgow – included art and were open to all. But other than that the provincial art lover had to rely on the good will of those local collectors who allowed local people to view their art. And although many bigger towns were graced with literary or philosophical societies which possessed an art collection of sorts, membership was largely confined to the professional middle classes.

By the end of the century, the situation had changed completely, to the extent that there was a veritable competitive frenzy of public art gallery development among the larger British towns. Furthermore, unlike the public galleries in London, these developments were the result of local decisions and local fund raising. This was because legislation had been passed which established modern elected municipalities with tax raising capabilities. The stream of reform Acts which were passed in the nineteenth century may be relatively little known nowadays, but the great regional art galleries would never have come into existence without them.

This legislation was in large part prompted by the world's first industrial revolution, when Carlyle's "industrialisation" was proceeding at a breath-taking pace. It created a new middle class and new conurbations which did not fit into the existing political framework, and they began to press for recognition. When that recognition came, space was created for amenities like public art galleries to flourish.

London had always been a major manufacturing area, but the development of the new steam-driven industry took place mainly in new fast-growing towns in the midlands and north of England. The new industries created immense wealth, but this was not translated into civic amenities like public art galleries until well after the peak of industrialisation in the 1830s and 40s. It was only when Parliament unified the way in which provincial towns operated that such major municipal projects became possible.

Historically, towns and cities had been run in a great variety of ways. The Municipal Corporations Act of 1835 swept all that away by establishing a uniform system of town councils to which existing boroughs were expected to conform sooner or later. There were to be annual council elections, with a third of councillors up for election each year. The councillors themselves elected a higher level of officers (aldermen) for a six-year term. Boroughs had to appoint salaried town clerks and treasurers, and were required to publish their financial accounts, which were subject to audit. Thus the modern system of local government was born.

178 existing boroughs adopted this system immediately, the rest were reformed or abolished by 1886 (except the City of London, to which the Act did not apply.) Even more significantly, the Act also allowed

unincorporated towns to petition to become incorporated boroughs. Many new industrial towns in the midlands and north had grown to become large conurbations, some of international significance, but they still could not manage their own affairs. They were now able to become incorporated under the Act and be self-governing for the first time. Birmingham and Manchester were pioneers in 1838, and Sheffield followed suit in 1843. In all, 62 new boroughs were incorporated.

All this meant that larger towns were now run by a body accountable to their ratepayers and open to financial scrutiny. Municipal affairs now had to be run to suit the wishes of the more affluent of those most directly affected. The new system also opened up avenues for local worthies to become involved in running their borough by becoming councillors, as well as marking the beginning of professional careers in local government. Both became significant avenues to middle class advancement, socially and professionally.

The Reform Act of 1833 further changed the municipal landscape by giving the vote to the new industrial middle class, in both local and national elections. This new group (all male, of course) gained local political power at the expense of the traditional urban elite of landowners, professionals and merchants. The old elite tended to be paternalistic, often with a desire to improve "their" town by funding civic amenities. Conversely, although the new middle class was a varied group – mainly small businessmen and manufacturers, frequently from one of the Nonconformist sects – it was usually united in an aversion to raising the rates (only payable by the better off, such as themselves).

This was unfortunate, as the industrial towns were in dire need of civic funds. From the 1730s to the 1820s life expectancy in England rose from about 32 to about 40 years. Life expectancy in rural areas continued to rise gradually, but a major mortality crisis occurred in the rapidly growing industrial areas in the 1830s and 1840s. Life expectancy in cities like Manchester and Liverpool fell to levels not seen since the medieval Black Death.

A constant influx of migrants from rural areas led to acute overcrowding. Coupled with the absence of clean water or sewerage systems, this led to high death rates from infectious diseases and regular cholera epidemics. (The new middle class avoided the worst effects because they moved to the outskirts, usually upwind, away from the slums.) By 1861 Manchester and Birmingham had hundreds of thousands of inhabitants but still no comprehensive water supplies or integrated sewerage systems.

This was in spite of the fact that the Public Health Act 1848 allowed boroughs to take out loans for water facilities. As late as 1871 most boroughs did not have water systems adequate to prevent contamination, even though it had been proved that the 1854 cholera epidemic had been caused by contaminated water. But at the same time many boroughs were undertaking major railway construction or huge city centre projects.

Fortunately, from the late 1860s public amenities became a higher priority. The Second Reform Act of 1867, the Municipal Franchise Act of 1869 and the Assessed Rates Act of 1869 widened the local franchise to many working-class voters, who were not ratepayers but now had to be cultivated by local politicians.[28]

Joseph Chamberlain, Mayor of Birmingham from 1873 to 1876, was the pioneer of what became known as "municipal socialism" (though he was a Liberal not a socialist). He argued that failure to spend on infrastructure was a false economy in terms of urban development, and found ingenious ways to pay for civic utilities. From the mid-1870s the leading cities actually began to compete to create healthy city environments. The results were spectacular - in the last three decades of the nineteenth-century life expectancy in the largest cities began to rise above that of the 1820s, before its calamitous decline.

During the 1840s, when industrial expansion was at a pace never before seen in human history, some provincial Liberal Party activists began to call for the provision of free cultural facilities funded by the state. They argued that amenities like libraries, museums and art galleries, hitherto largely the private preserve of the affluent, would not only be morally uplifting for the lower orders, but would, it was hoped, help to keep the working class out of the pubs in their (limited) free time. Not that these facilities would just be for the working class – they were intended for all the inhabitants of a town, a civic amenity for everyone.

The issue was brought up in Parliament. The concern with drunkenness is made obvious in the remit of a committee set up in 1835 to examine "the extent, causes and consequences of the prevailing vice of intoxication among the labouring classes of the United Kingdom". The committee was chaired by James Buckingham, MP for Sheffield, a member of the Parliamentary Radical Group which transformed the Whigs into the Liberals. He campaigned unsuccessfully to allow boroughs to fund libraries and museums through the rates. The cause was later taken up by two Liberal MPs of other northern industrial towns, William Ewart of Liverpool, and Joseph Brotherton of Salford, who introduced a bill to allow boroughs with a population of 10,000 or more to raise a halfpenny in the pound on the rates for the establishment of museums. This became the Museums Act of 1845.

Ewart and Brotherton then promoted the provision of municipal public libraries. At the time, the only lending libraries were by subscription, too expensive for the working class, and tending to be aimed at novels for middle class ladies. And it was unlikely that literate members of the working class could afford to buy books or have access to private libraries.

Edward Edwards was a major force in this campaign, a self-taught son of a builder who managed to become an assistant librarian at the British Museum. The campaign succeeded in introducing the Public Libraries Act 1850, even if the Act was rather limited in its effects. Only boroughs with populations over 10,000 could fund public libraries, two thirds of ratepayers had to consent, and only a halfpenny in the pound could be raised through the rates – and, amazingly, the funds so raised could not be used to buy books.

The first major free public library to open under the Act was in Manchester in 1852. Appropriately, Edward Edwards was appointed to run it, but this was not a happy ending as his irascibility and inability to work with others resulted in his dismissal in 1858. Too late, the powers that be eventually admitted that had he been of a higher social origin his eccentricities might have been tolerated, but as it was he had to eke a living from writing books for the rest of his life. He managed to obtain a small government pension, but he died in poverty on the Isle of Wight, found dead outdoors after wandering off in old age.[29]

Nevertheless, progress under the Act continued. In 1855 the rate which could be levied was raised to one penny and common-sense prevailed with boroughs now being allowed to buy reading materials for their libraries. Since this made it easier to fund libraries than museums, some boroughs subsequently created art galleries by adding rooms to existing libraries. A notable example of this is in Leeds, where the library was richly decorated with magnificent tiling and wood carving, while the poor relation art gallery had to make do with plainer walls and woodwork.

However, although incorporated boroughs were now able to fund museums, art galleries and libraries, they were not required to. There was still a long way to go for (usually Liberal) councillors to persuade their (usually Conservative) opponents that art galleries were an appropriate way to spend civic cash. But their persistence eventually won the day.

What inspired these determined local politicians and their supporters to keep going during their often-lengthy campaigns? Why was public access to art seen as important when there were so many other things which required attention? Trying to find an answer to this question requires a plunge into the intellectual currents swirling around Victorian Britain. This was an era of intellectual ferment when much which had been taken for granted was being questioned, and new ways of doing things were fiercely debated.

Nearly always, the ideas of the giant of the Victorian art world, John Ruskin, were a major factor in campaigns for art galleries, whether municipal art galleries for all, or projects to bring art to the slums. But many other lines of thought fed into the intellectual soup out of which the public gallery would emerge. As will be seen, they were not necessarily mutually compatible or of equal influence, but they all made their mark on the development of the art gallery.

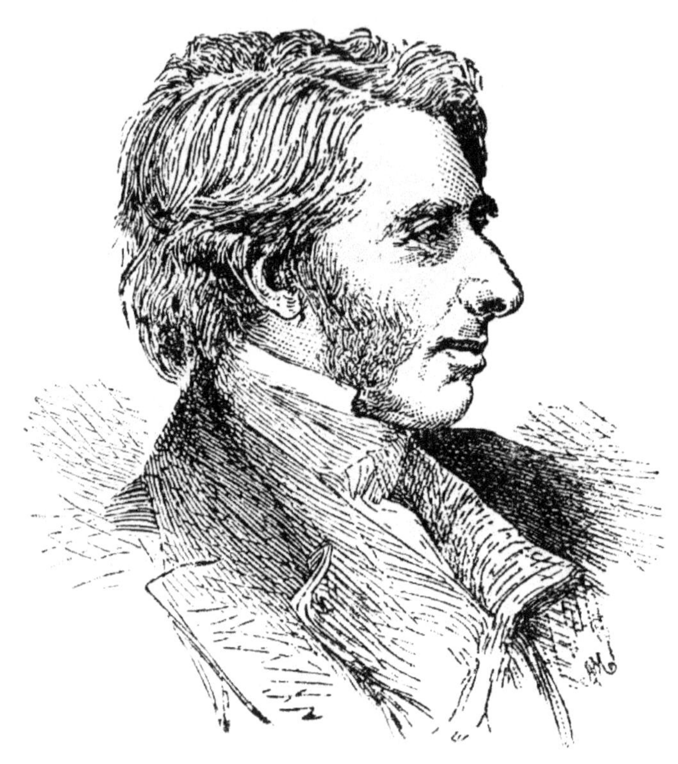

John Ruskin, giant of the Victorian art world

7. Intellectual Underpinnings

B
Y THE MID-NINETEENTH century municipalities had the authority to create public art galleries, and many of them had the money. But this did not mean that art galleries were high on everyone's agenda. The industrial revolution may have created unprecedented wealth, but there were plenty of other things to spend ratepayers' money on – clean water and a sewage system, for example – and a good proportion of those ratepayers were more interested in keeping rates low than in looking for more ways to spend the proceeds.

This meant that those who campaigned for municipal art galleries had to be prepared for a long fight, and needed solid arguments to support their case and keep up their morale. For most, the work of John Ruskin was the main impetus. The other major influence from the 1870s was Matthew Arnold's concept of "high culture" and the need to protect it. This chapter will mainly concentrate on these two, but there were numerous major thinkers in the Victorian era, and the direction of the public art gallery movement was influenced by a good many of them.

For example, Thomas Carlyle was not only the inspiration for the National Portrait Gallery; he was Ruskin's friend and mentor, and the starting point for some of Ruskin's most important ideas. The aesthetic movement of the 1890s challenged the earlier idea that art should have a moral purpose. William Morris' Arts and Crafts movement disputed the rigid demarcation between the fine and decorative arts. Throughout the nineteenth century the ideas of Utilitarianism affected the use of public money, and while the Evangelical movement may have encouraged sobriety and cleanliness, it also opposed Sunday opening. Most of these currents of thought are still surprisingly relevant.

Also significant is Augustus Pugin, because his admiration for the medieval and the Gothic style paved the way for Ruskin's similar interest in the Gothic and its artisanal working methods.

Pugin was an architect who got his chance when the Houses of Parliament burned down in 1834. This spectacular conflagration allowed him to make his name with his beautiful interior design work for its replacement. He came to the attention of the wider public with his book *Contrasts*, published in 1836 when he was only 24. *Contrasts* was a series of architectural drawings which unfavourably compared modern city buildings with their fifteenth-century equivalents. A typical example contrasted a benevolent monastic foundation with the grim conditions of a contemporary workhouse built under the New Poor Law.

Like many, Pugin saw the British city of the 1830s as an outward expression of self-interest and indifference to others. The new middle class built comfortable homes for themselves, while workers were housed in small shoddily built buildings, which soon became slums. There were few public amenities other than pubs. He compared this to a highly idealised version of society under the medieval feudal system, in which (he claimed) everyone willingly accepted responsibilities to those above and below, and the different social strata lived harmoniously together.

His admiration for the Catholic medieval architecture of northern France led to his conversion to Roman Catholicism. With the zeal of the convert he set about rebuilding Britain as a Gothic Catholic Christendom. By the time he was 30, he had built 22 churches, three cathedrals, three convents, half a dozen houses, several schools and a Cistercian monastery. All were built in a medieval Gothic style, which became much imitated by later architects. Like Pugin, they were trying to bring humanity and coherence to the modern city landscape, in an early attempt at town planning.

Pugin's frenetic workload wore him out and he died at 40, a few days after he created his most famous design, the clock tower of the Houses of Parliament (which houses "Big Ben"). But *Contrasts* left an architectural legacy of nineteenth-century town centres, churches, schools and family houses which became the signature Gothic look of Victorian Britain.[30]

Although Ruskin publicly attacked Pugin (probably because the workmanship of some of Pugin's buildings was below par), he was in fact in his debt. Pugin's pioneering advocacy of the medieval made it easier for Ruskin to gain public acceptance for his own views on architecture and medieval craftsmanship from the 1840s.

Ruskin himself first became known as an art critic. The first volume of *Modern Painters* appeared in 1843 and it revolutionised how art was perceived. Ruskin saw art as having a spiritual origin, based on a universal, divinely appointed order. Nature, the visible world, is an embodiment of God's truth; art must therefore be faithful to the visible world as it actually is; the embodiment of the divine world. Hence his dislike of Dutch landscapes which depicted views which manipulated actual scenery for artistic effect, and his championship of Turner who painted what he saw. Similarly, he praised the "primitive" art of early Italian artists like Giotto, and criticised the idealised art of the Renaissance (a factor in his later support for the Pre-Raphaelites).

Ruskin developed his ideas further in a stream of books and lectures. In *The Nature of Gothic,* he wrote that a society with a poor quality of life cannot produce great art, as a workman must have respect and autonomy to produce work of genius. His own industrialised Victorian society gave the workman neither. It was the first time aesthetic value and the producer's quality of living had been connected, and introduced the idea that art could not be studied in isolation from the society which produced it.

In *The Seven Lamps of Architecture* of 1849 he emphasised the need to respect the original fabric of old buildings. His criticism of the crude restoration of medieval churches then under way was the inspiration for the later conservation movement. *The Stones of Venice* regarded art and architecture as a direct expression of the social conditions in which they were produced – it now became quite normal to study art and society inclusively.

Ruskin may have repudiated Pugin, but he readily acknowledged Carlyle's influence. Carlyle was best known to the public for his "Great Man Theory". As he put it in *Heroes, Hero-Worship and the Heroic in History*:

> "For, as I take it, Universal History, the history of what man has accomplished in this world, is at bottom the History of Great Men who have worked here…all things that we see standing accomplished in the world are properly…the practical realisation and embodiment, of Thoughts that dwelt in the Great Men sent into the world: the soul of the whole world's history…were the history of these."

The likes of Hitler and Stalin put a bit of a dent in the Great Man Theory in the twentieth century, but fortunately Carlyle's main influence on Ruskin was his version of the Gospel of Work. This was a long-standing feature of Protestantism, and the origin of the concept of the "Protestant work ethic", which saw work as a positive part of the spiritual life ("work is prayer"), rather than a curse and a burden. Carlyle went so far in regarding work as intrinsically uplifting as to insist that the working class should be satisfied with their lot, and refrain from agitating for greater democracy (or "mobocracy" as he sourly described it).

Ruskin also regarded work as necessary and morally good, but he insisted that workers should be happy in their work. This could only be achieved if they had control over what they produced and how they produced it. If they did not, work was degrading rather than godly. In stark contrast, manufacturers of the day saw rigid discipline and lack of autonomy as essential to accustom workers to the new machine-led work methods.

It may seem, and indeed is, rather odd that the indulged only son of wealthy parents who never needed to earn a living should be so concerned with work. He did acquire one job in middle age, when he was appointed the first Slade Professor of Fine Art at Oxford. In this role he helped to establish art history as an academic discipline in the English-speaking world.

But the Ruskin who was the major influence on campaigners for cultural projects emerged from the 1860s onwards, when he began to develop a deep concern for social issues. As his art criticism had always been concerned with society, this was not the major shift it might seem. He shocked middle class Britain in 1860 when he published *Unto This Last*. The book attacked the free market economics of Adam Smith and John Stuart Mill and the visibly horrendous effects of unfettered competition. In spite of Britain's professed Christian beliefs, he thundered that it actually worshipped not God, but money.

The book subsequently became enormously popular with early Labour politicians, and read with admiration by Gandhi, Tolstoy, and Proust. But it horrified most of Britain at the time. Ruskin's professed support for free education, public libraries and care for the sick and elderly was one of the forerunners of a line of thought which eventually culminated in the welfare state. In spite of this, he was no leftist but remained a life-long Tory.[31]

His mentor Carlyle may have been an anti-democrat with a rosy view of the benefits of work, but he did not think workers should accept the relentless brutality of many contemporary working conditions. Ruskin agreed, but went further than his mentor in the book *The Crown of Wild Olive*, published in 1866. He argued that the rationalisation of work processes, mass manufacture and market culture were killing the intrinsic value of work, because they left no scope at all for individual input. It is an indication of how repugnant Pugin, Carlyle and Ruskin found much of modern life that they all looked back centuries to an idealised version of the medieval artisan as a model for how work should be organised.

William Morris read the 1854 reprint of Ruskin's *The Nature of Gothic* when it was produced as a pamphlet for the Working Men's College in London. It changed his life forever. He became Ruskin's greatest follower, fully agreeing with him that art is only as good as the society in which it is created. But he differed from Ruskin in one important respect: he regarded egalitarianism as essential for a good quality of life. The extreme social inequality of his time could never provide a decent standard of living for the majority. Politically, he was a socialist, not a Tory like Carlyle and Ruskin.

Like them, he idealised medieval work practices, and like them he knew the Gospel of Work was not possible under capitalism. Nonetheless, he fully recognised that industrialisation had led to a higher general standard of living than ever before. Morris was not a Marxist – he did not read Marx until 1883 – he was concerned with the independent artisan, not the wage-slave proletariat. Morris set out his position in *Useful Work versus Useless Toil*. Craftsmen and women must not only have control of how they worked, they should also be able to decide what was to be made. Which meant that they needed equal social and intellectual access to the means to make that decision.[32]

Medieval practice made little or no distinction between what would later be known as fine art and decorative art. Morris – who was an artisan himself – tried to dismantle the barriers which had grown up between the two. His company produced pottery, tapestries, furniture and other products of a very high technical and artistic standard, as did his printing press. But although they were commercially successful, they were too expensive for the ordinary working people whose lives he wanted to beautify.

The Arts and Crafts movement he inspired did raise the status of high-quality handmade craft work, but the gap remains between craft and art. About the only success on this front is that some kinds of studio pottery and photography have gained fine art status. Art galleries are usually the repositories of easel paintings and sculpture. More recent exhibited work may look different – it may be non-figurative or made of "found" objects – but it is still not seen as "decorative". Furniture and other decorative arts may be placed as "dressing" alongside paintings of the same period, but while fine and decorative arts may be displayed in the same building (as in the Wallace Collection or the Victoria and Albert Museum) they are usually displayed separately.

Morris was a major figure during his lifetime, both for his thought and for the Arts and Crafts products he produced, and he remains highly influential to this day. The influence of the aesthetic movement was rather more limited. The movement is associated with the idea of "art for art's sake". Its most famous advocate in England was Walter Pater, whose 1873 collection of essays, *The Renaissance*, focuses on his own subjective reactions to the paintings he writes about, rather than discussing the paintings themselves. It ends by stating:

"For art comes to you proposing frankly to give nothing but the highest quality to your moments as they pass, and simply for those moments' sake".[33]

As a movement, it was the antithesis of Ruskin's idea of art having social and spiritual purposes. Its point of view is well expressed by Kenneth Clark, a twentieth century Director of the National Gallery: "The only reason for bringing together works of art in a public space is that…they produce in us a kind of exalted happiness. For a moment there is a clearing in the jungle: we pass on refreshed, with our capacity for life increased and with some memory of the sky."

The aesthetic movement in England was at its peak in the 1890s, associated particularly with Whistler, Aubrey Beardsley, Oscar Wilde, and the painter of antique beauties in diaphanous drapery, Albert Moore. Aestheticism was a minority interest in its day, although the twentieth century modernist concentration on form, colour and abstraction owes much to its outlook. As an argument that art should not preach, it challenged the moral purpose art galleries were held to possess earlier in the century.

In practice artists did not stop preaching, though in the twentieth century they were often making a political rather than a moral point. The general aesthetic bias against narrative art, however, was a major critical blow to the reputation of much Victorian art. Although it remained popular with large sections of the general public, there was often little chance to see it, as many galleries relegated their Victorian art to the basement and some even talked of disposing of it altogether.

This was because Victorian narrative painting was not deemed to be "high culture". Art galleries are, if nothing else, repositories of that art which in its day is considered to be of the highest status. In Britain, the purest example of this is the National Gallery in London, an unparalleled collection of high-quality examples of all branches of Western European painting from the fourteenth century to the early twentieth century.

The concept of "high culture" was first popularised in Britain by Matthew Arnold in *Culture and Anarchy*, a collection of lectures published in book form in 1869. I will examine this in some detail, because it sums up the dominant attitudes of the cultural elite from Arnold's day until it began to be seriously challenged in the 1960s.[34]

In his preface to the book Arnold defines culture as "being a pursuit of total perfection by means of getting to know…the best which has been thought and said in the world", thereby "turning a stream of fresh and free thought upon our stock notions and habits". In other words, culture is a way of using the intellect to reassess the everyday in a new and thought-provoking way.

But this is not just for the benefit of the individual. The perfection to be pursued is "a harmonious perfection, developing all sides of our humanity; a general perfection, developing all parts of society". Developing cultural pursuits is to develop society as a whole. That is why Arnold's work is subtitled: *An Essay in Political and Social Criticism*. Arnold was practicing what he preached, as his notion of "culture" developed a tradition stretching back to Edmund Burke's work of the previous century on taste, beauty and the sublime, which sought "perfection" in a process of all round development of human faculties.

Arnold's culture combined beauty and intelligence, or "sweetness and light". Arnold regarded this culture as Hellenistic, deriving from the ancient Greeks. He contrasted this unfavourably with what he regarded as the Judeo-Christian tradition, which he characterised as emphasising relatively unthinking outward conduct and obedience.

To Arnold, culture is the product of a community, and becoming cultured is something which has to be done within a community. But Arnold regretted that few are capable of this journey. The aristocratic "Barbarians" are too concerned with their own selfish interests. The middle class "Philistines" (Arnold invented this description) are too self-satisfied. And the working class "Populace" are far too easily swayed by emotion rather than reason.

Fortunately for the future of humanity, a few individuals (who can be from any class) have the right intellectual curiosity to pursue perfection and bring its beneficial results to society at large. Their efforts would provide a counterweight to the materialism of the industrial age.

But this process could be threatened by the "anarchy" of working-class emotionalism and violent action, before it could complete the transformation of society. Therefore the state needed to be strengthened to enable it to protect culture so it can fulfil its role: "to act on the minds of those who take action so they think more clearly".

Arnold's fear of the potential for mass violence among the Populace, and thus its threat to culture, was not unusual among the mid-nineteenth-century middle classes. But it was largely unfounded, as working-class politics in England were rarely revolutionary. The Barbarians, in spite of the military basis of their interests and attitudes, were a major repository of high culture artefacts and important employers of professional expertise, however reluctant they might be to share either. Culture might well be more at risk from the attitudes of practical, commercially minded Philistines, likely to be averse to supporting non-profit making activities such as public art galleries.

The parsimonious attitude of the by-then middle class which dominated the House of Commons regarding the awarding of funding to the National Gallery seemed to bear this out. As did the many municipal councillors who gave more priority to low rates than to culture. In a final crushing judgement, which survives to this day, Arnold deemed "Philistines" too obsessed with "utility" to be capable of any real understanding of culture.

In *Culture and Anarchy* Arnold noted that he had been accused of promulgating a "religion of culture", which breathes "a spirit of cultivated inaction". The latter charge he easily refutes, as he was actually asking for political action to put his ideas into practice, not a life of pure thought. But he does not directly deny the former. And it is true that art galleries have sometimes been seen as examples of the secularisation of modern life, non-religious temples of art, publicly accessible areas which for some have replaced places of worship.[35]

This is more likely to be true of countries like the United States and France, which make secularism a core political value, than in England, where even today secularism only goes so far. Church and state have never been fully separated. England still has an established Church of England headed by the monarch, and religious education has always been compulsory in state schools. In the Victorian era, the restrictions on individuals who would not adhere to the Thirty-nine Articles of the established Church of England were not lifted until the later nineteenth century. But breaking the power of the church was never a major political objective in Victorian England.

In fact, the Victorian Evangelical movement to which Ruskin's mother belonged very successfully used the media of the Sunday school, religious tract distribution, and home visiting to encourage large numbers of people towards godliness, in the form of cleanliness, sobriety and churchgoing. A census of religious worship carried out in 1851 recorded 60 per cent of the population of England, Scotland and Wales as being in church on census Sunday, a pretty high figure. While they might not specifically support public art galleries, Evangelicals were unlikely to oppose them as they were a suitable alternative to the public house.

Unfortunately, Evangelicals were zealously opposed to Sunday trading, and campaigned for strict adherence to the Sunday Observance Act of 1781. The Act not only closed shops and public houses on Sundays, but also museums, libraries, art galleries, public parks and zoos. Middle class people usually had at least one half day off during the week, but the Act meant that nearly all leisure activities were unavailable to working people on their only free day. Admittedly, it also ensured that their free day remained free as they could not be forced to work on Sundays.

The law was vehemently opposed both before and after its enactment (similar provisions applied in Scotland and Wales). John Stuart Mill complained about the zealotry which tried to stop Sunday rail travel. Sunday observance was legally enforced well into the twentieth century. To most present-day citizens, it is almost unbelievable that museums, zoos and art galleries could not legally open to the public on Sundays until 1932, and not until 1972 that theatres could do so.

Admittedly, in spite of the successes of the Evangelical movement, the nineteenth century also saw a significant growth of secular liberal values not directly linked to organised religion. But it can be convincingly argued that these liberal values developed out of Christianity and retained Christian ethics. The idea of the individual is at the heart of Western culture. The individual is part of society but is not fully subsumed by it, and always has a degree of autonomy. Not only can the individual exercise his or her own moral will, it is actually expected. As Christianity espoused the idea that all human beings are fundamentally equal, the relationship between the individual and the divine became personal, rather than based on any particular community. Thus political liberalism, which is underpinned by individualism and democracy, can plausibly be seen as being derived from Christianity.

Another feature of Christianity is that it has historically absorbed elements of the cultures into which it spreads. First Hellenism deriving from ancient Greece, then northern European pagan practices, and most recently Western Europe's acceptance of science as the arbiter of objective truth rather than religion. This last was not without its problems, and Darwin's theories on evolution in particular came as a bombshell to Victorian religious thought.

Political Liberals reconciled these two strands of nineteenth-century thought by developing a dual mentality. They accepted the scientific method as a way of solving technological problems, but recognised that science cannot address ethical issues, so fell back on their traditional means of making ethical decisions, namely Christianity.[36]

To return to Matthew Arnold's alleged "religion of culture", it is clear that neither practising Christians nor liberals holding Christian-derived principles would need to look to culture to fill a spiritual void. But some conservative intellectuals who lost their faith, such as Matthew Arnold himself, might well look to culture as a repository for their residual spirituality. Arnold was a poet as well as an essayist, and his most famous poem, 'Dover Beach', is a description of the ebbing away of his religious faith. (It is a testament to Victorian earnestness that it was written on his honeymoon.) So it may well be the case that another argument for public art galleries is that for some people they do fill a spiritual void – which is fairly close to the position of aestheticism.

But in whatever way culture is deemed essential to humanity, it has to be paid for, and this was where Utilitarianism had a habit of putting on the brakes. Utilitarianism was the dominant creed of political Liberals in the earlier part of the Victorian era. To Jeremy Bentham, the founder of Utilitarianism, the test of any policy or action was the question "What use (utility) is it?". Furthermore, actions and policies should not only be useful, but should aim to give the greatest happiness to the greatest number of people. A policy which is of use only to a few should not be supported. This has implications for the public provision of cultural facilities like art galleries. If the question "what use is it?" is put crudely, public art galleries are unlikely to win wide support. They could be seen both as of no practical use, and of interest only to a small cultural elite.

Fortunately, it can be argued that cultural services are useful if they are intended to improve the aesthetic standard of manufactured goods so as to make them more competitive on the international market. Such was the viewpoint of the Utilitarian Henry Cole and his South Kensington Museum. Some provincial galleries were partly founded with these aims too, though that side of the original aims tended to fade over the years. Just as fortunately, public art galleries in their early days usually proved to have wide popular appeal with encouragingly large visitor numbers.

The founding of galleries on the grounds that they are morally improving could also pass muster. Although if they are to give the greatest possible happiness to the greatest possible number their audience would have to be universal, rather than being focused just on these groups who could be said to need them most. Then as now, the majority of the audience was middle class. Small surprise, then, that where the working classes were specifically catered to it was through private philanthropy rather than public funding.

Galleries can also be justified on purely economic grounds, in that they will boost business and tourism either directly or indirectly, by enhancing the reputation of the town or city in which they are placed. This was an important motivation for the provision of municipal art galleries. It is an argument which was successfully revived in the 1990s

Bentham saw no distinction between one kind of happiness and another, an opinion which has been strenuously disputed, and not one which the average art gallery visitor is likely to endorse. A later Utilitarian, John Stuart Mill, also disagreed. He was the son of a leading follower of Bentham, James Mills, but outshone his father to became the most famous and influential Utilitarian, with a reputation on a par with Ruskin and Carlyle.

Mills held that intellectual pleasures were more fitting than sensual ones – as he put it, it was better to be a dissatisfied Socrates than a satisfied fool. Unlike Bentham, he took account of feelings arising out of the social nature of humanity when deciding the public good: emotions like guilt, remorse and community-mindedness. Both these points could be used to lend weight to the provision of art galleries, as part of what would nowadays be thought of as a cost-benefit analysis. It was this softer form of Utilitarianism which led the Liberal movement to support reform projects while still supporting capitalism.

In spite of the Conservative supporter Ruskin being the inspiration behind so many art galleries, in the later Victorian era it was Conservative councillors who tended to be against spending funds on municipal art galleries, and such projects were more likely to be promoted by Liberals. But it is worth noting that, while both the Tory Ruskin and the socialist Morris supported art galleries for the masses, they criticised them as having a solely palliative effect – better housing, nutrition and sanitation would do far more to improve the lives of slum dwellers. Such considerations still form part of debates on the use of public funds for cultural programmes.

Of course, it was not only art gallery campaigners who took note or took issue with all these developments. All these intellectuals and activists were public figures who became well known through the expanding number of newspapers and magazines. Most middle-class people would have known something about their ideas, many would have read their books, and some would debate them in their literary or philosophical society. Self-taught or politically engaged working class people would seek out this kind of knowledge wherever they could find it. And people like Ruskin and Morris gave well-attended public lectures to a wide variety of audiences.

Senior art gallery employees and many visitors would have been familiar with most of these lines of thought, as would the public servants and politicians who founded and maintained these institutions. So it seems safe to assume that these were ideas which helped to shape the way art galleries were set up and used. And while their potency certainly began to fade in the 1960s, they have not entirely gone away.

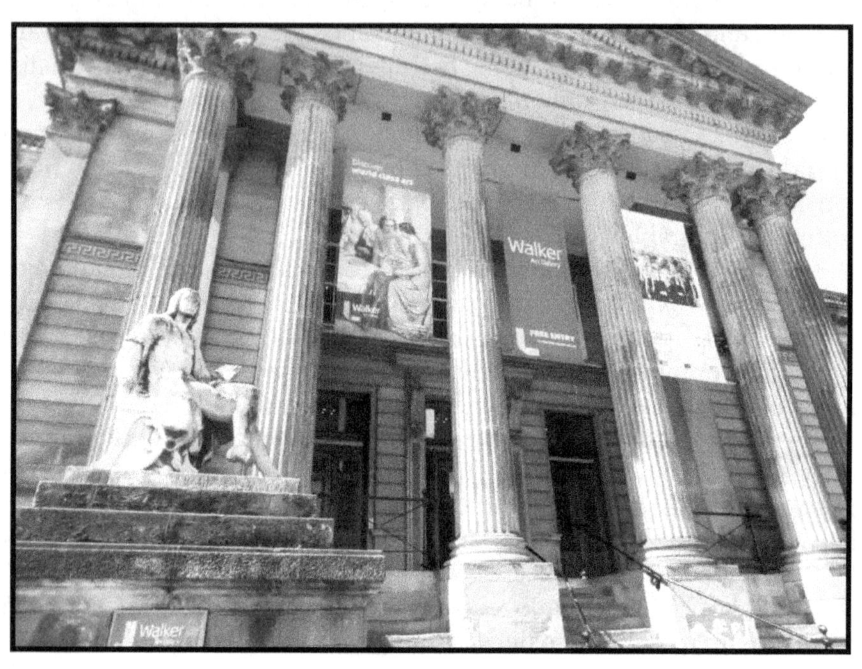

Walker Art Gallery, Liverpool (I. Wilkinson)

8. Art and the New Industry

A S A LONDONER born and bred, John Wilkes might well have
been indifferent to art in the provinces, other than encouraging
the local aristocrat to allow the public to see his collection. Be that
as it may, once the legal framework was in place and towns could make
their own decisions on cultural matters, by the end of the nineteenth
century virtually all towns of any consequence had their own public art
gallery. The trend started in the new industrial cities, where some of the
wealth created by the world's first industrial revolution ended up being
converted into art. Other places relied on funding from more traditional
elites.

Each town followed its own route. As the process frequently involved
strong-willed men with equally strong opinions, no doubt some of the
municipal meetings where the issue was debated were decidedly robust
demonstrations of the new local politics.

But in many cases these debates were only the final phase, as more
often than not the galleries brought into being by municipal decisions
built on existing private philosophical and literary societies. Many towns
had such organisations, set up by local professional men as a way of
expressing their keen interest in science and the arts. These societies
usually had collections – very varied collections, based on the "cabinet of
curiosities" kept in many upper-class houses. There were often a few
portraits or topographical paintings, but most of the displays were made
up of natural history specimens and scientific instruments. There was,
however, a notable exception to this relative indifference to art.

One of the earliest and most significant societies was set up in
Liverpool, a city whose richer inhabitants regarded themselves as
"gentlemen" of taste and discrimination, as opposed to Manchester
"men" – merchants, not manufacturers. Rather annoyingly, when it came
to art their snobbery had a sound foundation. In the eighteenth century,
the upper strata of Liverpool society established a range of private
cultural amenities, including a subscription library society, a College of
Art and Science, and a botanic garden. But probably the most significant

access to culture was just outside Liverpool, at Ince Blundell Hall.

This was the home of local landowner Henry Blundell, who allowed the public access to his collection of antique marbles. This was well worth seeing, as at his death he had the largest such collection in Britain. Like many eighteenth-century collectors, he was taken in by forgers from time to time, but his sculptures included many important antiques, restorations and fine copies. (Blundell was not the only major collector from northwest England – the antiquities collection of his friend and fellow Lancastrian Charles Townley ended up in the British Museum.) As a Roman Catholic Blundell could not hold public office, but he played an important role in Liverpool life nevertheless, and became the first patron of the Liverpool Academy of Art in 1810, the year of his death.

These strands of cultural activity coalesced in 1814, with the foundation of the Liverpool Royal Institution, which was explicitly set up for the purpose of "the Promotion of Literature, Science and the Arts". As Liverpool was already well known for its collectors of Old Master and contemporary paintings, it would have seemed only fitting that the Institution included an art gallery.

Liverpool's most remarkable collector was the banker and abolitionist William Roscoe, who started his collection in the 1780s. He collected prints, with what was then the highly unusual intention of demonstrating the development of art in Italy and northern Europe. His historical books on subjects like Pope Leo X and Lorenzo de Medici were extremely successful and highly regarded. But probably his most notable characteristic was that his collection of paintings owed little to the general taste of his time.

At the time it was almost unheard of to value so-called "primitive" works, that is, Western European paintings from before 1500. He wrote that these pre-Renaissance paintings were to be judged "by reference to the age in which they were produced", and not by modern standards of excellence. Their value lay "in the light they throw on the history of the arts"; an astonishing approach to art at a time when art was valued more as an aid to contemplation than as a history lesson. Roscoe pioneered an art historical approach pretty well unknown in the England of his time.

Tragically, when the bank of which Roscoe was a director went into liquidation in 1816, he was forced to sell his collection. It is a measure of his standing that 37 of the "primitives" were bought by supporters and presented to the Royal Liverpool Institution, where they were shown to the public from 1819. The way they were displayed was as pioneering as the collection itself. They were hung by school and chronology, the first time this had been done in Britain.

This sophistication arose from the importance of Liverpool as an international port, which provided both the overseas connections that fostered wide-ranging interests and the money to fund them. The city had profited hugely from the eighteenth-century slave trade, but the abolition of that inhumane traffic in 1807 made little difference to its economy. The growth of the new Lancashire steam-driven textile industry filled the gap, and led to Liverpool handling four fifths of British cotton imports (which maintained the connection with slavery, as the cotton was mostly slave-produced in the United States).

In 1826 the Liverpool Royal Institution's transatlantic connections led to the first European exhibition of the great American naturalist painter John James Audubon. Art got another boost in 1841 when a new art gallery was built to host the Institution's collection. Because of Roscoe and his circle, in the first half of the nineteenth century Liverpool was well ahead of London in its approach to art and its display.

Unfortunately, the general conditions in the city were not as progressive as its taste in art. Liverpool was a city of huge social contrasts – a tiny group of wealthy merchants and ship owners, a small lower middle class, and a vast pool of insecure casual labour. Living conditions for the workers and their families were among the worst in the country. To make matters worse, the working class was divided, because of the deep-rooted sectarian hostility between the large Catholic Irish immigrant community and the city's Protestant inhabitants.

In the earlier part of the Victorian era the state interfered little in such matters. As in the rest of the country, social reform was left to private institutions, through the efforts of Liverpool's relatively small professional and manufacturing class, who were often Nonconformists.

Liverpool did have reformers interested in art, some of whom campaigned for a municipal art gallery for all classes, but they were an isolated group. As the city lacked a large pool of skilled artisans whose work might be seen to benefit from aesthetic education, there was no significant movement to bring art to the poor. Art remained an upper middle-class affair.

The most vigorous advocate of municipal cultural projects was the Liberal councillor James Picton, a self-made architect from a poor background. Heavily influenced by Ruskin, Picton talked of the connection between art, beauty and nature and how they could improve the lives of the poor, spiritually and morally. Picton agitated in vain for the transfer of the buildings and collections of the Liverpool Royal Institution to the city, so they could be available to the working class. (By the time this eventually happened, in 1892, Picton was no longer alive to see it.)

In the meantime, the Earl of Derby gifted a natural history collection in 1852, leading to Liverpool council paying for a small "Library, Museum and Gallery of Art" (the art consisted of a few paintings already owned by the city). Picton tried but again failed to get the city to erect a purpose-built building, but another private gift, from the Liberal MP and wealthy merchant William Brown, paid for the Brown Library and Derby Museum of Natural History. Picton continued to call for a municipal art gallery, but the council continued to consider art a luxury which should be paid for by private finance. Picton's reasonable point that a gallery would need municipal backing to encourage donors and collectors to support it went unheeded.

The city then received yet another gift, the Mayer collection of applied art and ethnography. The whole issue of municipal support for culture became a matter of heated debate among Liverpool's small chattering class and the local press. Eventually, in 1870 the city's Library, Museum and Arts Committee set up an autumn exhibition in the Library and Museum building as a way of pressing its case for a public art gallery. The exhibition was a great success, with the profits used to purchase some works "for the permanent collection".

By 1873, the exhibitions were so successful that the council was forced to revisit its opposition to building an art gallery, but any decision was pre-empted by the Scottish-born brewer Andrew Barclay Walker, who announced his intention to give the city an art gallery in commemoration of his term as Mayor. It may seem a surprising act by a Conservative councillor, as Conservatives had been the main opponents to a municipal art gallery (with the notable exception of Edward Samuelson). But Barclay was already a well-known philanthropist, and his gift may have been partly intended to raise his reputation in the face of the success of the teetotal Temperance movement. (Several other brewers supported municipal art galleries elsewhere for similar reasons.)

Accordingly, in 1873 the foundation stone of the Walker Art Gallery was laid and the council allocated a small purchasing fund. So the city got its art gallery with little cost to the ratepayers, and with great fanfare the Gallery opened to the public in 1877. It was a resounding success. There were over 300,000 visitors in the first four months, and visitor numbers remained high, peaking at over 600,000 in 1881.

The gallery went from strength to strength, laying down the foundations for the nationally important institution it was to become. Walker paid for an extension in 1884. In the 1880s the gallery purchased important contemporary British art – works by Pre-Raphaelites and painters of the social realist Newlyn School. In 1893 the Royal Liverpool Institution's collection was transferred to the Walker Art Gallery on long term loan. In 1908 the gallery began a tradition of the study and support of local artists by holding the "Historical Exhibition of Liverpool Art", covering local eighteenth- and nineteenth-century artists.

By the end of the century, Liverpool's cultural projects had provided a unique row of handsome public buildings in the city centre – the Brown Library, the Derby Museum, and the Walker Art Gallery, the last also providing a prestigious venue for middle class social events and exhibitions.

The Walker Art Gallery was justifiably reckoned to be a considerable success on a number of levels. If there was one fly in the ointment, it was the continuing practice of holding selling exhibitions with an entrance fee. These undoubtedly helped to fund the art gallery, but they also restricted free access to the permanent collection. Perhaps partly because of this, working class attendance declined until by the First World War the Gallery was seen pretty much as a middle-class bastion, to the extent that in 1921 it was regarded as a suitable target for a sit in protest against the operation of the Poor Law.

The prestige of the Walker Art Gallery was one of the reasons Liverpool's near-by rival, Manchester, eventually established its own highly successful municipal art gallery. Manchester boasted another prominent example of a private cultural society, the Royal Manchester Institution, founded in 1823. Local artists had made a case for it as a place to show contemporary art, combined with a school of art, but they were canny enough to appeal to local business by stressing its potential as an economic benefit to the city. Sir George Beaumont, a patron of the National Gallery in London, welcomed the new Institution, though with a touch of metropolitan condescension. He was pleased "to find such alacrity among Mercantile Men in behalf of the arts, it shows the progress they have made".[37]

The foundation of the Institution was indeed largely due to the enthusiasm of Manchester businessmen, with little input from the local aristocracy. It reflects the energy of the new middle class of a city which was of huge international significance at the time, the "Cottonopolis" which was at the centre of the world's first Industrial Revolution but whose dirt and poverty horrified many visitors. Like most cultural buildings of the period, the Royal Manchester Institution was built in a classicist Greek Revival style, after an architectural competition won by a pupil of Sir John Soane, Charles Barry.

The Institution was well funded through membership fees and profits from the annual selling exhibitions of new works, some of which were bought to add to its permanent collection. The gallery later purchased a hugely popular collection of Pre-Raphaelite works. There was evening opening and sixpenny tickets, but the Institution was primarily a middle-class society for the appreciation of the arts rather than a body designed to bring art to the masses.

By this time Manchester was a bulwark of Liberalism, whose mouthpiece was the newspaper *The Manchester Guardian*, founded in the city in 1821. Once Manchester became self-governing, it municipalised the gasworks and waterworks and undertook massive city centre redevelopment projects. But it can be argued that what really put Manchester on the international map was the Manchester Art Treasures Exhibition in 1857. It has already been noted that the South Kensington Museum was established as a result of the Great Exhibition, but ironically the far bigger art exhibition in Manchester left no permanent legacy (though it had an indirect effect elsewhere, as will be seen).

The Manchester Art Treasures Exhibition reflected a desire to improve the taste and design of manufactures, as well as an assumption that fine art had an improving effect, especially on the working class. There were 16,000 exhibits, loaned for the occasion, covering Old Masters, modern paintings, drawings and engravings, photography, Oriental art and sculpture. They were arranged chronologically according to the approach advocated by the German art history pioneer Dr Gustav von Waagen, and the Old Masters were arranged by schools. The Italian and Northern European works were deliberately hung so as to be directly comparable, for the first time giving equal prominence to both. (The National Gallery had few examples of northern art at the time.) British art, including contemporary work, was well represented.

Over a million people visited over the course of five months, the fee being reduced on Saturday afternoons to encourage working class visitors, and the exhibition paid for itself. Employers in the north and midlands arranged excursions for their workers. The industrialist Thomas Fairbairn was the driving force behind the exhibition, and he arranged for 800 mechanics from his works to attend, while the mill owner Titus Salt took 2,500 of his employees. Special funds were set up to enable Sunday School children to attend.

However, the exhibition's ability to build a mass audience for art was limited by the decision not to label works or give free lectures, on the grounds that this would interfere with catalogue sales. Since visitors were also forbidden to draw or take notes, it is unlikely the educational goals of the exhibition were met. The curator of the Old Masters section felt that "the lower and uneducated classes did not go to the Art Treasures willingly", considering that they would have benefitted more from their visit if more information had been provided. It was noticed that labourers and families often preferred to picnic in the grounds and favoured the modern works over Old Masters.[38]

The influence of German scholarship was not limited to the display itself. The organisers of the exhibition used von Waagen's *Treasures of Art in Great Britain* of 1854 as a guide and inspiration. The book catalogued most of the great British private art collections, and the organisers planned to bring the best of the works mentioned under one roof "for the edification of their fellow man". They were largely successful in persuading aristocratic owners to lend very valuable Old Master paintings.

The exhibition was directed by George Scharf, the English-born son of a family of German artists, who was a follower of von Waagen's pioneering ideas on art history. (Both men had subsequent careers of great distinction: Scharf ran the National Portrait Gallery for 40 years, and von Waagen became the first Director of the Berlin Art Museum.)

To quote the English art historian Francis Haskell, the Manchester Art Treasures Exhibition was "...the first Old Masters exhibition directed by a qualified expert under the influence of German erudition and connoisseurship". Von Waagen's contribution was just one example of his vitally important role in linking the rapidly developing academic discipline of German art history with the vibrant but relatively chaotic British art world.

In view of all this, it seems astonishing that once the exhibition was over, the borrowed art works were returned to their owners, the building housing it was sold and demolished, and the event disappeared without trace.[39]

Nevertheless, the Manchester Art Treasures Exhibition had a huge impact in England, Europe and the United States. Many heads of government sent commissioners to report on it. It was visited by everyone from the King of the Belgians to Friedrich Engels, Florence Nightingale to Charles Dickens. It encouraged Old Master exhibitions everywhere, most notably in Leeds in 1868. This became the impetus behind the opening of Leeds Art Gallery, 20 years later.

The chairman of the exhibition attempted to use the stunning success of the Exhibition as a springboard to set up a city art gallery in Manchester, but this came to nothing and there was no permanent legacy of the event. One of the reasons for this rather surprising failure is probably a concurrent economic crisis in the cotton industry.

A different tack proved more successful. As its President, the architect Thomas Worthington spearheaded efforts to transfer the Royal Manchester Institution to city ownership and thus make its collections available to a wider audience. Worthington had been inspired by Ruskin to encourage architects to become involved in improving modern industrial society via architecture, and he worked on many projects to improve the lives of the poor. (Though his most famous work is Manchester's Albert Memorial, which predated Sir Gilbert Scott's more famous version in London by more than a year.)

Worthington's campaign was helped by the declining influence of the Institution and the perceived success of rival Liverpool's Walker Art Gallery. The reformers had a much easier time than in Liverpool, as they not only succeeded in persuading the Institution to hand over its entire property to the city, but obtained agreement from the city council to fund £2,000 annually for the purchase of works for the permanent collection. One third of new Art Gallery Committee members would be Institution members, and the new gallery would continue the annual selling exhibitions formerly run by the Institution.

Thus the Manchester City Art Gallery opened with the autumn exhibition of 1883. These selling exhibitions were accompanied by popular middle class social events but as in Liverpool they limited working class access to the permanent exhibition and led to the neglect of educational projects aimed at local artisans. The fine art collection grew considerably, however, thanks to the buying enthusiasm of the Art Gallery Committee and donations from wealthy Manchester industrialists. By the end of the nineteenth century the Gallery had built up a permanent collection which was impressive enough to match the importance of the city itself.

If Liverpool and Manchester were pioneers in turning private art collections into municipal art galleries, Birmingham was a pioneer of a different kind, the originator of a new kind of municipal politics. In the nineteenth century Birmingham grew to a large town of small workshops producing a famously enormous variety of goods, providing relatively stable employment. It was the first municipality to set up a public art gallery as part of a wider project to redevelop the city centre, which took place in the 1860s and 1870s.

In the mid-nineteenth century, Birmingham saw the birth of a new "civic gospel". Appropriately, it was promoted by three municipally-minded Dissenting ministers – Unitarians George Dawson and J W Crosskey and Congregationalist R W Dale. The last of these demonstrated his faith in local government by writing that "perhaps a strong and able Town Council might do almost as much to improve the conditions of life in the town as Parliament itself".

Dawson was a follower of Ruskin, described by the *Spectator* magazine as a literary middleman between Carlyle and Ruskin and the new middle class. Like Ruskin, he saw nature as a mirror reflecting God's glory, which gave an important new social meaning to the vocation of the artist who portrayed nature. It was everyone's duty to pursue the beauty of nature, and thus the duty of the municipality to educate the people to perceive beauty and provide them with beautiful surroundings.

Reformers among the Birmingham Liberal Party took up this call to civic activism by expanding both the power of the town council and increasing municipal cultural opportunities. They were prominent in the campaign which led to the Forester Education Act of 1870, which established free elementary education. As time went on, fewer small masters and shopkeepers served on the town council, to be replaced by more large employers and professionals, with less interest in keeping the rates low. Under the mayoralty of Joseph Chamberlain from 1873 to 1876, the gasworks and waterworks were municipalised and the centre of the city was redeveloped under the Artisans' Dwellings Act of 1875. The new school board expanded municipal powers into elementary education, including the architecture for the new schools. This locally driven progressive policy became known as "municipal socialism".

Birmingham's localised political organising became the model for the development of party politics nationally. William Morris was President of the Birmingham Society of Arts in 1879 and 1880, and presented many of his best known ideas as lectures to that body, which directly affected the planning, collecting and educational policies of the Birmingham Museum and Art Gallery.

Birmingham adopted the Free Museum and Libraries Act in 1860, developing a plan to provide a reference library, four lending libraries and a Museum and Gallery of Art. As elsewhere, this was done in conjunction with a private society, the Birmingham and Midland Institute. The municipality reached an agreement to attach rooms to the Institute's buildings, including a one room art gallery which was established in 1867. It was very successful from the start, attendance and the collection growing so much that by 1872 there were calls to increase its size. In 1880 a donation of £17,000 to the town council for art and industrial objects came with the proviso that the council had to provide a building to house them. By ingeniously using space above offices built by the recently municipalised gasworks, the council was able to provide a suitable space for the gallery, with free entry and without raising the rates.

A new permanent Birmingham Museum and Art Gallery opened in 1895. Its first curator was the partly German-educated Whitworth Wallis, previously employed in Paris and at the South Kensington Museum. His wide-ranging expertise and a generous £20,000 purchasing fund enabled him to build up an excellent collection of fine and decorative art objects, and organise frequent loan exhibitions. The gallery became famous for its Pre-Raphaelite collection and also housed an important Old Master collection.

The building's Italianate look consciously emulated Renaissance Italy, and, following Ruskin and Morris, visitors were encouraged to find beauty even in the manufactured exhibits. Unfortunately, the industrial objects originally intended to educate craftsmen were housed in poorly lit rooms and became relatively neglected.[40]

(For those who want to know more about the establishment of public art galleries in Liverpool, Manchester and Birmingham, Amy Woodson Boulton's excellent book *Transformative Beauty* gives a comprehensive account of what took place and its context.)

Although Birmingham was an important pioneer, the first completely free public library in Britain was in fact set up in Salford near Manchester. Salford Museum and Art Gallery opened in 1850 as the Royal Museum and Public Library. As in Birmingham, it was built in the Italian Renaissance style popular for commercial buildings in the mid-nineteenth-century, and designed with an early example of top lit galleries. A former Mayor, Edward Langworthy, left £10,000 to build an additional wing. The building and its collection of paintings, antiquities and casts was a great success, with 160,000 visitors in its first year.

Like Liverpool, many regional galleries were founded with the help of prominent local businessmen. For example, the Mappin Art Gallery in the great Yorkshire steel town of Sheffield was formed from the bequest of a local brewer. Unlike Walker, he was an enthusiastic collector, mainly of contemporary British works. It opened in 1877 and was successful from the start – 350,000 visitors in the first year – being both free and (unusually for the time) open on Sundays.[41]

The gallery in the midlands town of Wolverhampton was also funded by a local businessman, a local contractor called Philip Horsman, who built it on land given by the council. It opened in 1884, and continued to receive local business support in its early days through bequests from the likes of toy and hardware manufacturer Paul Lutz (mainly of nineteenth-century paintings).

In Bury's case, the art came first, as the impetus behind its gallery was a bequest by paper manufacturer Thomas Wrigley, which included paintings by Turner, Constable and Landseer. It opened to the public in 1901.

A number of galleries arose directly out of regular selling exhibitions by local artists. The experience of welcoming large fee-paying popular audiences to view art for profit and instruction encouraged these gallery founders to adopt an inclusive ethos not always evident elsewhere. Cartwright Hall in Bradford is a prime example, founded in this way in 1898 (though it was not open to the public until 1904). It was built in an opulent "Imperial Baroque" style and set in a new public park. This "palace for the people" successfully operated as a space for cultural activities, civic business and entertainment.[42]

Some towns ran temporary art exhibitions, inspired by the Manchester Art Treasures Exhibition. Leeds was then the world centre of the wool trade, and in a spirit of rivalry with Manchester it staged an ambitious, but smaller, exhibition of art treasures of its own in 1868. This was the catalyst for the foundation of the Leeds Art Gallery, although it did not actually come into being until 1888. By that time, it had become something of an embarrassment for a town of Leeds' importance not to have an art gallery (but this was a thrifty town in thrifty Yorkshire). Queen Victoria's Jubilee provided a suitable opportunity. Funds were raised by public subscription to build an art gallery in honour of the Queen, as a wing of the existing public library. (Though it has to be admitted that it is much plainer than the opulently tiled library it is attached to.) The Leeds Art Collections fund was established in 1912.

It could take a long time for campaigns for public art galleries to bear fruit. The inhabitants of Preston campaigned for a library and museum for nearly 50 years, continuously fundraising without success. At long last, local lawyer Edmund Harris bequeathed the enormous sum of £300,000 to found a library, museum and art gallery. This was enough to provide a purpose-built museum and art gallery, under the supervision of the architect James Hibbert.

Hibbert was a strong critic of the commercial activity of selling exhibitions in public art galleries, a widespread practice by the 1880s. He not only explicitly rejected this approach, but made sure the architecture of the Gallery made a deliberate statement to that effect.

Most provincial galleries of the later nineteenth century were built in the then fashionable Gothic or Italianate Renaissance styles. Preston's Harris Museum and Art Gallery stands out as the only late nineteenth-century gallery to be built in the northwest in a classical style. The classicism announced the alleged superiority of Greek culture and warned against the excesses of capitalism and mass taste. In a statement that would have been endorsed by Matthew Arnold, Hibbert declared that the gallery should be a "…means of educating and purifying public taste…Fashion should be carefully avoided…". The Gallery did not follow the fashion in its acquisitions policy either, pursuing an interest in art from all nations rather than the mainly British contemporary art bought by most other regional galleries.

Although Preston was a prime example of the wealth of the new industrial northwest, the motto inscribed on the building pointedly indicated what kind of wealth really mattered: "The mental riches you may here acquire abide with you always."[43]

Warrington was another pioneer which based its cultural projects on a local society, the Warrington Natural History Society. In 1848 the new borough founded 'the first Public Museum in a manufacturing district' and one of the earliest public libraries in the country. By the 1870s its collection had grown to include the fine and decorative arts. William Beamont, the first Mayor of Warrington and one of the founders of the Museum in 1848, laid the foundation stone of a new purpose-built museum in 1855 and declared the vision of creating 'a Home for the Muses: making Art, Literature and Science accessible to all'.

The building contained a successful School of Art organised by the Mechanics' Institute, but the initial art holdings were not very significant. The building was extended in the 1870s, and a purpose-built gallery was opened in 1877. The new gallery was mainly intended to house the work of the sculptor John Warrington Wood, who had trained at the School of Art under its dynamic tutor J. Christmas Thompson. Many municipal art galleries played an important role in supporting local artists by purchasing their works for their permanent collection.

A special exhibition to mark the opening of the gallery included works loaned by prominent townspeople, loans from the South Kensington and Indian Museums, and paintings by local artists who had exhibited at the Royal Academy (Luke Fildes, Henry Woods and James Charles – whose works were unfortunately not bought for the gallery). After paying for the building, there was little funding for paintings (a not uncommon problem for municipal galleries), and in 1878 it was reported that the art gallery was noticeably less popular than the museum, but there was a gradual build-up of art holdings over time.

Manchester acquired another significant art gallery as a result of a bequest of well over a million pounds from Sir Joseph Whitworth, an engineering magnate. He wanted the funds to be used for free educational schemes for workmen, leaving the details to the trustees. One of the trustees, solicitor Robert Darbishire, was able to fulfil a long-held dream by using the bequest to buy land and two mansions. One mansion was demolished and the other extended with an art gallery to create, with the surrounding land, the Whitworth Institute and Park. The Park proved expensive to maintain, and in 1904 all but five acres were leased to the municipal Corporation for a thousand years at a peppercorn rent. This put the Institute on a sound financial footing. The scheme was formally opened in 1908, though the Institute opened in 1896 and the Park had been public since 1894.

All these municipal galleries emerged from the money created in the new centres of manufacturing in the north and midlands of England, but in time art galleries sprang up in the major cities of other parts of the United Kingdom and Ireland (which was a single political unit at the time). These cities also benefitted economically, directly or indirectly, from the new industry, and shared similar social problems.

The two Scottish examples project the quite different popular images of Glasgow and Edinburgh to an almost stereotypical extent. One is the perfect example of a "Palace of the People", while the other reflects a more elitist view of culture and the arts.

Glasgow Art Gallery and Museum has always been part of Glasgow life in a way that is probably unique in Britain. Glasgow was the "second city of the Empire" in its day and the leading shipbuilding city in the world before the First World War. The Museum was founded in 1870 in the Kelvingrove Mansion House, mainly to house a bequest from Archibald McLellan.

McLellan was a successful coachbuilder and art collector. He was building a gallery to house his collection at his death in 1854, and he left the building and his collection to Glasgow. He also left huge debts, which meant his heirs had to put the collection up for sale. The Town Council bought it for £44,500. There was some criticism of this at the time, but it was probably a very good deal. His gallery has gone through various uses, but the 400 paintings formed the backbone of Kelvingrove's Old Master collection.

The present building was built from the profits of an International Exhibition in 1888 and by public subscription. Another International Exhibition in 1901 featured an exhibition of British art. Its success helped to create a purchase endowment of £39,000 for the Museum, which also benefitted from a number of important donations.

James Donald, a chemical manufacturer, bequeathed paintings which included the basis of the gallery's Impressionist holdings. The shipping magnate William Burrell donated 48 French paintings and drawings. The storekeeping Hamilton family provided a fund for the purchase of oil paintings in 1927 – it has bought around 80 works to date. The ship owner William McInnes not only left his art collection, including 33 important French paintings, but collections of silver and glass. He also championed the work of the groups of artists known as the Glasgow Boys and the Scottish Colourists. The number of oil paintings at Kelvingrove increased from 1,000 in 1914 to 1,500 by 1939.

As a general resource for Glasgow's inhabitants, the Art Gallery and Museum had a number of functions. There was a large ground floor hall for entertainment events and space for the museum collections, while the art gallery was upstairs. Its unique eclectic style was described by its architects as "an astylar composition on severely Classic lines, but with free Renaissance treatment in detail".[44] (There is an urban myth, fortunately false, that the architect jumped from one of its towers because the building had been put up back to front.)

The contrast with the establishment of Edinburgh's public art gallery reflects almost laughably the images of the two cities. Boisterous Glasgow with its large working-class population produced a Palace of the People. More sedate and upper middle-class Edinburgh produced a gallery via bodies which all contained the word "Royal", sufficient indication that the Scottish capital's efforts were very much an elite project. As does the fact that it was called the National Gallery of Scotland, befitting a capital city claiming to represent the whole country.

But Edinburgh was not just middle-class gentility. It too had developed flourishing industries, particularly in printing and publishing (the *Encyclopaedia Britannica* being its most famous publication). These were accompanied by paper and printing machinery industries, and a flourishing service and trading sector. Together with its intellectual reputation as the centre of the internationally famous Scottish Enlightenment movement and its status as Scotland's capital city, it was almost inevitable that Edinburgh would want a prestigious cultural symbol like an art gallery.

The rather complex story begins in 1819 when the Royal Institution for the Encouragement of the Fine Arts was founded. It began to acquire paintings. In 1826 the Scottish Academy split from the Royal Institution, becoming the Royal Scottish Academy in 1838. One of the Academy's main aims was to establish a national art collection and it started to collect its own paintings. In the meantime, the Royal Institution opened a new building in 1828. In 1835 the Royal Scottish Academy rented exhibition space in the Institution's building. In the 1840s the Academy decided to construct a new building next to the Institution. The royal connection was well and truly sealed when Prince Albert laid the foundation stone in 1850. The gallery opened to the public in 1859.

The new building was designed by William Henry Playfair in the style of an ancient Greek temple, with one half used as the exhibition area for the Royal Scottish Academy (RSA) and the other half housing the new National Gallery of Scotland (formed from the Royal Institution collection). In 1912 the RSA moved into the Royal Institution building (also designed as a Greek temple) and the building was entirely given over to the Scottish nation's permanent collection of Scottish and European art (now known as the Scottish National Gallery).

Dublin, the capital of Ireland (then politically part of Britain) also acquired a National Gallery, inspired by its Great Industrial Exhibition of 1853. An extensive display of art was included (organised by the railway magnate William Dargan), which attracted so much enthusiasm that it was decided to set up a permanent public art collection. A building designed by Frances Fowke was completed and opened in 1864. It initially contained only 112 works, but a purchase grant was set up in 1866 and by the end of the century space was tight. A gift from the Dowager Countess of Milltown of 223 paintings, plus silver, furniture and a library, prompted the addition of the Milltown wing, designed by Thomas Newenham Deane. Around the same time, Henry Vaughan donated 31 Turner watercolours. George Bernard Shaw also made a substantial bequest to the Gallery, in memory of his many visits in his youth.

The Director of the Gallery from 1914 was Hugh Lane, a noted expert and collector who died in the sinking of the *RMS Lusitania* by a German U-boat. He left a large art collection to the Gallery, along with monies to set up the Lane Fund for the purchase of art works. The story of Hugh Lane's other, and perhaps even more significant, contribution to Dublin's modern art world is described in Chapter 14.

In the nineteenth century Belfast, later capital of Northern Ireland, was famous for its shipyards and linen manufacture. Belfast Natural History Society was set up in 1821 and began exhibiting art in 1833. It included an art gallery from 1890. Originally called the Belfast Municipal Museum and Art Gallery, it is now called the Ulster Museum.

Cardiff, capital of Wales, did not acquire a national gallery until the mid-twentieth century. But it benefitted from one of the most significant donations to any British gallery, as will be seen in a later chapter.

New galleries continued to be created in manufacturing areas up to and beyond the First World War. Less industrialised areas had to rely more on financial support from the pre-industrial elite, such as the local gentry or successful professionals. These towns were usually well-established market towns or ports, but often with some new industrial activity. But the origins of their art galleries were no less varied and opportunistic than those in the new industrial towns. The next chapter continues the story.

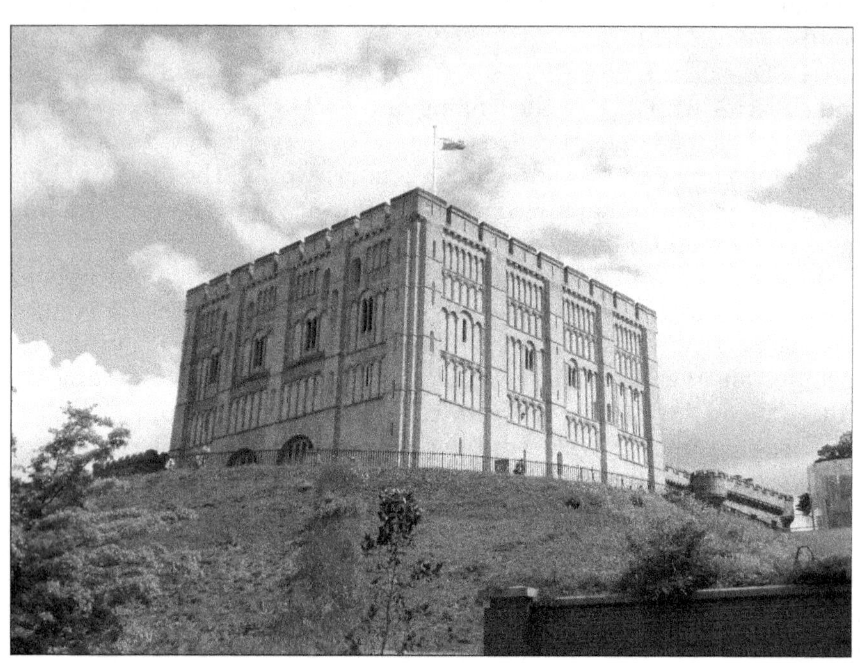

Norwich Castle Museum and Art Gallery

9. Art and Civic Pride

MOST OF THE early public art galleries outside London appeared in those parts of Britain where the Industrial Revolution had brought explosive economic and population growth. There was no shortage of money and energy if the local municipality decided an art gallery was what their town needed. While towns elsewhere might have fewer funds, they were not lacking in civic pride, and they could be just as innovative as the big industrial cities. In any case, as industrialisation spread beyond the initial pioneers of Liverpool, Manchester and Birmingham, other towns and cities found ways to benefit from the Industrial Revolution.

Campaigners in other parts of Britain could often put a very persuasive case for a public art gallery. It would add to the cultural reputation of their town and encourage the growing activity of tourism. It would help to support local artists through selling exhibitions or acquisitions for the permanent collection. It might not have been explicitly stated, but they could also act as an eminently suitable focus for local middle class social life in a town which did not have one. And, last but probably not least, they could argue that their town needed a gallery because a rival town already had one.

The municipal authorities of Oxford and Cambridge had no pressing need to follow suit as they already had university art galleries which were open to the public, though as will be seen those towns too undertook major expansion. As the rest of this chapter shows, those municipalities which built up public art galleries from scratch during the nineteenth century followed very varied routes to that end, and usually had to be pushed to do it. But they are also fine examples of local responses to local demands, and probably a uniquely British way of providing public art.

Sunderland provides a good example of what could be done with local skill and perseverance, with the help of what nowadays would be called good public relations. An established port, with an elegant eighteenth-century iron bridge which was the biggest single span bridge in the world at the time, Sunderland was a notable municipal pioneer. It was probably the first town outside London to establish an art gallery under the 1846 Art Unions Act when the Corporation took over the collection of the Sunderland Natural History and Antiquarian Society. The Corporation added to the Society's collection of a few oil paintings by commissioning a local artist, Mark Thompson, to record the opening of a new dock in 1850. This may well be the first municipal commission.

A key figure in these developments was Thomas Dixon (1831-1880), a local resident and cork-cutter with a keen interest in literature and philosophy. (Cork cutting involved cutting corks for bottles out of sheets of that material.) In spite of his working class background he was very widely read, partly because he lived in a house whose owner had a large library which he was able to use. He gained the respect of many notable artists and thinkers of the day, and corresponded with them on equal terms. As a result, they held him in very high regard – Ruskin called him "the highest type of working man" (which was not as condescending as it might seem today).

As well as campaigning for a new art gallery building, Dixon was energetically involved in efforts to promote public libraries and helped to set up a School of Design. He lived long enough to see his efforts rewarded with a new museum and library which was built in the year before his death. Ruskin himself designed a new art gallery for the building in 1880, to which Rossetti donated two drawings.

The collection grew and illustrates the way local art galleries can very effectively publicise notable regional artists. Ralph Hedley was a successful Victorian realist artist of ordinary life in the North East, who frequently exhibited at the Royal Academy. He was commissioned to paint the portrait of John Dickenson, the owner of a Sunderland marine engineering works. Dickenson was so impressed by the result that he became Hedley's major patron, and donated 31 of his paintings to the Museum on his death in 1908.

Derby Museum was also founded in 1879 (though the art gallery was not built until 1892) and it too came to provide a prominent showcase for its most famous artist. The name he is known by, Joseph Wright of Derby, indicates how closely he is associated with the town he was born (and died) in. Joseph Wright took an active part in 18th-century Derby's fascination with the new scientific discoveries and their application, the precursor to the Industrial Revolution. The town had links with Birmingham's Lunar Society, a hotbed of contemporary scientific enquiry and debate. Wright was the first major artist to record the new industrial and scientific landscape. He was particularly famous for his striking use of light and dark, especially in his candlelit scenes. Eventually, the

Museum honoured its local son by building a gallery solely for its collection of Wright's works. The Museum also acquired an extensive display of Derby's other major artistic achievement, Royal Crown Derby fine bone china.

Like so many others, Derby Museum and Art Gallery grew out of local middle-class societies. In this case, it was through a rather tortuous process of mergers and transfers. Derby Town & County Museum and National History Society was set up in 1836. Its initial collection came from Dr Forrester, the former President of Derby Philosophical Society (which had been set up by Charles Darwin's grandfather).

The Society moved to new premises and in 1856 offered its collection to the Corporation but the offer was rejected. Perhaps as a rebuke, the following year the Society opened its collection to the public. In 1858 the Society merged with Derby Philosophical Society. Finally, the whole collection transferred to Derby Corporation in 1870 and the museum eventually opened to the public in 1879.

Art galleries also appeared on the south coast, far from the main industrial areas. Hastings was a fishing village which by the end of the nineteenth century had become a major seaside resort. Hastings Museum and Art Gallery owes its existence to the railways, as it was established as part of Brassey School of Science and Art (the Brassey Institute) in 1892. The Institute was set up in 1878-80 with funds from Thomas Brassey, arguably the world's greatest railway engineer. During the nineteenth century he was responsible not only for building one third of British railways but for a great deal of the rest of the world's railways too. He had died in 1870 at his home in St Leonard's-on-Sea near Hastings. (The Museum relocated to a converted private house in 1927, and the original building is now the town library.)

The Hastings Museum and Art Gallery itself was originally set up by the Hastings and St Leonards Museum Association as Hastings Museum. The Association is a private voluntary organisation, formed in 1889 in support of local museum activity. It is believed to be the first "Friends" association in the country and continues as a Friends' Association to this day. The Association was responsible for running the Museum, including funding, collecting exhibits and mounting displays, until 1905 when Hastings Corporation took over.

The municipality of another south coast town, Plymouth, had been collecting objects since 1897, and finally opened a purpose-built Edwardian baroque style Museum and Art Gallery in 1910. Plymouth has a long seafaring tradition and strong connections to the Royal Navy, and is of course where the Pilgrim Fathers set sail in the Mayflower on their way to the New World and what became Plymouth Rock.

Plymouth Art Gallery has an important fine art collection, its major highlight being the Cottonian Collection. This collection began in the 1740s with Charles Rogers, who amassed a large collection of prints and drawings. The collection grew in size and scope as it was bequeathed though the Cotton family. The family was sufficiently civic minded to open it to the public in 1853. An Act of Parliament was needed to pass the collection to Plymouth Corporation in 1915-16. This was well worth it, as by then it consisted of several hundred Old Masters, plus ceramics, bronzes, watercolours and several thousand rare prints.

Moving to the East Midlands, Leicester was a long-established centre of hosiery manufacture which grew considerably in the nineteenth century. Like Sunderland, its Corporation was one of the first to set up a museum, now known as New Walk Museum and Art Gallery. Its neo-classical building started life as a school. When this closed in 1836, the town's Literary and Philosophical Society persuaded the town Corporation to buy the building in 1847 and turn it into a museum. The Society then presented its various collections to the town in 1849, continuing its association with the new amenity by holding its meetings in the lecture hall. The art gallery was added later.

The collection retains the eclecticism typical of philosophical society collections, based as they were on the haphazard collections of the aristocratic "cabinet of curiosities". Its present collection owes much to several significant donations, and includes dinosaurs, an important collection of German Expressionist paintings, and a large collection of Picasso ceramics. The Museum's location is also notable. The "New Walk" of its present name arises because it is in a wide pedestrian walkway built in the eighteenth-century for middle class families to see and be seen. It is flanked on both sides by substantial contemporary houses erected for newly affluent Leicester citizens.

The aristocracy was generally conspicuous by its absence from local efforts to establish a public art gallery, and rarely donated to municipal art galleries, never mind provide building funds. The Grosvenor Museum in Chester in an exception. As its name suggests, it was paid for by Hugh Lucas Grosvenor, 1st Duke of Westminster. This ancient city was evidently well supplied with private cultural institutions, as the Museum was built in 1885-6 to house the collections of Chester Archaeological and Historic Society, Chester Society of Natural Science, Literature and Art, and the Schools of Science and Art. The artworks thus brought together were mainly works on paper rather than paintings.

Nottingham Museum and Art Gallery, on the other hand, owes its existence to a riot. It is sited in Nottingham Castle, a seventeenth-century mansion on the site of the original Norman castle. When the House of

Lords rejected the 1831 Reform Bill, which would have extended the right to vote for Members of Parliament, serious rioting broke out in the town. The mansion was burnt and sacked, because its owner was the Duke of Newcastle, an opponent of the Bill. The Duke was awarded £21,000 compensation the following year. Nottingham Corporation took the opportunity to lease the ruin from the duke for a period of 500 years, and turned it into a museum which opened in 1878.

Other galleries were established by the local bigwigs. One of the most interesting is Charles, Baron de Ferrières, the man behind the Cheltenham Art Gallery and Museum in the West Country (now The Wilson). He was a former Mayor of Cheltenham and its Liberal MP, born in the Netherlands in 1823. His family was of French Huguenot origin, but his mother was English and he lived in England from infancy. He was naturalised British in 1867 by an Act of Parliament and succeeded to his Dutch title a year later. The Baron's father (a former Chairman of the Dutch East Indies Company) had an important art collection. He left 43 paintings he inherited from his father to the town, mostly Belgian and seventeenth century Dutch works, and donated £1,000 towards the building of a gallery in which to display them.

During his lifetime, Charles had exhibited some of his inherited collection at the 1868 National Exhibition in Leeds, and gave others to the Victoria and Albert Museum, the Rijksmuseum in Amsterdam, and other art galleries. On his death, he left 24 paintings to the Reverend Thomas Sheepshanks, which were on long term loan to the Victoria and Albert Museum until 1929. Subsequently, the Museum acquired other works from the collection. The influence of the Baron's inheritance was thus spread remarkably widely.

The new gallery building opened in 1899. The building next door became available and was taken over as the museum in 1907. The Baron gave generously to many other causes in Cheltenham, maybe partly because he did not feel fully accepted by English society. A degree of social insecurity can be a motive for philanthropy, but no art lover is going to complain about that.

Norwich, on the other hand, emulated Leicester by taking over an existing building as an art gallery. Norwich in East Anglia is an ancient city, and a major medieval port (in spite of being inland) because of its importance to the English wool trade. It was old and important enough to be the site of a twelfth century Norman Castle, which many centuries later ended up being converted to a museum and art gallery which opened in 1894.

This was only the latest of public uses for the building. For a long period it was used as the county jail. Work to convert the Castle to a

Museum and Art Gallery began in 1883. Ironically, the conversion involved removing the jail remodelling work done by Sir John Soane – one of the many works of the great architect of Dulwich Picture Gallery which failed to survive.

When the City and County jails amalgamated on a new site in 1884, Norwich Castle was put up for sale. No one was interested and it was decided to let the Castle become a ruin (imagine the outcry if that happened today!) Fortunately, the Quaker banker and philanthropist John Henry Gurney proposed that the building should be converted to a museum. The proposal was agreed by the relevant City Committee and the building was officially opened in 1894.

The new Norwich Castle Museum and Art Gallery took in the collections of the earlier Norfolk and Norwich Museum of 1825. The Friends of Norwich Museums' website explains that this was a private gentleman's club where members displayed their personal collections in two small rooms. As the Museum grew, it moved to a larger building, but it outgrew that too within five years. A new building was constructed, where it was decided to open the Museum to the public to celebrate Queen Victoria's wedding day in 1840. This was such a success that from then on the Museum was open to the public permanently, free of charge.

The Norwich Castle Museum and Art Gallery is another example of a local gallery recognising local artists. The City gives its name to the Norwich School of painters, particularly known for a group of landscape artists, who worked both in oil and watercolour.

The School also included several successful female flower painters. Both types of painting show the influence of Dutch art, unsurprising given the long trading links between Norwich and the Netherlands. The Art Gallery has become the most important collection of their work, housed in a gallery paid for by a member of the Colman family of mustard fame. Norwich silver and Lowestoft porcelain are also well represented. All of which, of course, is very well protected by extremely solid Norman architecture.

The Norwich Castle Museum and Art Gallery is another example of a local gallery recognising local artists. The City gives its name to the Norwich School of painters, particularly known for a group of landscape artists, who worked both in oil and watercolour. The School also included several successful female flower painters. Both types of painting show the influence of Dutch art, unsurprising given the long trading links between Norwich and the Netherlands. The Art Gallery has become the most important collection of their work, housed in a gallery paid for by a member of the Colman family of mustard fame. Norwich silver and

Lowestoft porcelain are also well represented. All of which, of course, is very well protected by extremely solid Norman architecture.

Bristol was another wealthy medieval city and international port, later associated with the African slave trade and American tobacco imports. It is also another city which developed an art gallery out of private associations. The Bristol Institution merged with the Bristol Library Society in 1871 and the following year the new body moved to a new combined museum and library building built in a striking Venetian Gothic style. It was designed by Sir Charles Robert Cockerell, who later completed the Fitzwilliam Museum in Cambridge.

The new building was extended in 1877, but by the 1890s the Museum and Library Association was struggling financially, to the extent of being unable to pay its curator, Edward Wilson. The Association and its premises transferred to Bristol City Corporation in 1894, and Wilson remained as (paid) curator until his death. The Museum was saved, but it continued to have quite an eventful history.

In June 1899 the site of the Salisbury Club was offered for sale to the city. The tobacco baron Sir William Henry Wills gave £10,000 to help buy the site and build a new City Art Gallery on it. Designed by Frederick Wills in an Edwardian Baroque style, work started in 1901, and the gallery opened to the public in 1905. It was built in a rectangular open plan in two sections each consisting of a large hall with barrel-vaulted glazed roofs, separated by a double staircase. It incorporated a Museum of Antiquities, as it had been decided during the planning stage that Assyrian, Egyptian, Greek and Roman antiquities should be grouped with art in the new structure, rather than remaining with the natural history collections that remained in the old building.

In 1913, a drill hall at the rear of the Art Gallery was purchased jointly by the Gallery and the University of Bristol. Unfortunately, the outbreak of war in 1914 put paid to any plans for new building. However, after being used for storage for over a decade, the drill hall was demolished and an extension of the Art Gallery was completed in 1930, funded by Sir George Wills, a cousin of Sir William Wills.

Tragically, the Victorian Museum was gutted by fire in the Bristol Blitz of 1940. The Art Gallery extension was badly damaged by bomb blast but managed to partially reopen in 1941. The art works then shared space with the remains of the Museum collection. Proposals to fund a new museum building came to nothing, but in the 1970s the existing building was extensively refurbished. It celebrated Bristol artist Banksy in 2009 with a large exhibition of his works.

Another ancient city, Exeter in the West Country, was able to take advantage of Royal connections. In 1863 it founded the Royal Albert

Memorial Museum, which shared a building with a School of Art. Yet again, its origins lie with a private society, the Devon and Exeter Institution, founded in 1813 with the aim of "promoting the general diffusion of Science, Literature and Art". The Institution had a collection of artefacts and a flourishing library.

The President of the Exeter School of Art was Sir Stafford Northcote, a Devon MP. He had been one of Prince Albert's secretaries for the Great Exhibition and when Albert died in1861, he launched an appeal for a memorial. This was to be the Devon and Exeter Albert Memorial Institution, a building housing a museum and art gallery, a free public library, a school of art and a mechanical institute. The public responded generously, giving around £15,000, a substantial sum for a non-industrial district without hugely wealthy potential benefactors.

Richard Sommers Gard, Exeter's MP at the time, presented a site for the proposed building, and additional land was purchased for £2,000. An architectural competition to design the new building was won by John Hayward. Inspired by Ruskin, the design was heavily influenced by the thirteenth century Early English style. The work was finished in 1868, with an official opening in 1869 in the presence of members of the British Association. The building contained the museum, a free library and reading room, and a school of art; a lending library was added in 1870. Another wing was added in 1887 to celebrate Queen Victoria's jubilee, and the word "Royal" was added to its title. (The educational and library aspects of the museum moved out in the twentieth century.)

Brighton, on the south coast, has even stronger Royal connections. It was one of the earliest seaside resorts, benefitting from its proximity to London. The building which houses Brighton Museum, founded in 1873, is part of the Royal Pavilion Estate. (The highly distinctive Royal Pavilion was originally built in a then-fashionable "Oriental" style for the Prince of Wales, later George IV, and was completed in 1805.) The site of the museum was initially intended as a tennis court but it was never finished, and it later served as cavalry barracks.[45]

George's successor King William IV also stayed in the Pavilion on his visits to Brighton, but after Queen Victoria's last visit to the town in 1845 the Government planned to sell the building and grounds. However the Brighton Commissioners and the Brighton Vestry successfully petitioned the government to sell the Pavilion to the town for £53,000. This required an Act of Parliament, the splendidly named Brighton Improvement (Purchase of the Royal Pavilion and Grounds) Act 1850. From 1851 part of the Pavilion was used for annual exhibitions of the work of local artists. The stable building of the Pavilion estate (now the Brighton Dome, a performing arts venue) was used as a museum as early as 1856.[46]

Henry Willett, a founding father of Brighton Museum and a successful local businessman, gave the Museum its distinctive emphasis on the decorative arts. He was a major collector, whose collecting activities were heavily influenced by John Ruskin, the American Oliver Wendell Holmes, and an influential curator at the British Museum, Sir Augustus Franks. His collections reflected his wide-ranging interests, including fossils, natural history specimens and local artefacts. He is best known however for his collections of pottery and porcelain, which were chosen to illustrate British political, social and cultural history, and included mass produced pieces of little regard at the time. His collections were first loaned to the newly opened Brighton Free Museum in 1873, then enlarged and developed until they were presented as a gift to Brighton in 1903.

Newcastle-on-Tyne was surprisingly late in setting up a public art gallery. An ancient city, for centuries it had been so important as a coal exporter that "taking coals to Newcastle" became a description for a pointless activity. Furthermore, that coal powered the world's first industrial revolution. But in spite of its prominence, and the example of Sunderland just down the coast, it did not establish an art gallery until 1904.

As in Liverpool, it was a local brewer who came to the rescue in 1900. Alexander Laing made an offer to the City Council to build an art gallery to commemorate his half century of successful business. It was largely a public relations exercise, as he had little interest in art but the gallery was to be named after him. The City accepted and the Laing Art Gallery opened in 1904. Unfortunately, the new gallery had virtually no contents.

This gave the first curator, C. Bernard Stevenson quite a problem (he is said to have joked that he would have to exhibit wood shavings left by the joiners), but he solved it with aplomb. He arranged for loans from local collectors and national institutions to set up the *Special Inaugural Exhibition by British and Foreign Artists*. It concentrated on works by British artists from Hogarth onwards, and was a triumphant success. This reaction prompted the council to build up a permanent collection, which also focused on British art. Over time, the gallery received a large number of important gifts and bequests, many from prominent local industrialists and other public figures.

The Laing Art Gallery is another local gallery which acknowledges a local artist, in this case John Martin, nineteenth-century painter of large-scale apocalyptic scenes. In the twentieth century his work was generally not highly regarded by critics, but he has regained favour more recently. In fact, given the considerable influence of his artistic vision on Hollywood and video game designers, he can fairly be regarded as one of the most widely influential British painters ever.

The enthusiasm for municipal art galleries even filtered back to the metropolis of London. Inspired by the success of the new galleries in Liverpool, Manchester and Leeds, the City of London was prompted to set up the Guildhall Gallery. The first Guildhall Art Gallery was built in 1885 to display the City of London Corporation's growing art collection. It aimed to cater to an 'increased taste for Art' evident in Victorian society. Under the leadership of its first Director, Alfred Temple, from 1886 until his death in 1928, the Gallery ran a series of popular and influential exhibitions and expanded its collection of contemporary nineteenth-century paintings.

Like Henry Cole of the South Kensington Museum, Temple was a bureaucrat who became a successful gallery director. He followed his father, grandfather and great-uncle into the Town Clerk's Department of the City of London Corporation. He had taken art classes at the Lambeth School of Art and South Kensington Museum as a young man, and when he changed direction to become the director of an art gallery he built up one of the best collections in England. (As well as the South Kensington Museum, he has a connection to Dulwich Picture Gallery, as he lived nearby in later life.)

The original Gallery was destroyed in the London Blitz but eventually a new building opened in 1999. The present building rivals Norwich Castle Museum and Art Gallery for the use of ancient building works, as the remains of a Roman Amphitheatre were found on the site in the 1980s, and these are incorporated into the new building.

The university galleries also continued to develop in the nineteenth and early twentieth centuries. In Oxford, the University needed a new art gallery, but there were no funds. Two bequests were combined to provide a building which was part art gallery, part modern language institute, which opened in 1845, built in the Greek Revival style by Charles Robert Cockerell. It included a major collection of drawings from the collection of the artist Sir Thomas Lawrence, bought by public subscription, and a gallery was established as well as a centre for the study of such works. Ruskin donated Turner watercolours. There were further donations of prints, drawings, early Italian paintings and bronzes, and Pre-Raphaelite paintings.

When the university opened a natural history museum in the mid-nineteenth century, the Ashmolean specimens were transferred to the new body, and the Ashmolean itself now turned to archaeology. It already contained Anglo-Saxon antiquities; local, Roman, Egyptian and Near Eastern antiquities followed.

There was a large increase in acquisitions when Sir Arthur Evans was

Under Keeper from 1884, including the Fortnum collection of classical and Renaissance bronzes. Sir Arthur was famous as the excavator of the Palace of Minos at Knossos in Crete, and a pioneer of archaeological research.

In 1894 a new extension was built at the rear of the University galleries, funded by Fortnum. The two bodies were combined in 1908, as the Ashmolean Museum of Art and Archaeology. As a result of its origins, it covers art from a wide range of cultures.

When Glasgow University became overcrowded and moved to a less polluted part of Glasgow in 1870, the Hunterian Museum moved with it. The new building was by Gilbert Scott in the Gothic Revival style. This was controversial, as no Glasgow architect was offered the work and locally it was a Greek style which was preferred. The collections were originally crammed together, as was usual at the time, but the different categories were later moved to various specialist locations. The art collection was eventually housed in a purpose-built building on the university's campus.

Fitzwilliam Museum in Cambridge went through numerous changes in the nineteenth century. The collection was first housed in the Perse School. Eventually, land belonging to Peterhouse College was found for a permanent building. In 1834 Perse School asked for its building back, so an architecture competition was held for a new building. It was won by George Basevi, a pupil of Sir John Soane. His neoclassical building was monumental rather than practical. There were 18 steps to the narrow entrance hall, and a further 24 steps up to the gallery, or 16 down to the lower floor.

Tragically, before the project was completed, Basevi fell to his death from one of the towers of Ely Cathedral. The building was completed by Cockrell and Barry, and there have been several extensions since.

As a result of the Gothic Revival movement, in its new location the collection strengthened its focus on medieval and early Renaissance works. Later, works associated with the Arts and Crafts and the Aestheticism movement were added.

Initially, the university did not really understand what to make of the art collection, as art history was not then on the curriculum. As a result, the gallery was used as a venue for tourists, state visitors and Royal visits, and there were continuous controversies over how the institution was run.

The Museum was managed by a syndicate chaired by the Vice Chancellor. Originally it was not fully public as it was only open to university members for four and a half days out of six. However, by the mid-1870s only Friday was exclusive to university members. An important use of the collection was as subjects for artists to copy, including students of the Cambridge School of Art which was founded 1858. (They had to apply for tickets.)

There were also issues over what was hung and how. Perhaps not surprisingly, in the Victorian era there was controversy over the propriety of some pictures, such as voluptuous nudes (Eastlake had the same problem at the National Gallery). The original hanging style in 1855/6 was picturesque, which was crowded and lacked academic focus. Syndicate member William Whewell unilaterally re-hung the paintings to deal with these problems, with the result that the other members all resigned. Whewell held his ground, as otherwise there would have been interminable committee meetings. His work was accepted in the end. It was an example of the perennial issue of learning versus catering for a wide range of visitors.

The establishment of the Slade Professorship of Art – found at UCL and Oxford too – helped to introduce a more professional approach to the collection within the university. Syndicate members successfully lobbied for the appointment of a director, and the first director was appointed in 1876 (who had in fact been the second Slade Professor). From then on the museum developed more fully for teaching purposes.

The Fitzwilliam continued to develop as a university resource. In 1884 additional space was added for a separate building to house a classical cast collection to be used as a major learning resource. Classical art and architecture was now a Cambridge subject, and the first Reader in Classical Archaeology became the second director. The museum supported archaeological excavations from the 1880s. Its best-known director to the general public is undoubtedly M R James, famous for his supernatural stories.

This is not an exhaustive list of all the regional public art galleries established up to the First World War. A number of others were founded in the 1880s and 1890s in Lancashire and West Yorkshire, and new municipal public galleries continued to open well into the new century in many parts of the country. But this chapter gives a fair picture of the wide assortment of fortuitous circumstances behind these projects, the many people with a range of different motives who were involved, as well as the different responses in different towns. There was no national policy or funding, nor were they set up by a single person's charitable foundation. They were local responses to local circumstances.

But as civic activities they did have one flaw. They rarely reached the most deprived communities, who could fairly be said to need the inspiration of art the most. The next chapter shows how some individuals tried to rectify that.

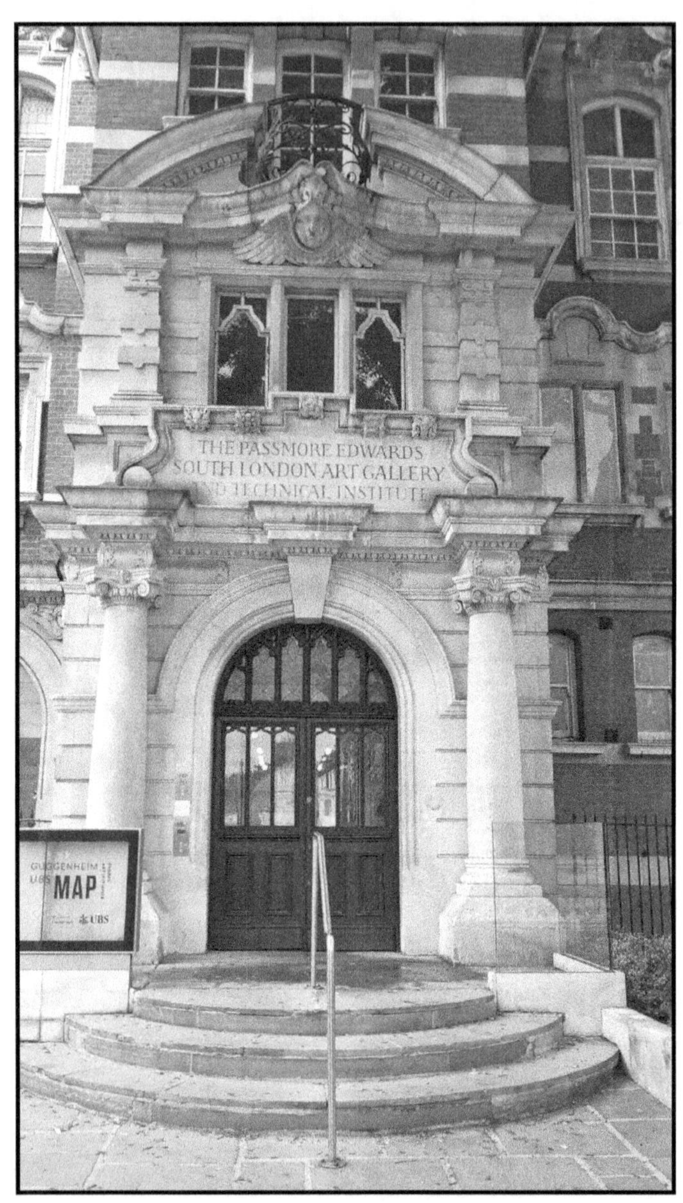

Entrance to South London Gallery (I. Wilkinson)

10. Bringing Art to the Masses

AS THE NINETEENTH century reached its last quarter, some middle-class social reformers began to think of ways of bringing art to the poorer parts of major cities. Although by that time these cities might well have a public art gallery, it probably would not be accessible for the working class, either because of the opening hours or because they were not within easy reach from poorer areas. If they were to have access to art, the art would have to be brought to them.

The idea was to bring contemporary art to the working classes by setting up art galleries in the areas in which they lived. The people behind these projects were usually inspired by John Ruskin, particularly around his views on the links between beauty, art and nature. There was rarely much nature or beauty to be seen in working class areas, but art could provide an avenue to both. Since, to Ruskin's followers, nature was to be revered as an embodiment of God's work, art would also bring the working class closer to God. The galleries would cater to the spiritual wellbeing of the urban working class, then largely ignored by both church and state.

The pioneer was South London Gallery, which opened in 1887 with a small collection of loaned pictures. The dream of its founder, William Rossiter, was that the gallery should be "…the National Gallery of South London…placed where it is most wanted, where the daily lives of the people most need such refreshment, and where the great artisan class, whose work beautifies the wealthier part of the metropolis, live with so little beauty either natural or derived from art".[47]

The South London Gallery was in Camberwell, a mainly working-class area with a well-developed retail sector, and many inhabitants who worked in the hat making and printing trades. Rossiter had realised this would be a suitable area for his philanthropic work through his teaching at the Working Men's College, founded by Christian Socialists in 1854 in the East End of London to provide an education for artisans. He noticed that many of the students lived in South London: "…which is, as I then perceived for the first time, the vast dormitory of the great majority of the men who work in central London".[48]

He began with the South London Working Men's College, opened in 1868 in Blackfriars Road. When the college moved to Kennington Lane in 1878, a free library was added – the first in South London. The art gallery was born when Rossiter borrowed pictures to cover the walls of the library in summer. This action then took on a life of its own, as Rossiter later explained: "... so many friends lent pictures, and so many were allowed to remain, that the exhibition intended for a few weeks has now been in existence for about 14 years, and has become so important that the name of Free Library has been replaced by that of South London Fine Art Gallery." In 1882 a series of Sunday lectures was inaugurated which remained an important feature of the gallery's work. The number of visitors increased enormously, from 27,000 in 1881 to 86,500 in 1887.

In 1889 the gallery moved to the Peckham Road, and in 1891 a purpose-built gallery was opened at Portland House. Its architecture was highly significant, as the red brick building was deliberately non-classical. The founders wanted to create a look which would be more welcoming to its audience than the usual classical style.

The 1891 Trust Deed stated that its opening hours should be those "most suitable for the convenience of the artisan and poorer classes of South London, care being taken to encourage women and children to visit".[49] This policy was a success, as even in its early days the gallery attracted 4000 visitors during the week plus 2000 a week on Sundays.

The project was paid for by public subscription and overseen by the eminent Victorian artist Lord Leighton (who at the same time was attending the annual Royal Academy receptions at Dulwich Picture Gallery a few miles to the south). The philanthropist John Passmore Edwards later paid for a library and lecture hall. When the Camberwell Vestry took over the enterprise in 1896, it became the first local authority in London to run an art gallery under the 1850 Public Libraries Act.

In 1898 Passmore Edwards paid for the building of the Camberwell School of Art, as an integral part of the gallery, also intended primarily for the local working-class population. The project had now become a combined cultural and educational complex. The school worked closely with local employers to meet their needs for new courses, and students' work was shown at the gallery, along with other contemporary artists. The contrast with Dulwich Picture Gallery could not be greater, but ironically the explicit aim of catering for the working class made the South London Gallery if anything even less socially inclusive than Dulwich, as the middle class attended philanthropic galleries only in the role of voluntary "helpers".

The School of Art played a major part in the Gallery's role in technical education and its development of popular taste. The School primarily aimed to give practical craft training to builders, decorators, and designers of wallpaper, textiles, furniture and embroidery, although drawing was also taught. The students copied the exhibits in the gallery, which arranged educational exhibitions.

If the South London Art Gallery was highly successful in fulfilling its aims during the last two decades of the nineteenth century, this was thanks in no small part to its parallel success in attracting an active group of Liberal philanthropists. Led by Rossiter, the Gallery's benefactors included artists in the circle of Leighton, Burne-Jones and prominent politicians.

Rossiter and Leighton's support was strengthened by a network of well-connected philanthropists and politicians. Apart from Baroness Burdett Coutts, these included Sir John Lubbock (later created Lord Avebury), who was a Liberal MP, Vice-Chancellor of the University of London, a banker, and President of the Society of Antiquaries and the Royal Society. Octavia Hill, the famous pioneer of housing reform, who was Secretary of the Working Men's College from 1856, and a joint founder of the National Trust, was also actively involved.

The fund-raising activities of the gallery also brought in illustrious names. The report of a Public Meeting held in 1890 on behalf of the gallery listed three Rothschilds among the contributors. Another was the Duke of Westminster, an enthusiastic art collector, who regularly opened Grosvenor House, his London home with its outstanding art collection, to parties of craftsmen on educational visits.

The Camberwell institution's success in gaining the support of prominent people would be the envy of any charitable body. These included glamorous representatives of the stage (a newly respectable profession) including Herbert Beerbohm Tree. The most advanced artistic circles of the time took an active interest in the gallery – Walter Crane and Edward Burne-Jones were involved – and drew in prominent patrons of the Arts and Crafts Movement, notably the Earl of Carlisle and the Hon. Percy Wyndham. Other eminent supporters were J C Robinson, the highly esteemed former curator of the South Kensington Museum, the collector Alexander Ionides, who left his pictures to South Kensington Museum, Mr and Mrs Rudyard Kipling, and J W Cross, who made a donation in memory of his wife, the novelist George Eliot.

Unusually, the Gallery provided opportunities for women to play a prominent role, probably because it was relatively informal and did not threaten conservative institutions like the Royal Academy. Nine out of 38 artists who donated work in 1895 were women. There were similar effects in other philanthropic art gallery ventures, as their obvious respectability meant women could take significant public organisational roles without affecting their reputations. Not only did they gain useful practical experience, they also acted as visible role models at a time when females were rarely seen in such a capacity.

At roughly the same time as the South London Gallery was flourishing, another philanthropic gallery project was taking shape in the East End of London. The Reverend Barnett had been Vicar of St Jude's since 1873. He was a well-known social activist, having set up Toynbee Hall in 1884. This was the first university settlement, where students lived and worked alongside the inhabitants of slum areas.

Barnett claimed that "Amid lives cramped by continuous toil, there lingers a craving for the ideal and a capacity to respond to the manifold thought of beauty in form and colour." He saw the severe poverty of much of his flock at first hand, and hoped to "lessen the dead ugliness of their lives". The way he put this into practice was by organising exhibitions of contemporary British art in St Jude's Parish Church School from 1881 to 1898, using his communication talents to persuade established artists to lend paintings. The explicit intention of the exhibitions, which were free to local inhabitants, was to promote Christian spirituality.

Influenced by Ruskin, Barnett saw religion and art as being intertwined. To him, like Rossiter in Camberwell, the beauty of art derived from its ability to be a route into spiritual development. The church was losing contact with the working class; art could help to heal the rift from the sacred caused by modern urban life. Conversely, the middle class gained spiritually by lending paintings and through voluntary work. Barnett was also influenced by Matthew Arnold's concept of "high culture". Arnold saw the arts as the embodiment of the most worthy social and moral values, and a force for public improvement. Barnett was not just aiming to provide pleasure for the individual, like the contemporary followers of the aesthetic movement. His philanthropy was underpinned by the heavyweight moral force of Ruskin and Arnold.

Rather surprisingly, the Reverend Barnett was not only tone deaf but colour blind. Nevertheless, the talks he gave at the exhibitions, emphasising their spiritual aspect, were apparently well attended and well regarded. Evidently there was genuine interest in art, as a third of the visitors bought the inexpensive guide to the pictures. For those who could not afford to buy, it was loaned free on Sundays and Passover (the area had a large Jewish immigrant population). To make the exhibitions accessible to those with long working hours or domestic responsibilities the opening hours were extensive – 10am to 10pm during the week, 2pm to 10pm on Sundays.

Although the inaugural exhibition in 1881 contained a wide range of exhibits, thereafter only paintings were shown, on the grounds that this was easier and cheaper. The Reverend Barnett and his supporters must have been highly gratified by the growing number of visitors over the years. From 9,000 in 1881, numbers tripled to 26,500 the following year, and reached a peak of 73,000 in 1892. The crowd trying to get in was sometimes so great that the police had to close the gate.

However, there was one disappointment. While those organising the exhibitions could impose what was displayed and how it was hung, there was no guarantee that the target audience would absorb the intended message. Unusually, visitors were asked to vote for their favourite paintings. The number of those doing so was small and weighted to males, but there was a clear preference for sentimental and genre pictures over the overtly moral pictures prominently displayed and promoted, much to the Reverend Barnett's chagrin.[50] It was a hard lesson many an enthusiast has had to face, but doubtless it was faced with good grace.

The popularity of the exhibitions led to the architect Charles Townsend being commissioned in 1897 to design a purpose-built gallery for exhibitions of contemporary art on Whitechapel High Street. One of the first publicly funded galleries for temporary exhibitions, it opened to the public in 1901. Before the First World War, the Gallery frequently presented the work of a group of Jewish artists from the local community known as the Whitechapel Boys. The adjoining Whitechapel Library was the meeting place of these pioneering modernists, among them Mark Gertler and David Bomberg. Most of the group achieved little success in their lifetimes. But without the Whitechapel Gallery and Library (the latter known as the "Jewish university") it is more than likely they would not have flourished at all.

Not that the Whitechapel Gallery was the only public art in East London aimed at the working class. Bethnal Green Museum opened in 1872 as an offshoot of the South Kensington Museum, and served as a home to the National Portrait Gallery for a while. It also held French paintings on loan from Sir Richard Wallace (from the Wallace collection, which later found a home in central London). But in the nineteenth century Bethnal Green Museum primarily held various technical and scientific collections, aimed at the artisan, and it was not really suitable for paintings (since the 1950s it has been the Museum of Childhood). It was a government project like its parent, not part of the philanthropic movement to bring contemporary art to the working class.

Ruskin was not only an inspiration for others. When the South London and Whitechapel galleries were founded he had already set up his own museum near Sheffield in 1875, writing that he was…

> "… ready to arrange such a museum for their artizans as they have not yet dreamed of; - not dazzling nor overwhelming, but comfortable, useful … making the interior a working man's Bodleian Library ..."

Ruskin provided the exhibits from his own collections of exquisite objects. He wanted to "deindustrialise" his intended visitors – Sheffield's ironworkers and miners – by bringing them back, through sensory connection with the exhibits, to their original direct response to nature and art. The aim was to teach aesthetics, ethics, even politics, through the study and enjoyment of beautiful objects – both man-made and natural – by provoking insights that revealed aesthetic, ethical and spiritual truths.[51] The fact that he considered his audience to be capable of such insights was one of things that distinguished Ruskin from many, if not most, of his contemporaries.

There was certainly a morally uplifting element in his belief that handling beautiful objects could have a transformative effect, but the fact that the objects were to be handled rather than just viewed is closer to a practical educational model. This is of a piece with his objections to the separation of the manual and the intellectual:

> "We are always in these days endeavouring to separate the two; we want one man to be always thinking, and another to be always working, and we call one a gentleman, and the other an operative, whereas the workman ought often to be thinking, and the thinker ought to be working, and both should be gentlemen, in the best sense."[52]

His museum was an enactment of this ideal.

Whether his audience of industrial workers wished to be "deindustrialised" is open to question. After all, the work might have been hard and dangerous but it provided for a better standard of living than their previous rural occupations. All the same, they probably appreciated the opportunity to experience objects they were unlikely to see again. Ruskin's museum no longer exists, but the collection is housed in the Sheffield city centre Millennium Gallery.

Manchester was the site of another prominent philanthropic gallery, yet again inspired by Ruskin. It was one of the results of a reform movement which swept the city in the 1860s and 70s, probably the reaction to a severe economic crisis. The crisis was two-pronged: the overproduction of cotton cloth leading to manufacturers suspending production, plus the absence of baled cotton from the United States because of the blocking of southern ports by the north during the

American Civil War. Thousands of textile workers lost their jobs, but many nevertheless supported the north and the abolition of slavery. (Britain had abolished slavery in its empire 30 years previously.) As a result of this reform movement, a number of cultural projects were established in the poorest parts of the city, one of them being Ancoats, an area so deprived it was known as "the Bethnal Green of Manchester".

The Manchester Art Museum at Ancoats was explicitly set up by T C Horsfall to put Ruskin's ideas into practice. He saw it as a force for social cohesion as the study of art, nature and human life would, he thought, stimulate the moral capacity and skills of the local inhabitants. His motto was "Knowledge shall be used by those who have it for the good of those who have less".

Horsfall was successful in attracting financial support, via a pamphlet, from around one hundred local philanthropists and cultural leaders, including the Manchester Literary Club. He succeeded in attracting the attention of Ruskin himself, through a letter he wrote about Ancoats to the Manchester Guardian. Ruskin approved, to the extent that he praised it in his book *Fors Clavigera*. The project had moral support from the likes of Lord Leighton and William Morris as well as Ruskin, although the latter two made it clear that they regarded such projects as palliative only (not surprisingly, since physical conditions for the working class were still very poor).

Horsfall got the project off the ground by setting up a committee, which arranged art loans to schools and small exhibitions in local spaces. He publicised his project with great energy and skill. No doubt he benefitted from the advice of his friend Reverend Barnett, of the Whitechapel Gallery. He certainly agreed with Barnett that "it is impossible to make the poor rich, but it is possible by nationalising luxury to make more common the better parts of wealth".

Eventually in 1881 the council allotted two rooms to Horsfall's project in the newly built Queen's Park Gallery, and the first exhibition was held in 1884. But times of access were not convenient for working class visitors, entrance was not free and the space was insufficient. In the end the committee took Ancoats Hall at £30 a year.

Horsfall followed the advice of the Egyptologist Flinders Petrie to make the museum "an illustrated text book". Exhibits were carefully labelled and explanatory texts gave extracts from works by eminent authorities. Books on art from Ancoats Free Library were recommended. Efforts to encourage an interest in nature were evidently less successful, as the Museum's Rambling Club did not get much support.

A Model Workman's Room was offered as an example to be followed, but low wages meant local people could not afford the exhibits. So it was later refitted as a sitting room and bedroom which could be afforded by residents – Horsfall regarded this as one of the project's successes. The "Mother's Room" was very popular with children and was copied by the Brooklyn Museum in New York. The Room aimed to attract women by exhibiting textiles and a "Model Dress" with a 2p paper pattern. The press coverage was positive, comparing it with Toynbee Hall in London. Although the local middle class was lukewarm, the Mutual Improvement Society and the Working Men's Club were encouraging and supportive.

Entertainment was provided, it being understood that local residents would only attend if it suited them, not the organisers. About 2,000 visitors a week attended, including around 300 a week for evening sessions of songs, readings and recitations. When museum attendance counted as school attendance from 1895, numbers doubled to over 77,000 in 1895/96 compared with 1890/91.

The curator recorded in his diary that local children were very enthusiastic. The concerts were popular with both children and adults. But there was a continuing shortfall of funds which had to be plugged by Horsfall and donations. And in spite of the good attendance figures, the interest of local residents in the art gallery was always limited, mainly coming from those with an existing interest in self-improvement. The museum was taken over by the Manchester University Settlement, after which the focus moved to social research and the museum became neglected. On the other hand, some of the Settlers were women and they attracted local women, who were attending in good numbers by 1899.

A curator, Bertha Henshaw, was appointed who reinvigorated the art museum, which transferred to the council in 1918 (Ruskin's centenary, as Horsfall noted). It was renamed Ancoats Horsfall Museum and survived until 1954.

The Museum never really succeeded in "cultivating the masses", but it did influence similar projects elsewhere. The practice of loans of art to schools was copied, as was the exhibition and pricing of furniture and domestic objects. 1500 schoolchildren a week were visiting by 1917, and parents were found to be much in favour in a survey five years later. Bertha Henshaw reported that children returned on Saturdays, holidays and even when they had left school. So she was probably right in her insistence that the Museum brought "some light and pleasure into the lives of children in poor districts".[53]

These art gallery projects of philanthropic middle class social reformers were intended to raise moral wellbeing by encouraging the local inhabitants to make visual improvements to their surroundings. Undoubtedly they were partly a civilising movement to try to make the working class conform to middle class manners and tastes, but the motivation was usually Christian and moral, even if this might not be made explicit. The South London and Whitechapel Galleries were both founded by vicars, and the university settlement which eventually submerged the art aspect of the Ancoats gallery was certainly Christian in practice and intent. Ruskin's motivation for his own museum also had a firm moral basis.

It is more than likely that none of these projects succeeded in their aims as well as their founders would have liked, but it is also more than likely that there was at least partial success. It is noticeable that the London projects have had more durable success, but as will be seen this was because later their audience became largely middle class. But given that projects like this, then and now, require a high degree of clear-headed realism as well as idealism (both usually in short supply), the fact that they succeeded at all is probably as much as their founders could have hoped for.

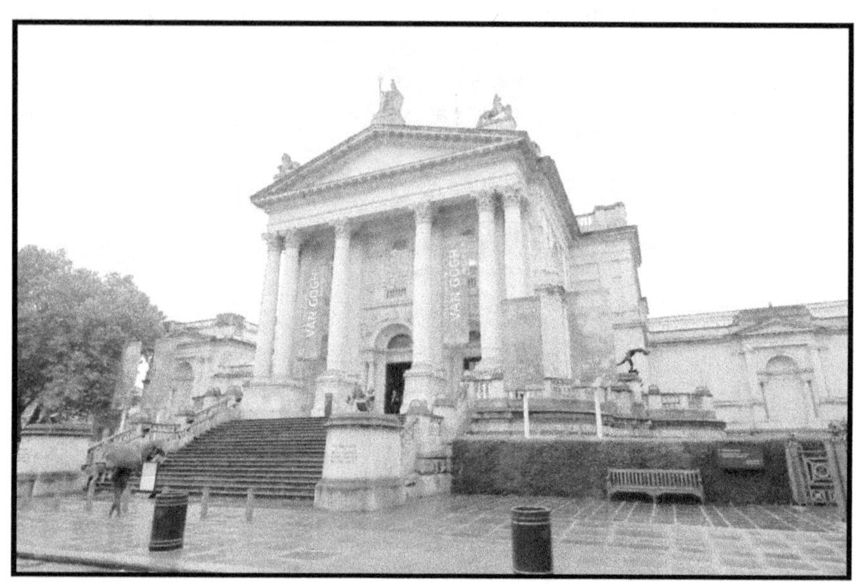

Tate Britain

11. A Home for British Modernity

AS THE PRESTIGE of British art rose during the eighteenth and nineteenth centuries, the thoughts of patriotic art lovers turned to the idea of an art gallery solely for the works of British artists. The first known person to put this idea into practice was Sir John Leicester, who in 1806 built a private gallery in his London house for living British artists, opening it to the public twelve years later. But when he offered his collection at a reasonable price to the then Prime Minister, Lord Liverpool, as a foundation for a national gallery of British art, he was turned down. He was only the first of a succession of nineteenth-century collectors who wanted to showcase British art for the national benefit – with very mixed results. It was not until right at the end of the century that a national gallery of British art finally came into being.

Part of the problem was that the aristocracy did not have much interest in contemporary art. In the 1830s the German art historian Dr Gustav von Waagen undertook a survey of 94 British aristocratic art collections, which found that only 22 contained contemporary works, and of these none had more than ten examples. Aristocrats developed their aesthetic taste on leisurely tours of the continent, with their opportunities for unhurried contemplation of sixteenth and seventeenth century Old Masters.

Middle class businessmen had neither the time nor the temperament for this kind of thing, nor were they particularly keen on Old Masters. As *The Art Journal* warned them, that world was full of fakes, and in any case the new middle class did not wholly identify with the aristocracy, certainly not to the extent of wishing to emulate their artistic preferences. Their own preference was for landscape, genre, and historical costume paintings by living British artists, and when they collected, this was usually the kind of work they bought. When the first volume of Ruskin's *Modern Painters* came out, his praise for contemporary native works over Italian Renaissance painters added serious critical opinion to their existing taste.

Fortunately, potential collectors had plenty of opportunities to view contemporary British art in the Victorian era: at the 1851 Great Exhibition, the 1857 Manchester Art Treasures Exhibition, the annual Royal Academy shows, and in the commercial galleries. The new municipal art galleries contained a great deal of contemporary British art, mainly because this was all most of them could afford to buy, but also because many of them bought from their own selling exhibitions.

For the collector as well as for the general public, paintings now had the added attraction of a new palette of vivid colours. During the nineteenth century industrial colour chemical works were set up which not only produced bright new colours like cadmium yellow, but produced paint at reasonable prices in reliable quantities. For the less affluent, the introduction of inexpensive engravings from the 1840s made the visual arts available even to the artisan and the rural cottager. For the first time, art became a part of life for almost the whole of society.[54]

The status of contemporary British art grew even higher, and gave further encouragement to middle class collectors. Not that this collecting was arbitrary; the middle class had its own standards of taste. Early and mid-Victorians valued art for its moral and educational possibilities. This could amount to "looking through the picture" to see God's work in the beauty of nature. Or the painting could serve as a lesson in proper behaviour through the illustration of an ethical point, or have the practical value of helping to improve the visual sense of artisans and manufacturers.

Not surprisingly, middle class collecting reflected middle class life. They preferred small cabinet size genre pictures, to suit the size of middle class rooms and reflect the domesticity of their surroundings. (This did not go unchallenged: *Fraser's Magazine* in 1882 urged its readers to broaden their horizons, largely to no avail.) Thus the newly rich Victorian collector tended to differ from his aristocratic peers not only in the subject matter of the paintings, but in their size.[55]

A further incentive to collect British art became apparent when the collection of Elhanan Bicknell was sold on his death. Like Sir John Leicester, he had intended to leave his collection of British works to the nation (he favoured landscapes and owned Turners), but changed his mind for family reasons. To widespread public astonishment, his heirs sold the paintings for three times what Bicknell had paid for them only 30 years before. The investment possibilities of buying art so startlingly revealed did not go unnoticed, and the market for British art expanded yet further.

Another serious attempt to establish a national collection of British art occurred in 1840, but from a rather different angle. In that year the highly esteemed sculptor Sir Francis Chantrey wrote a will bequeathing a fortune and the income on it for the purpose of buying British art, hoping to encourage the establishment of a public national collection of British painting and sculpture. The fund was administered by the Royal Academy and the first work was bought for the collection in 1877, following the death of Lady Chantrey. (There was criticism of the choice of the Royal Academy to select the works, as there was the danger that the Academy would favour its own members; nevertheless, the arrangement continues to this day.) The works bought with the bequest were housed in the South Kensington Museum, as nothing at all was done to set up a gallery to house British art.

The nation received more British art in 1847, when the Quaker druggist Robert Vernon donated 157 paintings from his art collection to the nation. His collection was quite systematic, as he aimed at a representative collection of British art from Reynolds and Gainsborough onward. It was quite varied, including history painting, poetic subjects, portraits and genre. He had begun collecting shortly after making a fortune by supplying horses to the army during the Napoleonic wars.

As a self-made man, he may have been partly motivated by social climbing, but he became close to the artists he commissioned, entertaining them at his homes in London and in the country. This was unusual, as collectors usually bought from dealers, auctions and exhibitions. He was definitely motivated by his religious beliefs, seeing art as a way to promote social and moral improvement. He made his collection more widely available when he opened his house in Pall Mall to the public in 1843. From his death in 1849 up to 1854, *The Art Journal* arranged to engrave and publish each work in the collection – complete with an uplifting description – so the lower classes could benefit from Vernon's generosity.

In view of this sustained commitment to the promotion of British art and artists, it is almost tragic that the authorities seemed to have no idea what to do with Vernon's bequest. It was housed first at Marlborough House, then in the South Kensington Museum, then moved again to the National Gallery, where the works languished largely in obscurity until the opening of the Tate Gallery in 1897, to which many of the paintings were transferred.

The collection of John Sheepshanks, the son of a wealthy Leeds cloth manufacturer, had a more settled fate. He moved to London at the age of 40 to make it easier to indulge his passion for collecting, mostly buying small cabinet paintings of genre subjects which he displayed at his house in Blackheath. He was regarded as eccentric, being noted for treating his servants as equals and wearing working class dress. Like Vernon, he formed friendships with some of the artists he collected and commissioned work directly. In 1857 he gave his collection of 233 paintings and a similar number of drawings to the Schools of Art at the South Kensington Museum (where they remain), at the same time asking that they be accessible on Sundays.

Another collector who wanted to draw attention to British art was Thomas Holloway. He had made a fortune with his patent medicine, Holloway's Pills, and engaged in a number of philanthropic works, but his most famous project is Royal Holloway College, which he founded in 1879 when he was 80 "to afford the best education suitable for Women of the Middle and Upper Middle Class".

Although he had a large collection of Old Masters at home, he decided to celebrate the triumphs of British art for the College. From 1881 to 1883 he spent £84,000 on 77 paintings. These included rural landscapes, figurative narrative or historical works, and scenes of London life like Frith's *The Railway Station*. (Originally there were also a Turner, a Gainsborough and a Constable, but these were sold in 1992-3 to support college funds.) The collection was open to the public by arrangement.[56]

A new kind of collector began to emerge from the late 1850s. The aesthetic movement began to spread the idea that art should be valued solely for its beauty and the pleasure it brought, discarding the earlier view of art as a vehicle for moral or social purposes.

This created a new motive for collecting art. The Liverpool banker George Rae is a leading example of the aesthetic collector. He bought 21 Rossettis, then well ahead of popular taste, and whose works famously celebrated beauty. In approved aesthetic fashion Rae wrote of the "electric shock of beauty" he experienced on viewing *The Beloved*. Another collector, William Graham, was an important benefactor of Rossetti and Burne-Jones, and Frederick Leyland's London drawing room was devoted exclusively to Rossetti and Burne-Jones.

These collectors supported British art in a different way, not by supporting the careers of established artists but by enabling their favoured protégés to pursue their own vision rather than be forced to be more commercial. In the last two decades of the century there was a proliferation of the construction of private galleries by wealthy men – art was to be worshipped, a result of the cult of beauty and high art prices (kept high because of new Continental and American buyers). This was a personal reaction to art, art to be worshipped privately. These collectors made a valuable contribution to the development of British art, but they were not likely to sponsor a gallery for the general public.[57]

Whatever the twentieth century may have thought (and a 1940s Royal Holloway College committee recommended disposal of many of their works as they were from "an unusually bad period of British art"), in the later nineteenth-century British art had a high national and international reputation. Artists like G F Watts, Frederick Leighton and Edward Burne-Jones exhibited internationally to great success. Britain saw its art as the height of modernity, a reflection of the new industrial age from which it emerged, both the good and the bad, as well as producing works of high moral and intellectual significance.

By the later nineteenth century, the increasing number of public galleries meant it was now easier to compare national schools. An "English School" was now defined as beginning with Hogarth, and mainly about landscape painting (especially in watercolour) and genre works. Favouring British art also appealed to the popular nationalism of the time. The French had a gallery devoted to their own art (at the Palais du Luxembourg), but the British didn't, therefore many felt British art was not getting its due.

Finally, right at the end of the century, a public gallery was founded in London to house British art, both contemporary and historic works. The Tate Gallery opened in 1897, with funding provided by the sugar magnate Henry Tate, initially as an offshoot of the National Gallery. Works bought with the Chantrey Bequest (which remained the main purchasing fund until the 1920s) and works from Henry Tate's own collection of Victorian art formed the basis of the collection.

The route to this result was, however, far from straightforward and involved a long campaign and much debate in the rapidly proliferating mass market newspapers and new specialist journals. Both the press and periodicals expressed their dissatisfaction about the public display of contemporary British art. But although from the 1880s there was increasing demand for a gallery to house British paintings, there was little agreement as to how this should come about.

The new mass media ensured that, even if final decisions would continue to be taken behind closed doors, the debate about British art would be conducted in public. From the 1880s the steam press and railways speeded up the production and distribution of newspapers, enabling mass market newspapers to develop and grow. In turn these newspapers benefitted from the increased public literacy which resulted from the introduction of free elementary education. Expanded correspondence pages gave opportunities for a wide range of the public to offer their views, and new specialist art journals were published.

The various proposals and arguments for and against were thus well known to those who were interested and this played a part in developing a consensus. The press could now affect the course of public development. Most newspapers were Liberal, both in London and elsewhere, except for *The Times* and a few Conservative regional papers.

Political parties used the press to disseminate their policies. Liberals wanted more government spending on social and cultural services for the working class. The press played a part in efforts to develop a national culture all classes could enjoy.

Numerous points of view were aired in the press, both before and after Henry Tate offered funding in 1890 for a new building to house his collection of British art. Should the National Gallery house works by living British artists? Should there be a gallery of British art in London, the equivalent of the Palais du Luxembourg in Paris – and, if so, should it be funded by the government or with private money? Was the South Kensington Museum suitable for showing British art or not, bearing in mind its purpose related to industrial design, not fine art?

What about the danger that a gallery for contemporary British art might be open to corruption, especially as the Chantrey Bequest was administered by the Royal Academy? (In 1890, Lord Leighton was openly accused by a letter in *The Times* from the headmaster of the Royal High School in Edinburgh of wanting a British art gallery for the benefit of himself and his friends.) And who would run such a gallery? British art was easily available in the provinces – would they support a London gallery? Tate's offer focused the debate, but it was another eight years before the gallery finally opened.[58]

Henry Tate was a rather unlikely figure to be the centre of a major cultural debate. Always a modest and unassuming man, he was born in Chorley in Lancashire in 1819, the seventh son of a Unitarian minister. At thirteen, he went to work in an elder brother's grocery shop in Liverpool, then moved into the sugar refining business, producing the tall sugar loaves then in use, which had to be broken into pieces for sale in grocer shops. In 1872 Tate was shown a method of cutting the loaves into convenient small cubes; he bought the license and made his fortune. He used his money to donate large sums to philanthropic projects in Liverpool and London, and to build up a collection of British art, mainly Victorian narrative paintings, paintings of animals, and landscapes.

Tate decided to found a public gallery of British art with his own pictures. His offer of his collection of contemporary British art to the National Gallery in 1889 had been rejected on the grounds of a lack of space. Undaunted, Tate made another proposal the following year: he would fund a new gallery if the government provided a suitable site and an annual grant. The offer was leaked to the press and aroused great public interest. The satirical magazine Punch started calling him 'the Potent Tate', while other commentators criticised his "sugary" taste in art. A *Times* article noted that British art was dispersed around the National Gallery, the South Kensington Museum and the British

Museum, and strongly advocated that the works should be brought together in a new gallery.

The authorities moved at a snail's pace, but eventually a site was found: Millbank Prison on the banks of the Thames was to be demolished. The new gallery building was paid for by Tate and designed by his favourite architect, Sidney R.J. Smith. It was opened in 1897 by the Prince and Princess of Wales. Tate's shyness meant he hated public speaking, so he took the precaution of writing out his speech beforehand. There were 65 pictures from Tate's own collection, with others acquired under the Chantrey Bequest, now allocated to the new gallery. The eminent painter G F Watts also donated pictures.

At Tate's suggestion, the new institution was officially named the National Gallery of British Art, but much to his dismay it rapidly became known as the Tate Gallery, as it has ever since. Tate continued to support the project by paying for extensions to the building which doubled its space. He also gave more pictures and his widow presented a famous Millais, *The Childhood of Raleigh*, after her husband's death at the age of 80.

After an infancy as an offshoot of the National Gallery, the Tate Gallery became an independent body in 1917, when it was given responsibility for modern foreign works as well as British art. As British art was regarded as "modern" at the time the Tate was founded, it was already seen as a gallery for modern art, so in effect the new role was just an extension of its existing remit.

However, even at its founding the small group which supported aestheticism disagreed with the national nature of the Tate. Whistler, for example, insisted art was international, not national, an early hint of the cosmopolitanism of modernist art which would cause tensions when the Tate became responsible for international modern art as well as British art. It is certainly difficult to see Henry Tate as an advocate for the *avant garde*.

A century later, these tensions were eventually resolved by retaining the original building as Tate Britain and founding a new Tate Modern gallery further along the Thames. There were still questions over Tate Britain's role, however – it has never been fully resolved whether it is primarily a showcase for contemporary British artists, or a historical record of British art. The debate is not over yet.

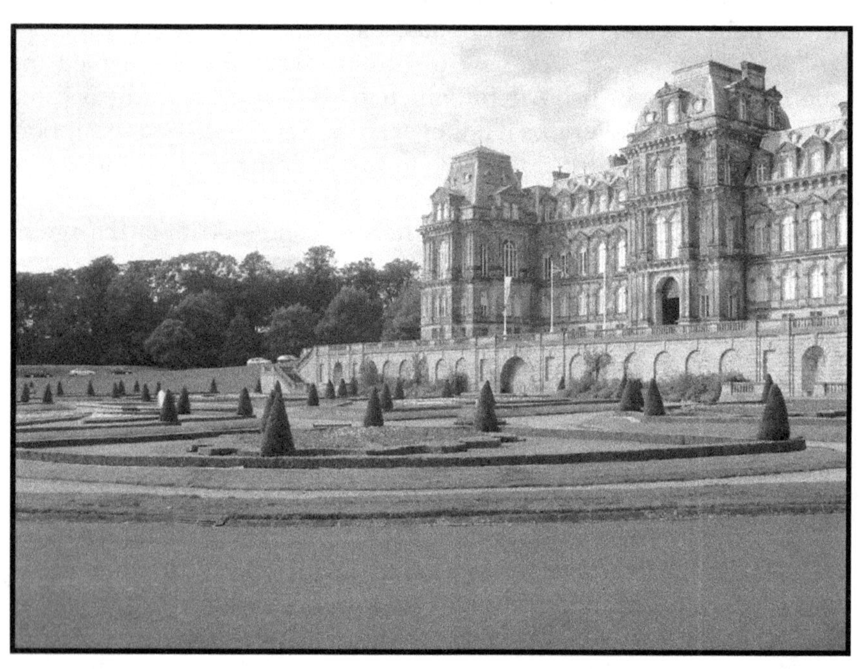

Bowes House, Northumberland (I. Wilkinson)

12. In Memoriam

MOST NINETEENTH-CENTURY PUBLIC art galleries can be easily classified – a gallery for the national collection of fine art paintings, a gallery for portraits of famous people, a gallery for the decorative arts, galleries intended to grace our hometown.

A few are not so easy to categorise. They owe their existence to private benefactors rather than public funds. As such, they reflect the tastes and interests of the founders, who typically carefully select the contents of the gallery and lay down the rules on how the Trustees should operate. Not surprisingly, as often as not they also bear the name of the benefactors.

These galleries have a double purpose. Firstly, to act as memorials to their founders and secondly, to make the kind of art favoured by the donor available to the public.

A prime example is the Bowes Museum, situated in northeast England but built to look like a French chateau. Its style may look rather incongruous in the middle of the northern English countryside, but it chimes exactly with its donors' intentions and interests. The Museum was founded in 1869 by the illegitimate son of the tenth Earl of Strathmore, John Bowes, and his French wife. Bowes' fortune came from the coal mines on his land, but from 1847 he abandoned coal to move to France, where he met his actress wife, Joséphine. Both were fervent collectors, and they decided to build a museum to house their collections at Bernard Castle, a town near Bowes' main English residence.

The "chateau" was designed by a French architect, and is actually thought to be based on Le Havre Town Hall rather than an aristocratic dwelling. Joséphine laid the foundation stone in 1869, fully expecting to run the museum after John's death as she was much younger than her husband. Tragically, she died only five years later. With the loss of the partner to whom he was so ideally matched, John's interest in the joint project waned, and the building was still unfinished when he too died in 1885. Completion was left to Trustees appointed by John and Joséphine under their wills, and Bowes Museum finally opened to the public in 1892. Although it was not publicly funded, its founders' intentions were much the same as those of municipal galleries – to bring the beauty and craftsmanship of art to the local population.

From the beginning, John and Joséphine had great ambitions for their museum. Its scope was considerable: European fine and decorative arts from the middle ages to their own day. They employed several art dealers to hunt for suitable purchases, all personally approved by either John or Joséphine. The Paris International Exhibition of 1867 and the London International Exhibition of 1871 were fruitful hunting grounds. At the Paris exhibition Joséphine proved she had a good eye by spotting a young china and glass dealer, Emile Gallé, a good 20 years before he became famous as an Art Nouveau glass maker. She commissioned a glass cabaret set, one of the earliest commissions he received. They also bought jewellery from several sources in Paris. The daughter of one of those jewellers, Amélie Bassett, became curator of the collections in 1874.

Before his marriage John Bowes had amassed a small collection of Old Masters (including a work now recognised as part of an altarpiece of 1423 by the Sienese artist Sassetta). Marriage to Joséphine in 1852 broadened his taste to include seventeenth- and eighteenth-century artists like Boucher and Tiepolo. In 1869 they acquired what is possibly the largest collection of Spanish paintings in Britain, including two Goyas and an El Greco. They also bought a cross-section of contemporary French paintings of the 1860s on the Paris art market, including works by Fantin-Latour, Courbet and Boudin. Their ceramics and textiles collections included French faience, French and German porcelain, tapestries and needlework seat covers. It has to be admitted that their most expensive purchase and most famous exhibit, an eighteenth-century automaton of a life-size silver swan, is less admired by art experts (but it remains very popular with visitors).

According to the Sunnyside Local History Society, the couple intended to be buried in the grounds of their museum. This would have echoed the burial of the Dulwich Picture Gallery donors in a mausoleum within the gallery itself. A chapel was started but never completed. In the event, that building was pulled down and rebuilt outside the grounds. The couple were reinterred there in 1928. The Museum is still a private body run by a Trust.

If the story of the Bowes Museum reads like a romance, the backstory of the other prime example of a donor museum is closer to a cross between a family saga and a soap opera (albeit a soap opera in the best possible taste). The Wallace Collection is Britain's most prominent private donor gallery. Like the Bowes Museum, it too beautifully showcased French fine and decorative arts, though there was much else besides. It opened in London a few years after its northern counterpart, in 1900. The gallery is named after Richard Wallace, another illegitimate son of an aristocrat, in this case the fourth Marquis of Hertford. But it is actually a monument to several generations of collecting by legitimate and illegitimate heirs of the Hertford family.

The first Marquis of Hertford acquired a small collection of high-quality paintings, including a Canaletto and two Reynolds portraits. The second Marquis was the one who bought the lease of the home of the Wallace Collection, Hertford House in the West End of London. He collected English portraits, along with French furniture and porcelain.

The third Marquis, however, was the one who really started the family habit of major collecting in a big way. This was largely enabled by the considerable fortune he gained by marrying the illegitimate daughter of an Italian dancer. This marriage might seem surprising, but her father was the Marquis of Queensbury, and he left her a large bequest.

The third Marquis was a knowledgeable and energetic collector, picking up a Titian, seventeenth-century Dutch paintings, French furniture, gilt bronzes, and Sèvres porcelain. His expertise attracted the attention of the Prince of Wales. The marquis bought a large number of paintings for the prince, 40 of which are now in the Royal Collection. Both of them took full advantage of the break-up of major French collections as a result of the French Revolution and the Napoleonic Wars. As always, one man's loss is another man's gain.

His heir, the fourth Marquis, was born in London but his mother separated from his father and raised her son in Paris. After a relatively brief spell in England as a young man, he returned in Paris where he put together a collection which was the envy of Europe. Though he never married and became eventually something of a recluse, he was a major figure in Paris society during the Second Empire. His huge wealth allowed him to add to existing family pieces to form one of Europe's largest and most admired collections.

His taste was almost more French than the French, as he followed the upper-class French nostalgia for the ancien regime by buying a great deal of French eighteenth-century painting, furniture and decorative art. But he also bought Old Masters, Dutch paintings, contemporary nineteenth-century art and a wealth of decorative pieces, including Sevres porcelain, tapestries, gold boxes and sculpture. His taste for Oriental arms and armour demonstrated, perhaps, a slightly more quirky preference than his French peers.

The Marquis had an unacknowledged illegitimate son, Richard, by Agnes Jackson (a distant descendent of the Scottish patriot and warrior William Wallace). Agnes had separated from her husband, but eventually she returned to Mr Jackson, at which point she left her son by the Marquis with his widowed grandmother in Paris. Fortunately, she doted on her grandchild (unlike his father, who was said to be reluctant to have the child in Paris). Richard was originally known as Richard Jackson, but for unclear reasons subsequently changed his name to his mother's maiden name of Wallace. On the fourth Marquis' death, a second cousin inherited the title but Richard was left the unentailed property (that is, property not legally limited to the legitimate heir) and the collection.

Richard had become a serious connoisseur by acting as his father's salesroom assistant and adviser. This may well be why he inherited the collection, as his father knew he was attached to it and would be unlikely to sell it off. The income from his inheritance (mainly estates in Ireland) enabled Richard to add further to the already magnificent collection. Although his taste was generally similar to his father, he was now able to follow his interest in medieval and Renaissance works, buying several major collections in the 1870s. He acquired the collection of medieval and Renaissance decorative arts owned by Comte de Nieuwerkerke (Napoleon III's Director of Fine Arts), part of Sir Samuel Rush Meyrick's collection of arms and armour, and the Vicomte Both de Tauzia's collection of early Italian painting and illuminated manuscripts. Gold boxes and miniatures also caught his eye.

Richard received great praise for his humanitarian work during the violence and chaos of the 1870 Paris Commune, for which he was honoured by the French government. But the upheavals made him decide to move most of the collection to the safety of London. He managed to buy the lease of Hertford House from the legitimate heir as a home for the collection. While Hertford House was being made ready, the collection was exhibited at Bethnal Green Museum, where it caused a major sensation and drew huge crowds. It was then installed in Hertford House, by now skilfully remodelled as a recreation of eighteenth-century French aristocratic refinement.

Like John Bowes, Richard had a French wife, who had been his long-term mistress until he married her after his father's death. They had a son, Edmond. Unfortunately, neither his wife nor his son took to English life. His wife never spoke English, and would or could not support her husband's social activities. His son may well have been disenchanted by England because his parents' marriage did not make him legitimate under English law. (Illegitimate children were not legitimised by their parents' marriage until 1926, and even then children remained illegitimate if either parent was married to a third party at the time of the child's birth.)

Edmond was forced by his parents to become a British citizen, but he was a Frenchman at heart and he returned to France. This was much against his parents' wishes, but he had followed family tradition by entering into a love match which had produced four children whom he did not wish to abandon. Bizarrely, in view of his own status, this is said to have provoked his father to exclaim "Good God, how many bastards has this family produced!"

Edmond died at the young age of 47, completely estranged from both his parents. On his son's death, Richard returned to France without his wife and died three years later. His wife remained at Hertford House, replacing Edmond with Richard's secretary Sir John Murray Scott, who became virtually an adopted son.

Before he died, Wallace had indicated he wished to leave the house and contents to the British nation, on condition that the collection was kept intact and nothing would be lent. His wife loyally followed his wishes, with Sir John as her adviser. Hertford House opened to the public, free of charge, in the year of her death.

The aristocratic style of Hertford House and its contents was very attractive to the nineteenth-century Gilded Age American millionaires who saw it, to the extent that it was the inspiration for similar projects on the other side of the Atlantic. The best known is Henry Clay Frick, whose private residence, Frick House in New York, was opened to the public as a museum (in 1935, well after his death in 1919, but he had always intended to make the house a museum). Like Hertford House, Frick House imitates the style of French aristocracy.

Another type of donor gallery is the Watts Gallery in Surrey, the first gallery in England to be dedicated to the work of a single painter. It was a purpose-built gallery to house works by the Victorian artist George Frederic Watts (1817-1904), funded by Watts himself and opened in the year of his death. Watts was the first English artist-celebrity, critically acclaimed and hugely successful at home and abroad during his lifetime. A brief summary of his life demonstrates how, in the end, he was not just the universally acknowledged embodiment of British art – he *was* British art.

Watts' family was poor but he made money from an early age from portraits in chalk and pencil. He was inspired by the Bible, Homer's *Iliad*, the works of Walter Scott, and later by the Parthenon Marbles in the British Museum. He entered the Royal Academy Schools in 1835 but attended only intermittently, and his relationship with the Academy was always uneasy. Portrait painting established his reputation, his most important patrons being the family of émigré Greek shipping merchant Constantine Ionides (a noted collector who made a major donation to the Victoria and Albert Museum in 1901).

In 1842 Watts' painting *Caractacus Led in Triumph through the Streets of Rome* won a competition relating to the decoration of the new Palace of Westminster. The prize of £300 took him to Italy, where he stayed for several years and began to practice sculpture. He returned to England with an entry for another competition for the Houses of Parliament, *Alfred Inciting the Saxons to Prevent the Landing of the Danes*, and won £500, confirming his status as a grand history painter – which unfortunately was going out of fashion.

He began to mix with the influential men of the day, including John Ruskin, who borrowed a large work, *Time and Oblivion*. He became a close friend of fellow painters Lord Leighton and Edward Burne-Jones. Mixing with famous men gave him the idea of painting their portraits for his own collection and eventual donation to the nation. As well as poetic works, he produced paintings illustrating contemporary social problems – not for sale but on view at his studio. He was an enthusiastic muralist, finally managing to receive an actual commission to paint a mural in the Palace of Westminster (a scene from Spenser's *Faerie Queene*), as well as painting a mural for Lincoln's Inn which received high praise.

During the 1880s Watts contributed to international symbolism with his own invented subjects, such as *Hope* (said to be Barack Obama's favourite picture) and the enigmatic *Dweller in the Innermost*, a personification of the idea of conscience. His work became an inspiration to younger artists at home and abroad. In the winter of 1881-2 a show containing more than 200 works was the first full retrospective of any living British artist.

He was now an international star, thanks to his links to the Grosvenor Gallery and the Paris art world. He exhibited abroad with great success: the Paris Salon in 1880, the newly opened Metropolitan Museum in New York in 1884 (a show which ran for six months), Munich in the same year, Paris again at the Universal Exhibition of 1889 (where both he and Burne-Jones triumphed). By 1900 he was the most famous living British painter, and more than a dozen articles about him had appeared in the British press.

His interest in social concerns continued and Watts became a close friend of Canon Samuel Barnett and his wife. He supported their activities to help the poor in the East End of London at their church, St Jude's in Whitechapel, by lending paintings for their hugely popular local art exhibitions from 1885.

In 1895 he donated a group of his portraits to the National Portrait Gallery; he became a trustee in the following year. In 1897 the new Tate Gallery opened with 17 paintings forming the first instalment of the Watts Gift. Specially displayed in two rooms (later one), this bequest formed a significant portion of the new gallery. (With the advent of modernism, Watts' reputation plummeted and the Tate Gallery closed the room in the late 1930s. A similar fate befell Lord Leighton's work, though the work of his other close artist friend, Edward Burne-Jones, maintained its appeal. It was not until late in the twentieth century that Victorian art began to be rehabilitated.)

Watts even made his mark at Lord's cricket ground. He made a set of drawings of cricket positions for cricket authority Nicholas Felix, which were published as lithographs in 1837. In 1895 he presented five of them to the Marylebone Cricket Club. Another intervention in the non-art world is the *Memorial to Heroic Self-Sacrifice*, which Watts funded. It was unveiled in Postman's Park in Central London in 1900. In 1887 Watts suggested a plan to celebrate Queen Victoria's Golden Jubilee by erecting a monument to "heroism in every-day life", commemorating individuals who had lost their lives while attempting to save another. The monument is still in use.

Watts had married the 16-year-old Ellen Terry in 1864 when he was 47, but they separated the following year (later, of course, she became a famous actress). More than 20 years later, he married a trained artist, Mary Seton Fraser Tytler. A few years after the marriage he bought land in Compton, near Guildford in Surrey, for a house to be built for the two of them. In 1902 he bought more land in Compton for a picture gallery. Named the Watts Gallery, it was built in the Arts and Crafts style, with top-lit natural lighting, and opened in 1904, the year of his death.

His wife complemented the gallery by designing and decorating a mortuary chapel for the village, complete with a nearby memorial to Watts. She gave most of her husband's work to the Watts Gallery, forming a significant collection. As already noted, Watts' reputation declined dramatically after his death, along with Victorian painting generally, and the gallery fell into some neglect, though it has subsequently been restored. But it is still quite easy to see why this internationally renowned artist who involved himself in such a wide area of artistic and social life should be regarded as a suitable recipient for a monument to his work.

On the face of it, Leighton House, the former Kensington home of Watts' friend Frederick, Lord Leighton, is also a memorial gallery, but the gallery was only created a long time after his death. In his day, Leighton was equal to Watts in public estimation – news of his ill health abroad shortly before his death was reported in *The Times* – and the house with studio that he built was famous for its extravagant aestheticism, borrowing objects and décor from many cultures, though most famous for its elaborately tiled Arab room. Middle-class visitors were allowed to view the house, paintings and decorative objects on Sundays, and working-class visitors were allowed in during the summer when Leighton was abroad. (The house contained paintings by Leighton's friends, such as Millais and Watts, as well as by himself.)

Leighton had no wife or children (there has been much speculation about the precise nature of his love life, if any, the latest being that he had a long-standing relationship with one of his female models). On his death his sisters needed to raise money for the bequests in his will. They were unable to sell the house as it only had one bedroom (a small ascetic room entirely at odds with the rest of the house), so the carefully acquired contents had to be sold in a three-day sale at Christies.

The house was taken over by the local authority, and it did not become a museum until the 1990s. The evident lack of interest was because after his death Leighton's reputation fell even more dramatically than that of Watts. In fact, his meticulous academic technique and antique subject matter was becoming out of date even before his death. The result was that what is now his most famous painting, *Flaming June,* failed to sell in Britain when it came up for sale in the 1960s and now (rather shamefully) resides in Puerto Rico. Leighton House has been restored to the state it was in during Leighton's life, and some contents have been reassembled on loan, but although it memorialises a famous artist it is a municipal gallery, not a donor gallery.

On the other hand, the Royal Holloway Gallery of British art can justifiably be regarded as a donor gallery, as Holloway provided the building and the paintings, and the gallery bears his name (see Chapter 11). But it is an integral part of a larger organisation, originally intended for the education of the female students of the College which he also funded, rather than the general public. All the same, it is a fitting memorial for the man.

As already noted, three university galleries were named after founding donors who gifted collections. The Ashmoleon Museum of Oxford University, founded in 1683, was based on the cabinet of curiosities collection of the Tredescant father and son of London. The son's will specified that the collection should be given to Oxford University after his wife's death. It was actually donated after their deaths by their neighbour Elias Ashmole, who arranged to have the museum named after himself rather than the actual collectors. It was a condition that the museum be open to the public, though a fee was charged. It was the first public museum in the world. (As happened with the National Gallery in the nineteenth century, this led to middle class complaints about the behaviour of crowds of ordinary people who sometimes frequented it.)

The second gallery was founded in Cambridge in 1816, based on a bequest by the 7th Viscount Fitzwilliam of his library and art collection. The bequest included £100,000 for a purpose-built museum and 144 pictures, including Dutch paintings, and Old Masters by Titian, Veronese and Palma Vecchio acquired at the Orleans sale in London. More than 500 albums of engravings were also donated, as well as music manuscripts by Handel, Purcell and others, and 130 medieval manuscripts. Initially, the collection was housed in a school building, then in what was at the time the University library. The current building did not open until 1848 (an entrance hall was added in 1875).

The last example is the Hunterian Museum in Glasgow University. Opened in 1807, it was the first public museum to have a gallery of paintings. The distinguished anatomist and collector William Hunter left all his varied collections to his alma mater. This included a major art collection, making it the first museum to have a dedicated gallery for art.

Like the Royal Holloway, the university galleries are part of a larger independent organisation, but as they were intended for the general public as much as students in a way the Holloway was not, they can be regarded as donor galleries.

On the other hand, England's first purpose built public gallery, Dulwich Picture Gallery, does fall into the category of a private donor gallery. The Bowes Museum was intended to contain the remains of its founders within its grounds, and Watts is interred in a mausoleum near his museum, but Dulwich Picture Gallery is unique in being the only English gallery which fully integrates a mausoleum dedicated to the donors within the gallery. However, Dulwich is a donor gallery almost by default, as at the time the arrangement with Dulwich College and Sir John Soane was the only way to create the gallery at all. Its founders would have been content for the state to take over the project (with due acknowledgement).

As will be seen later, the donor gallery has not died out. In the twentieth century there were Birmingham University's Lady Barber gallery, the Lady Lever Gallery at Port Sunlight near Liverpool, the Sainsbury Centre at the University of East Anglia in Norwich, Pallant House Gallery of twentieth-century British art in Chichester, and the Courtauld Gallery, part of the University of London. None of these are private, but both buildings and contents were heavily influenced by the donor. The composer Andrew Lloyd Webber and the artist David Hockney are proposing to set up private galleries, the first for Lloyd Webber's collection of Victorian art and the latter for his own work. Nevertheless, the donor gallery of any type is a relatively rare phenomenon in Britain.

Perhaps its true home is across the Atlantic, where Frick is only one of a number of fabulously wealthy individuals who created art galleries from their own collections and which bear their names. California hosts two famous twentieth-century examples: the Henry E Huntington Library and Art Gallery in San Marino, and the J Paul Getty Museum in Malibu. But the doyenne of them all is surely the Isabella Stewart Gardner Museum in Boston. Like the Bowes Museum, it was specially built to house her collection, assembled out of a collection of Renaissance and medieval architectural pieces imported specially for the purpose. It was finished in 1902. In her lifetime there was only limited public access, by ticket on selected days, but it became a fully-fledged public museum on her death in the 1920s. Her will stipulated that nothing must be changed – even the flower arrangements – an iron control that even the Wallace Collection cannot match.

American donor galleries are usually former residences, or built to look like former royal or aristocratic residences. The effect is of a visit to an idealised version of the donor, who, regrettably, was often in life an unusually successful Gilded Age robber baron with dubious ethics. This reality might be disguised behind a façade of Old World nobility: Frick hung his pictures in the same aristocratic style as the Wallace Collection, Huntingdon bought and displayed portraits of English aristocrats, and Gardner built a Renaissance palace. All this might seem a little too much display of ego on this side of the Atlantic, but these projects were an important impetus for the growth of public galleries in the United States (and anyway, if you've got it, why not flaunt it?)

America's National Gallery in Washington is also in effect a donor gallery, as prominent businessman and former United States Secretary of the Treasury Andrew Mellon designed and paid for it and provided its core collection. It still receives support from his descendants.[59]

In Britain it was more common for generous wealthy donors to establish and name galleries or new wings in existing institutions (and Tate, who funded a whole gallery, did not even want the building he paid for to be named after him). Thus few British galleries are bound by the restrictions that donors or later trustees can impose. The original limited public access to the Dulwich Picture Gallery and the continuing ban on lending by the Wallace Collection are cases in point.

The typical public gallery in Britain is run by the state or a local authority and relies on public funds. This makes them more open to public scrutiny and public concerns, but also more vulnerable to political and financial forces. The donor gallery, like the commercial gallery, can, in theory at least, follow a more individualistic path, which makes it a model well worth preserving.

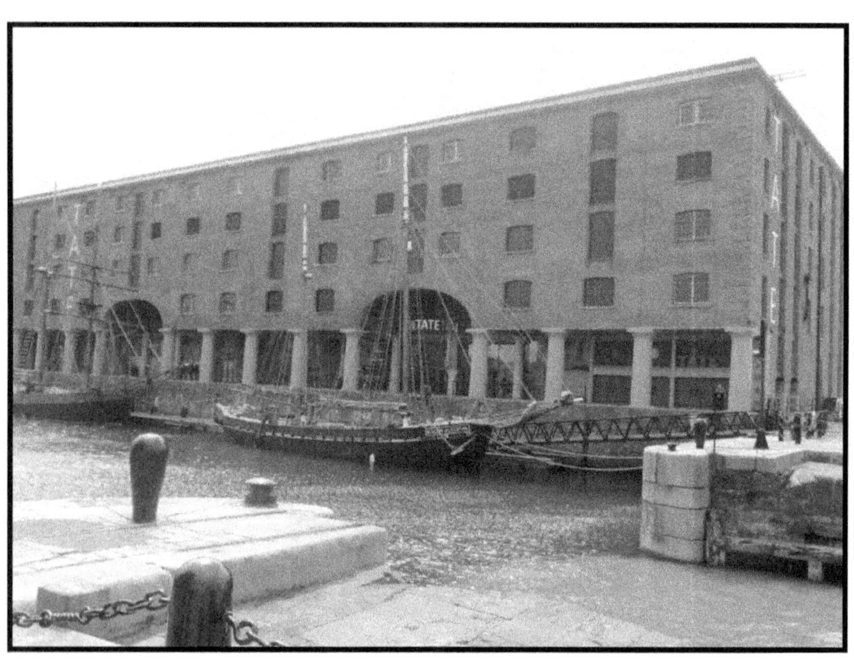

Tate Liverpool, Albert Dock (I. Wilkinson)

13. First World War
to the Aftermath of the Second

BY THE FIRST World War, Britain had an enviable network of public galleries, both in London and in the regions, catering for a wide range of the population. The First World War and the 1929 financial crash put a dampener on the creation of more new art galleries during the inter-war years. However, a few managed to see the light of day, until the Second World War not only put a stop to new galleries but seriously damaged some of the existing ones.

The centenary of Dulwich Picture Gallery fell during the First World War. Great progress had been made since the opening of the first purpose built public art gallery. Now London had art galleries of international significance, which could match anything to be seen in major cities abroad. Most towns of any consequence had a public art gallery. Some struggled to fill their gallery once they had acquired one, but many of the big cities were developing collections of national or even international importance.

What was more, the wide variety of galleries in London and the regions meant that they could cater for a very broad range of visitors. Each gallery had its own unique origins, with varying inputs of private, charitable and public money. Each had its own unique blend of human input from a variety of politicians, philanthropists, ratepayers and art professionals. This therefore meant that each had the capacity to develop its own unique audience.

The National Gallery held a relatively small, but well thought out, collection of masterpieces of Western European painting, representing all periods and schools up to around 1850. It was the home of paintings deemed worthy of the "canon", a consensus reached by art establishment experts about what were considered to be the best works by the best painters with the highest artistic prestige. (Reputations could go up and down, of course, but inclusion of an artist's work in the National Gallery was a good indication that an artist would remain within the canon.) It catered well for an educated upper- and middle-class audience. Not only for those with a general love of beautiful objects, but visitors with an academic interest in the development of European art, and those whose who knew their favourite paintings were on display for viewing whenever they liked.

But by the outbreak of the First World War, the National Gallery had lost its mass working class audience. No doubt this was linked to increasing affluence and the growth of other leisure possibilities like the cinema, cheap publications, and inexpensive day trips. But the Gallery was now far more helpful to those working-class visitors who did turn up, as it provided much more information on the exhibits than it did in its early days. Nevertheless, the National Gallery was by now fundamentally a middle-class institution, rather than the "art for all" space it was originally intended to be.

Did Edwardian visitors experience the spiritual uplift that the gallery's Victorian founders hoped for? A difficult question to answer as visitor feedback was rarely recorded. It is quite possible that many visitors to the National Gallery would have experienced a quasi-religious reverential attitude to the high-status art on display. But with the growth of secularism during the previous century, the proportion which might have seen paintings as a route to God was probably pretty small.

The Victoria and Albert Museum continued its success in attracting the self-improving upper working and lower middle classes. Unlike the National Gallery, its purpose was to improve practical skills and impart knowledge rather than to raise moral awareness. A visit to the Museum amounted to free education, and furthermore an education during which students could pursue their own interests at their own pace. Even today over forty per cent of visitors to the Victoria and Albert Museum work or study in the creative industries.[60]

But it also appealed to a more affluent middle-class audience with an interest in the decorative arts. Its location in one of the most well-heeled areas of London was a real asset in this respect. Its jumbled beginnings were now disguised by decades of building work, giving the Museum an almost palatial look – perfectly suitable for an institution named after royalty.

The Museum's collections ranked slightly lower than the National Gallery in the art hierarchy then still prevalent. The decorative arts had lower prestige than Old Master easel paintings. As did sculpture, because its practitioners had to get their hands dirty with clay or dust, and use workman's tools like chisels. But this largely did not apply, because the Museum held so many artworks from parts of the world where European ideas about art were irrelevant.

In any case, the V & A's collection of paintings contained a very large holding of works by Britain's greatest painter, Turner. And a good proportion of the three-dimensional exhibits were exquisite by any standards. Moreover, the Museum had kept up to date with modern image-making. It was the first Museum in the world to develop a photographic collection, and in 1858 was the first to host a photographic exhibition, when the Photographic Society of London exhibited in the upper Refreshment room. It will come as no surprise to learn that this stemmed from Henry Cole, who developed a close working relationship with the photography pioneer Julia Margaret Cameron. He even allowed her to use space in the Museum as a studio. With such an encouraging attitude, it's no surprise that by the First World War the Victoria and Albert Museum had one of the world's most important collections of photographs.

The National Portrait Gallery occupied a niche which attracted patriotic visitors with an interest in their own history, as well as the art lover. It was just as well that its chronic lack of space was eased when the art dealer and philanthropist Joseph Duveen funded a new wing, which opened in 1933. The tradition of scholarship initiated by Scharf quietly continued.

But while most galleries could begin to settle down into a sense of steady consolidation, for one gallery 1917 proved to be a pivotal year, and one which changed it forever. In that year, the remit of the Tate Gallery (officially the National Gallery of British Art) was widened to include historic British art – that is, from 1500 to 1790. Most British works in the National Gallery were transferred to the Tate, though the National Gallery retained many of the best works.

Even more momentously, modern foreign art was also added to the Tate Gallery's remit in 1917. This was the first time a national public gallery had been given specific responsibility for this kind of art. That it happened in 1917 was largely a response to the 1913 bequest to the National Gallery of 39 French Impressionist works by the Irish-born art dealer Hugh Lane. They were allocated to the Tate Gallery (still an offshoot of the National Gallery) and exhibited there in 1917, two years after Lane went down with the *Lusitania* at the age of only 39. (There is much more to this story, which will be explored in the next chapter.)

The final important event of that year was the setting up of a separate Board of Trustees for the Tate Gallery, which thus gained a degree of independence from the National Gallery (full independence did not come until the mid-1950s). Not only was the Tate Gallery's responsibility widened significantly, it had greater freedom in how it carried out that function.

Its role of showcasing British art meant it could, like the National Portrait Gallery, attract both the patriot and the art lover. Now it could cover the whole span of British painting. And it marked the beginning of its concern for modern and contemporary art, which 83 years later resulted in one of the most popular galleries of modern art in the world.

Unfortunately, the next major event in the Tate Gallery's history was not an innovation but a calamity. In 1928 the Tate Gallery paid the price of its riverside location when the Thames burst its banks and flooded the lower galleries. The situation was made worse by the incomplete infilling of the vaults of Millbank Prison when it was demolished to create the site for the gallery, as this allowed water to seep in through the floors. The Director Charles Aitkin heard of the flood at 5am and immediately set out to oversee the rescue work. Not only did he have great difficulty in reaching the gallery because of the widespread effects of the flooding, he ended up having to be rescued himself when he fell through a flooded manhole.

Of works on paper and oil paintings, 18 were completely ruined and nearly 300 were damaged. Alarmingly, Turner watercolours in the basement were saturated and caked in mud – to everyone's huge relief it turned out the colours had not run. Rex Whistler had just completed the mural which is still in the café; amazingly, although it was submerged it proved to be undamaged. (Given that many now heavily criticise that work for a section seen to be racist, no doubt some wish it had been obliterated.) Later work to the gallery and the Thames Barrier makes a repeat of the flooding highly unlikely.

The terms of the Wallace Collection's bequest meant it was never going to have to change direction like the Tate Gallery. Its approximate facsimile of an aristocratic lifestyle meant it had an enduring appeal to those who admired or wished to emulate it. The quality of its collections meant it had an equal appeal for connoisseurs of art. It provided the main opportunity in England to study French art of the eighteenth century (the Bowes Museum in Northumberland being less accessible for most). More frivolously (or more appropriately, in view of the abundance of Boucher on view), the Wallace Collection was well placed for a visit before or after a West End shopping trip. But there were many other things of interest, such as extensive displays of arms and armour, which further widened its appeal.

The Dulwich Picture Gallery remained a one off. Its beginnings lay partly as a middle-class offshoot of the artistic and literary establishment. The initial collection reflected eighteenth century aristocratic tastes, now made available to a mainly middle-class audience. By the time of the First World War it had less appeal for artists and writers, and its architecture as a model to be emulated was beginning to be challenged. In the inter-war years the white-walled gallery with paintings hung in a single row at eye level became increasingly fashionable. But Soane's work was still recognised as a masterpiece.

The Whitechapel Gallery continued to bring temporary exhibitions of contemporary art to the local working-class population. In the inter-war years it played a significant role in providing a venue for modern art, including the *Exhibition of works by Jewish Artists* in 1923. This showed works by the Whitechapel Boys, a group of local working-class artists which included David Bomberg and Mark Gertler. It also exhibited Picasso's *Guernica* in 1938 during a tour of the painting as a protest against the Spanish Civil War. It continued outreach work with the local population, but its main audience gradually became more middle class.

The South London Gallery had a similarly educational role to the Victoria and Albert Museum. Its relationship with the attached college of art was very interactive. The college students were expected to relate the exhibits to their work in the college, and artworks produced by college students were shown in the gallery. This meant some visitors to this public gallery had the rare opportunity of seeing their own work on its walls. Many of these artworks were judged to be of high quality, so general visitors presumably gained a positive aesthetic experience as well.

The City of London's Guildhall gallery proudly reflected City wealth and cultural interests, at a time when the City was at the height of its influence and power. Its collection of Victorian paintings reflected the taste of the City businessmen who sponsored it, and made it one of the few public galleries in London where this kind of art was on show.

Largely fortuitously, many provincial galleries responded to the growing public taste for contemporary British art in a way that London, on the whole, did not. Regional galleries sometimes acquired Old Masters through bequests, gifts and loans, but they could not afford to buy them. Instead, they acquired some of the best work by contemporary Victorian artists, bought from Royal Academy shows or their own selling exhibitions. This particularly benefitted Pre-Raphaelite painters, eagerly collected by the richer regional galleries at a time when the group was held in very little esteem in the capital. More Victorian art was acquired through donations by local businessmen. All these riches were very popular with local audiences, even if the metropolis still preferred Old Masters.

Thus the regions became the major repository of the native art produced in Britain's heyday, not London, the empire's capital city. Admittedly, it may have been frequently stored in basements when

Victorian art went out of fashion in the inter-war years, but it was still available to be put back on the walls when it eventually regained some of its appeal.

The social role of provincial galleries also differed from the London galleries. They often played an important part in providing the venue for the social events of the local elite, a function not needed in London where there were plenty of other places to meet. Their selling exhibitions in particular were significant social occasions, and art galleries sometimes also acted as venues for civic events.

Provincial galleries had a political and economic role as well as the cultural and social role which predominated in London. The social and civic events which they hosted fostered civic cohesion, and their potential for increasing local business was often a factor in their foundation. True, there were business and manufacturing motives behind the Victoria and Albert Museum and the South London Gallery, but they were not intended to attract customers to local businesses, nor did they provide commercial gallery space for local professional artists.

These provincial galleries often aimed to educate the masses and give them the opportunity to glimpse the possibility of a better life through the medium of art. Ruskin was the biggest influence, although the educational role promulgated by Henry Cole was also present. This was in a context where both Evangelicals and Utilitarians supported state education, if not necessarily for the same reasons. Purely cultural and aesthetic motives might not always have been enough to drum up public funding for art galleries, but the educational benefits could reliably attract wide support.

Unlike most London galleries, provincial galleries usually provided leisure services like refreshments as an extra inducement to those who might be reluctant to visit. Rather than forbidding temples to high culture, it was hoped they would be community resources freely enjoyed by all. A provincial art gallery was often closer in style to London's Vauxhall Gardens (which until 1859 offered art exhibitions as one of the many entertainments open to all), than to the National Gallery.

In the event, the interest of the working classes gradually declined as the First World War approached. Universal access to cultural facilities tends to favour the largest audience, which is always the middle class, and their interests tended to prevail. Other audiences were less well catered for, whatever the original intention. Exhibits originally aimed at workers became dusty and neglected. The philanthropic galleries, the only ones specifically aimed at the lower orders, began to fade away. The working classes were now more inclined to see art galleries as not for them and reacted accordingly. The exceptions were those regional galleries, such as Kelvinside in Glasgow, which had always been intended to be "palaces of the people".

On the other hand, although the network of government art schools was purely vocational in intention, it enabled some working-class students to acquire a certain amount of higher education, just as teacher training colleges did. These art students were likely to develop cultural interests and visit art galleries, and many would become designers or artists with a continuing professional interest in art.

By 1864 there were 90 art schools in Great Britain, teaching over 16,000 students, and many more children were being instructed. This must have helped visitor numbers generally, especially as from the 1870s art galleries were often established in the same building as an art school. The model for this was, of course, the South Kensington Museum, also government funded and eventually to be split into the Royal College of Art and the Victoria and Albert Museum.

By the 1920s the main pattern of public art gallery provision had been established. New galleries were established, but within the parameters which had already been laid down. Smaller municipalities continued to set up public art galleries where they did not already exist, especially in the industrial northwest, but the main impetus was over. Existing galleries were expanded, and collections continued to grow.

Nevertheless, there were two major new projects in the inter-war years, both the result of private funding. The Lady Lever Gallery near Liverpool can be seen as the final hurrah of the philanthropic gallery, as it was built for the workers of the Lever factory at Leverhulme. William Lever was the son of a wholesale grocer, who made a fortune by being the first to sell branded pre-wrapped soap. (Previously, soap was cut to order from a large block.) He began manufacturing soap, setting up a factory on Merseyside and building a model village for his workers, Port Sunlight. The enterprise grew into a huge multinational company.

Lever supported many progressive projects. He became a serious art collector when he met James Orrock, a campaigner for a British National Gallery, in 1897. He began to collect British eighteenth- and nineteenth-century painting, unusually growing his collection largely by buying other people's collections. An interesting feature of his collection was that he made a point of collecting art which had influenced British artists and designers - Chinese porcelain, Roman sculpture and Greek vases. The collection grew so big he eventually decided it needed its own building. He was familiar with American business methods, and may well have been inspired by those American tycoons who founded their own galleries. If so, the inspiration stopped there, as few other British businessmen have followed suit.

Lever personally selected the works from his collection destined for his gallery, which he named after his deceased wife. He demonstrated his American-learned marketing skills by buying arms and armour for his gallery, for visitors who "do not particularly admire pictures or statuary", and other objects which widened the appeal of the gallery, as "I have to cater for all tastes".

The building is noteworthy in that although it is in a classical style which emulates contemporary American galleries, it is actually a concrete construction, covered in cladding and plasterwork. (Though, as a Roman invention, concrete is perfectly suitable for a building in a classical style.) Lever's gallery was opened to the public in 1922 by the youngest daughter of Queen Victoria.

While the Lady Lever Gallery reflects the taste of its founder, the collection at the Barber Institute at Birmingham University has no connection at all with the person who paid for it. The heiress who set up the Barber Institute was born with the rather unfortunate name of Martha Onions. She married Henry Barber, a wealthy property developer who was one of the original supporters of Joseph Chamberlain's fund to set up the University of Birmingham. The couple wanted to make a permanent contribution, so in 1932, the year before her death and five years after the death of her husband, Lady Barber bequeathed her entire fortune to the University. It was to fund a building containing a concert hall and an art gallery "for the study and encouragement of art and music". Her own art collection largely consisted of numerous commissioned portraits of herself, but for the art gallery she specified that the art must be of a comparable quality to that in the National Gallery and the Wallace Collection.

The building was designed by an architect, Robert Atkinson, famous for his Art Deco cinemas, with an auditorium on the ground floor and the art gallery above. The Institute was fortunate in its art buying. Prices were low because of the Depression, and it received the expert advice of the young Kenneth Clark, then making a name for himself as the Director of the National Gallery. From these beginnings, the Institute eventually built up a nationally important collection which covered all the main schools, styles and genres of Western European art from the late medieval period. It was opened by Queen Mary in 1939, and is recognised as one of the few regional galleries which has a collection of outstanding international importance (the others being the Ashmoleon in Oxford, the Fitzwilliam in Cambridge, the National Gallery of Scotland in Edinburgh, and the Walker Art Gallery in Liverpool).

This muted progress came to an end with the outbreak of the Second World War, which brought challenges to many galleries which could never have been foreseen by their founders. Not least, a number of galleries were severely damaged by aerial bombardment.

The National Gallery's location made it a prime target, and it was hit nine times. Eventually every pane of glass on the roof was broken. The Director Kenneth Clark had had the presence of mind to remove all the paintings days before the outbreak of war on 3 September 1939. There was some talk of sending them to Canada, but the U-boat threat was too great (and anyway, Churchill vetoed it). They were eventually stored underground in a disused slate mine in mid-Wales. The controlled conditions meant valuable research could be carried out, to be put into practice after the war, and a new catalogue of the permanent collection was produced. Many of the paintings were cleaned while in storage.

Clark also looked for ways to keep the gallery open. Hugely popular concerts of classical music were held, led by the pianist Myra Hess, which nearly always sold out. One lunchtime concert was interrupted by a time bomb, but contemporary accounts say the musicians did not even miss a beat. Temporary art exhibitions were staged, including contemporary work by war artists. Once bombing lessened, one painting a month returned to London. This became a big news event, and the practice of showcasing individual paintings continues to this day.

The department store next to the National Gallery was destroyed in the bombing. The site was eventually bought by the Gallery for an extension, which became the Sainsbury Wing, opened in 1991. This, along with a Northern Extension which was completed in 1975, greatly increased the floor space and exhibition facilities of the Gallery.

Rebuilding work continued for some time after the war, but in 1945 it was possible to show a selection of masterpieces in relatively undamaged areas. Rebuilding included air conditioning, and a new Conservation Department. The latter was introduced by a new Director, Philip Hendy, who took over in 1946. He brought with him a new approach picked up from working experience in the United States, recognising that visiting an art gallery was part of a wider social experience. His innovations ranged from making the galleries more open and accessible to upgrading the restaurant service. His modernising efforts were not always supported by the Trustees, but they were welcomed by the general public. The Gallery now secured a more pivotal role in British cultural life, which it has maintained ever since.

Dulwich Picture Gallery had also anticipated aerial attack by evacuating many of its most important paintings to Wales. After bomb damage to the roof in 1940, more pictures were sent to Wales and the gallery closed. This was fortunate as a flying bomb caused very extensive damage in 1944. In view of its architectural importance, no-one was going to argue against its rebuilding. In 1945 the Governors of Dulwich College noted that "The decision to rebuild Dulwich Picture Gallery will be endorsed by anyone who has the slightest respect for architecture as a fine art." But delays caused by funding gaps, difficulties in obtaining building licences, and in reaching agreement on the rebuilding programme meant that the gallery did not officially reopen until 1953.

The Victorian building of the Guildhall Gallery in London was completely destroyed and the gallery did not reappear until 1999, when it was reborn in the new Guildhall building. The artworks themselves were relatively unscathed, as the most valuable works had already been hidden away elsewhere.

The Tate Gallery suffered so much damage during 1940 that it had to be abandoned. The roof was damaged, all the glass in the building was destroyed, and the flooring of one gallery was burned by incendiary bombs. Matters were made worse by heavy rain falling through the gaps in the roof. Some of the damage to the exterior is still visible. The gallery was not able to reopen until 1946.

Outside London, the original building of Bristol Art Museum was gutted in 1940 in the Bristol Blitz. The art gallery extension was also damaged, but it was able to reopen in 1941. The museum and art gallery were now combined in one building: the lower floor became the museum and the upper floor the art gallery. The archaeology and anthropology collections held by the art gallery were now transferred downstairs to the museum. This was meant to be a temporary arrangement, but the anticipated new building failed to materialise.

Kelvingrove Art Gallery and Museum in Glasgow also suffered bomb damage in 1941, but fortunately the most valuable works had been hidden away around Scotland. It is of course enormously to their credit that all these galleries showed such foresight and dedication to the wellbeing of their precious charges.

One gallery actually gained from the London bombing. The Duke of Sutherland's London house, Bridgewater House, was bombed and in 1945 the collection it housed was given on loan to the Scottish National Gallery in Edinburgh.

By the late 1940s Britain had begun to recover from the effects of the Second World War, and the time was right to start thinking about the areas of art where Britain still lagged behind the Continent and America – modern and contemporary art. Developments in this area took place in the now familiar pattern of lukewarm officialdom and one-off projects set up by energetic individuals. When success came decades later, it was surprisingly stellar.

But before this, the new dynamism displayed by the National Portrait

Gallery needs to be noted. It was down to the modern management and public relations methods introduced by its new Assistant Keeper, Roy Strong, appointed in 1959. The Gallery drew in large crowds through imaginative exhibitions which linked historical figures with present day concerns. A succession of highly popular events significantly raised the gallery's profile and attendance figures. Even more public interest was aroused by the BP Portrait Award which began in the 1970s (and which subsequently became somewhat problematic when climate change activists questioned the link with a major oil company). There was building work too, culminating in a new wing which opened in 2000. Visitor numbers rose to 1.8 million in 2011. The post-war history of the National Portrait Gallery showed that, while additional space is always welcome, making a mark can be done by making the most of what is already there.

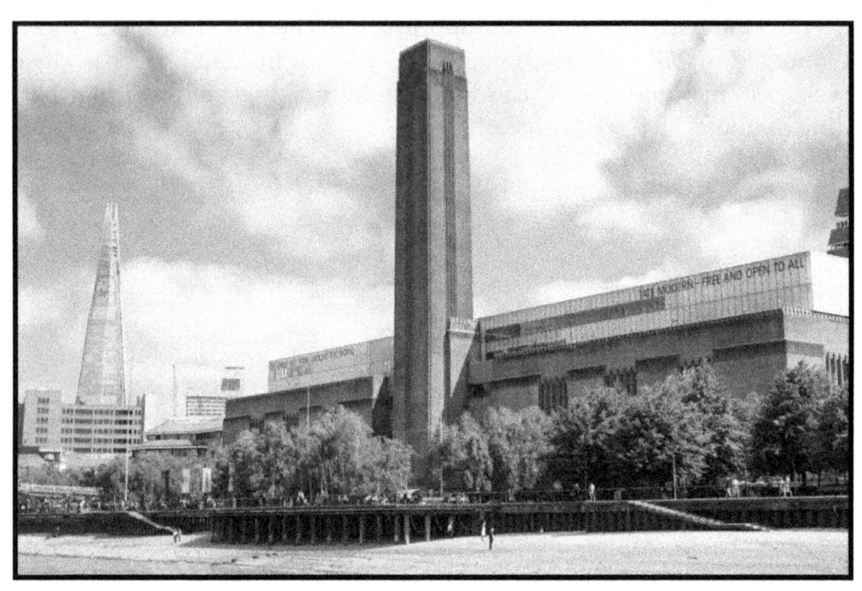

Tate Modern

14. Just One More Thing…

AS BRITAIN RECOVERED from the Second World War, the most glaring gap in Britain's public art collections began to loom larger and larger. Or at least it loomed large with those who were on the cutting edge of Britain's cultural life. The country's public art collections were sorely lacking in international modern and contemporary art. That is, art from French Impressionism to the American Abstract Expressionists.

Not that the British public was completely unfamiliar with this kind of art. Way back in 1905, the French art dealer Paul Durand-Ruel had shown over 300 Impressionist paintings at the Grafton Gallery in London. A few years later the art critic Roger Fry, a longstanding supporter of contemporary French art, curated two ground-breaking exhibitions at the same gallery. *Manet and the Post-Impressionists* in 1910 was followed by the *Second Post-Impressionist Exhibition* in 1912. These exhibitions were a real eye-opener for some, but most of the general public and significant sections of the art establishment were hostile to contemporary French art. One result was that British public galleries failed to buy much of this art when it was relatively cheap, leaving the field to private collectors like textile magnate Samuel Courtauld.

This makes it all the more bizarre that the National Gallery acquired ownership of 39 French Impressionist paintings in 1913, even though the Gallery did not in fact think very highly of most of them at the time. They were a bequest from an art dealer, Hugh Lane.

Lane was born in Ireland but brought up in England and maintained connections with both countries. His origins were fairly humble, but he proved to have an excellent eye for a good picture and he became an extremely successful art dealer. He developed a longstanding interest in both French Impressionism and Irish contemporary art. In 1908, he combined the two by persuading Dublin Corporation to give him a townhouse and a grant of £500 a year to set up the Municipal Gallery of Modern Art (now known as the Hugh Lane Gallery). This was one of the first public galleries of modern art in the world. Dublin's innovation was not followed in the rest of the British Isles until much later.

Tragically, as mentioned in the preceding chapter, on returning from a business trip to America he went down with the *Lusitania* in 1915, aged only 39. Lane had made a bequest in his will leaving 39 Impressionist paintings to the National Gallery in London. He then changed his mind and added a codicil leaving them to Dublin. The codicil was, however, signed but not witnessed. The paintings ended up in London with the National Gallery, which allocated them to the Tate Gallery (which was under National Gallery control at the time).

By the time they were eventually exhibited in London two years after Lane's death, Impressionist paintings had vastly increased in value and desirability. Not surprisingly, the Friends of the National Collections in Ireland vigorously disputed the London claim, as Lane's intentions had been perfectly clear. The dispute rumbled on, though over the years arrangements were made to share the paintings. Until recently, although the National Gallery in London still claimed ownership, 31 of the paintings remained permanently in Dublin. The remaining eight, the recognised masterpieces, were divided into two lots of four which were regularly exchanged between Dublin and London.

Finally, in February 2021 an agreement was signed by the two institutions which set up a partnership approach. Two paintings were added to the rotating loans making two groups of five, which will spend five years in each capital, and the two galleries will collaborate on care and display. Perhaps most significantly, the paintings will be relabelled to acknowledge the new arrangement.

In a final twist to the tale, a body called the French Impressionist Fund had wanted to give a Monet, *Lavacourt*, to the National Gallery in London in 1905, but it was not considered acceptable. This same Monet ended up as one of those exchanged and disputed masterpieces of the Hugh Lane bequest, which until the new agreement was described as owned by the London National Gallery.

On a more positive note, the 1917 National Gallery exhibition of the paintings from the Hugh Lane bequest prompted the Gallery to give the official responsibility for modern foreign art to its offshoot, the Tate Gallery. Lord Duveen (the son of Joseph Duveen, supplier of Old Masters to American plutocracy) funded two new Modern Foreign Art galleries, which opened in 1926. (He also paid for the Tate Gallery's Sculpture Galleries, the first in England dedicated to sculpture, which opened in 1937.) Thus modern art did secure an official home at the Tate Gallery, which continued to acquire European modern art. But it was not a gallery of modern art as such.

The real story about modern and contemporary art in the inter-war years is actually about a group of outstanding private collectors. Fortunately for the rest of us, they not only built up major collections of nineteenth-century and early-twentieth-century French art, they chose to leave their collections to the public. And not just to London: including Hugh Lane, these individuals benefitted all four corners of the British Isles – eventually. Unlike the relatively impecunious Lane, the rest of them were all very rich.

The Welsh sisters Gwendoline and Margaret Davies were rather unlikely collectors of modern art. They were the heiresses of an industrial fortune, brought up as strict Methodists and expected to use their huge inheritance for good works, not the indulgence of their own interests. Nevertheless, they built up a hugely important collection of Impressionist, Post-Impressionist and twentieth century paintings (not to mention other major works, including seven Turners).

The sisters discovered the French *avant-garde* while touring Europe. They were already familiar with modern art, as their governess's brother was a museum director with a passion for French Impressionists and Post-Impressionists. But their taste was much bolder than his – they became enthusiasts for the kind of modern art which was then baffling to British taste, Cézanne being a particular favourite. These works were cheap then, so their money went a very long way.

Their Cézannes had important influences. Kenneth Clark, later a Director of the National Gallery, came to see their Cézanne exhibition in Bath. Roger Fry showed Cézannes from their collection in London in 1922, inspiring Samuel Courtauld to collect Cézanne too. In sorry contrast, the Cézanne paintings he offered to loan to the Tate Gallery in the 1920s were turned down.

The Davies sisters began to lose the collecting bug after 1920 as their Methodism kicked in and they began to feel they should use their money for social purposes rather than art. It was entirely in keeping with this that after their deaths in 1951 and 1963 they bequeathed 260 works from their collection to the National Gallery of Wales. Their lasting monument is therefore one of the most important public collections of modern art in the country.

The next major collector left an even wider legacy. The Cézanne-collecting Samuel Courtauld was a very rich man because his family's textile business had developed rayon, a highly successful substitute for silk. (They were originally French Huguenot silk manufacturers.) Initially, he had no great interest in art. He reckoned the National Gallery had an off-putting atmosphere of "education and sanctity". All the same, his interest was piqued by the exhibition of Hugh Lane's collection of modern French art at the Tate Gallery in 1917. But he only started collecting in earnest when he visited the *Exhibition of French Art* at the private Burlington Fine Art Club in 1922.

His newfound interest meant he soon noticed the absence of modern art in public collections. Determined to rectify this, Courtauld set up a fund in 1924 to acquire Impressionist and Post-Impressionist art for the nation. It was used to buy paintings by Manet, Renoir, Suerat, and Degas, which were originally given to the Tate Gallery but were moved to the National Gallery in the 1950s and 1960s when these works were no longer seen as "modern". Lucky National Gallery – again!

Between 1926 and 1930 Courtauld built up a wonderfully comprehensive collection of modern art, although his interest waned after the death of his wife. Roger Fry was on hand to offer advice and expertise, but Samuel's taste was very much his own.

His keen eye also noticed the absence of graduate and postgraduate education in art history in Britain. He filled this gap by founding (and largely funding) the Courtauld Institute in London. It is now a highly successful part of the University of London. When his wife died, he not only gave his London house to the Institute but bequeathed his collection to it. The Courtauld Gallery opened to the public in 1958 on the top floor of its sister organisation, the Warburg Institute, and moved with the Courtauld Institute to Somerset House in 1989.

The era's other major collector of modern art (and much else), William Burrell, came from the place probably most receptive to modern art in the whole of the British Isles – Scotland. But this owed much to the course of Scottish art from the late nineteenth century to the 1930s, and to one of Britain's most significant art dealers.

Scotland had long had strong links with France, and this included art. Many Scottish artists from the 1880s to the Second World War were far more closely associated with France than was usual elsewhere in Britain. There were two significant movements in Scottish art around this time, both of which looked to France.

The so-called Glasgow Boys were active from the 1880s, and were greatly influenced by contemporary French realism. They painted unpretentious scenes of ordinary life. They often studied and worked in France, or worked in one of the artists' colonies in the French countryside. Members of the group known as the Scottish Colourists also spent much time in France, their work strongly associated with the Fauvism of Matisse and Derain. They were particularly known for the vibrant colours of their work. They mainly produced still life and landscape paintings in the first half of the twentieth century, receiving as much recognition in France as in Britain. The renowned Scottish designer and architect Charles Rennie Mackintosh and his group also looked abroad, his work being in response to the Continental Art Nouveau movement.

Translating this French connection into collecting habits fell to the Glasgow art dealer Alexander Reid. Reid had always had an interest in French art, and went to Paris in 1896 to study the French market at first hand. There he worked for Theo van Gogh and briefly shared a flat with him and his brother Vincent. Vincent's portrait of him confirms that the two men were so much alike that people sometimes could not tell them apart. In spite of this, Reid, to his later regret, failed to recognise the real genius of Vincent van Gogh.

This was not true of other artists he encountered for the first time. He was immediately entranced by the likes of Degas, Monet, Sisley and Pissarro, and was eager to introduce them to his home city. He returned to Glasgow in 1889 to set up his own gallery. He found that the best route to introducing French Impressionism to Scottish collectors was via Degas. Manet and Monet had their admirers too, the latter mainly for his seascapes, but the locals were conservative and sales were sparse. William Burrell bought a Monet, however, and became seriously interested in Degas after 1917.

In fact, Burrell bought continuously from Reid from the 1890s to the 1920s. In later life, he said of Reid that "He did more than any other man has ever done to introduce fine pictures to Scotland and to create a love of art."

In spite of his relative lack of success with modern French paintings, Reid did not starve, as he successfully sold earlier French art and contemporary Scottish works. But real success with modern art came in the 1920s. This was mainly because he staged a number of Impressionist exhibitions in various localities, the most important being *Masterpieces of French Art*, which attracted a new generation of collectors. Not only was he commercially successful, his aesthetic judgement proved to be extremely sound as well - many of the pictures he sold are now in major international collections.[61]

William Burrell was only one of many Scottish ship-owners and industrialists of the time who were serious collectors. But he was the biggest and probably the best. He had an interest in pictures from an early age, and the fortune he made from the family shipping business allowed him to retire in his fifties to devote himself to collecting. He eventually put together collections of national importance in a number of areas: Chinese ceramics, bronzes, Oriental rugs, Northern European late medieval and early Renaissance art, as well as a major collection of Western European easel paintings.

He was already an important collector by the turn of the century, to the extent that he was able to lend over 160 works to Glasgow's

International Exhibition of 1901. This was held in Kelvingrove, and marked the opening of Kelvingrove Art Gallery – the "Palace of the people".

As might be expected from a successful businessman, he was no pushover as a client. He was pretty strong-willed and inclined to caution and haggling. This meant he missed out on some fine pieces, but he also picked up some notable bargains. His business background probably also explains his helpful habit of keeping unusually detailed records of his purchases.

He seems to have had the idea of leaving his collection to Glasgow in the 1930s, and made arrangements to do so in 1944, as well as providing £450,000 for a building to house it. But Burrell still carried on collecting. There were around 6,000 items in his collection when he made his donation; by the time of his death in 1958 there were over 8,000. The additions included stained glass and medieval stone fittings to be incorporated into the gallery building.

Burrell never saw the gallery he paid for. He had insisted on a rural location well away from Glasgow's pollution. It was only in 1967 that a suitable site became available, years after his death. The Burrell Collection finally opened to the public in 1983. It was worth the wait, as it is a stunning building in a beautiful setting.

All this activity meant that eventually modern art up to the Post-Impressionists was reasonably well represented in British public collections. There was very little later work, though. The other modern art movements of the earlier twentieth century – Cubism, Italian Futurism, Russian constructivism, Dadaism – had little or no representation. Abstract art in general remained pretty unpopular with both the general public and much of the art establishment. This meant there were still significant gaps, and no obvious route to filling them.

In these circumstances, it is hardly surprising that the most famous attempt to blaze a trail towards contemporary art came from people slightly on the sidelines of the art world. A small group of well-known cultural commentators, including the artist Roland Penrose and the art critic Herbert Read, set up the Institute of Contemporary Art in 1947. It was not intended to rival New York's Museum of Modern Art, but to be a forum for international cultural ideas in general. Nevertheless, in the 1950s it was the major home of contemporary art in Britain. Its influence went beyond its membership, as non-members were admitted for an entrance charge.

Its intentions were clear from the title of its first exhibition – *40 Years of Modern Art*. Later, it played an important part in the origins of the art movements known as Pop Art and Op Art. The Institute also championed the British style of architecture called Brutalism (named after the modernist French architect Le Corbusier's choice of material, béton brut or raw concrete). It operated from prime West End premises: Oxford Street, then Piccadilly, and finally its current home in The Mall, which it reached in 1968.

The need for such an organisation was made obvious a couple of years after the ICA was founded. In an incident which has become notorious, Alfred Munnings, President of the Royal Academy, railed against modern art in a speech to an Academy banquet which was broadcast by the BBC in 1949. Munnings had made the mistake of having a drink or three beforehand. (Ironically, in spite of his criticisms, he himself had clearly been influenced by Impressionism).

The resulting furore did no good to either his reputation or the Royal Academy's. The cartoonist David Lowe produced an image showing Munnings charging up the steps of the Tate Gallery, with the caption "General Munnings' lowbrow cavalry charges the Tate Gallery. Picasso taken prisoner! Matisse severely wounded!" (Despite this, Munnings continued to be very successful on both sides of the Atlantic, being an English horse painter second only to Stubbs.)[62]

The steps were those of the Tate Gallery because it was the major official home of Britain's permanent collection of international modern art. It also held temporary exhibitions of modern art. But this was only one of the Tate's multiple identities – which included the historic collection of British art, and exhibitions of the work of contemporary British artists of any style.

The gallery did introduce the British public to contemporary American art, though almost by accident. The gallery's first exhibition in 1946 after its restoration from bombing damage was *American Painting from the Eighteenth Century to the Present Day* which included some modern art. This aroused a great deal of interest as American abstract expressionism was at the forefront of modernism at the time. But the Tate Gallery was not able to follow this up until 1956 when it mounted *Modern Art in the United States*, followed in 1959 by *The New American Painting*.

The real turning point was the Tate Gallery's Picasso exhibition in 1960. This marked the beginning of public acceptance of art after Post-Impressionism. Roger Penrose had put on two small Picasso shows at the ICA, but he had half the Millbank galleries at his disposal for this one. He managed to bring together Picasso works from multiple locations, including Russia and Picasso's own collection.

The exhibition was a spectacular success, with huge queues and over half a million visitors. The visitors were quite varied: society ladies, teenagers, bohemian types – even the Queen visited and apparently enjoyed it immensely. David Hockney went eight times, noting the example of an artist who could work in many different styles. Picasso himself, however, did not bother to attend, being "bored" with his old work. The society magazine *Tatler* came up with a new description for this huge success – it was "an art block-buster".

Things began to progress after that. The Arts Council helped this new enthusiasm along with its funding for two significant gallery projects. The Council had been founded in 1946 to invest public money in art and culture across Britain, through a network of national and regional councils. In the later 1960s it gave crucial support to two galleries which were landmarks in the exhibition of modern art.

One was an addition to the site of the Festival Hall, the only building remaining from the 1951 Festival of Britain. The Hayward Gallery opened in 1968 under the management of the Arts Council (it is now run by the Southbank Centre). Its Brutalist architecture was not to everyone's taste, but this was also a significant endorsement of modernism and an important statement of intent. The Hayward exhibited a rolling programme of modern art, showcasing the work of important international modern artists.

Outside London, the Ikon Gallery in Birmingham had opened in 1965 as a voluntary-run gallery for contemporary art, in a kiosk at the Bullring shopping centre. Also in 1968, it too gained Arts Council support to move to a decommissioned mortuary. Originally it promoted the work of local artists, but later it showcased national and international modern art. It remained a not-for-profit independent charity. Again, this project was an important statement of intent, but neither the Hayward nor the Ikon held a permanent collection.

The next significant development was also in the regions. The Tate Gallery decided to open an offshoot in Liverpool, a gallery for permanent and temporary exhibitions of modern and contemporary art. Tate Liverpool, as it was dubbed, was an important part of that city's major redevelopment in the 1980s, situated in a former warehouse on the now disused Albert Docks by the River Mersey. It opened in 1988, joining the Walker Art Gallery as the second major British art gallery in Liverpool.

In the 1990s, the Tate Gallery opened another offshoot for modern and contemporary art. This one was in the former twentieth century artists' colony of St Ives, Cornwall, whose leading lights were the sculptor Barbara Hepworth and the painter Ben Nicholson. Cornwall already had a reputation as a centre for artists, as there had been an earlier artists' colony on the other side of Cornwall, known as the Newlyn School. Like the Hayward and the Ikon, Tate St Ives put on a rolling programme of temporary exhibitions. It opened in 1993, on the site of a former gasworks.

St Ives was Barbara Hepworth's final home, after she had gained an international reputation for her abstract sculpture in the 1940s. The Tate Gallery had previously taken over her house and garden, already open to the public. She was one of a group of artists who were becoming internationally known and beginning to raise the reputation of British art abroad. They included sculptors Henry Moore, Lynn Chadwick, and Elizabeth Frink, and the painters Francis Bacon, Graham Sutherland and John Piper, as well as Hepworth's one-time husband, Ben Nicholson. This growing acclaim was another incentive to pay greater attention to contemporary art in public collections.

The Tate name had now become a brand. The final element was renaming the enterprise simply "Tate", and dividing the Tate Gallery into Tate Britain and Tate Modern. Tate Britain remained in the original building at Millbank, while Tate Modern was created from the conversion of Bankside Power Station. It was on the south bank of the Thames, quite near the Hayward Gallery. Like Tate Liverpool, it re-purposed a now disused industrial building. In this case the building was architecturally significant, designed by the distinguished architect Giles Gilbert Scott (who also designed the iconic red telephone box, which was partly inspired by Soane's work at Dulwich Picture Gallery).

Tate Modern opened in 2000 and was immediately enormously successful. It became one of the most popular modern art galleries in the world – an amazing achievement given Britain's history of backwardness in this area. And also rather surprising, as lack of interest before the second world war meant there were large gaps in its modern art collection. By the time British taste caught up, the best pieces were either already in public art galleries abroad, or too expensive to buy. It made up for this though by running major exhibitions of the work of modern artists.

Fortunately, the Estorick Collection of Modern Italian Art, a gallery which opened in 1998, helped to fill the gaps around Italian Futurism. Eric Estorick was an American, an academic sociologist before he became an art dealer and collector and founded the Grosvenor Gallery in Mayfair. He fell in love with twentieth century Italian art and built up an important personal collection. He persuaded the Tate Gallery to exhibit his collection in 1956, and it was on loan to the Gallery from 1966 to 1975. The Italian government and several museums offered to buy the collection, but in the year before his death he decided to set up a foundation to create his own gallery as the permanent home for his collection. It is in a converted Georgian house in Islington, north London, and stages temporary exhibitions as well as housing the permanent collection.

Scotland had already created a gallery for modern art (well, of course). The Scottish National Gallery devolved its post-1900 works to the new Scottish Museum of Modern Art, which opened in 1959. Bigger premises were needed as the collection grew, so it moved to a former children's home in 1984. This building was named Modern One. A second gallery, named Modern Two, was built opposite in 1999.

The Scottish Museum of Modern Art also has an outdoor sculpture park, but the first in the United Kingdom was the Yorkshire Sculpture Park founded in 1977 in the grounds of a country house near Wakefield. It was based on the open-air exhibitions in London parks organised by the Arts Council and the London County Council (later the Greater London Council) from the 1940s to the 1970s. The location is fitting, as Yorkshire was the birthplace of Britain's most famous modern sculptors, Henry Moore and Barbara Hepworth. The 500-acre Park proved very successful and hosts changing exhibitions of work by international modern and contemporary artists. It was founded (and is still directed) by Peter Murray as an independent charitable trust.

Scottish art also had an outpost in London. The Fleming Gallery of Scottish Art was set up when the Edinburgh bank Robert Fleming & Co was sold. The Fleming family (whose most famous scion is Ian Fleming, creator of James Bond) set up a foundation to buy the bank's art collection. It holds the most important private collection of Scottish art, containing works by the Glasgow Boys and the Scottish Colourists, and the gallery also showcased living Scottish artists. It opened off Piccadilly in 2002, but closed in 2017 and now functions as a lending organisation, with the intention of bringing Scottish art to the widest possible audience.

Camden Arts Centre is another significant venue for contemporary art. It is situated in a traditionally "arty" area of London, a local authority building which has been successfully re-purposed. It started out as Hampstead Central Library, then became Camden Arts Centre in 1965. Initially a venue for art and craft sessions, it added a remit for temporary exhibitions of international contemporary art, showing the work of many established and up and coming British and international artists over the years.

Like Tate Liverpool, Gateshead's Baltic Centre of Contemporary Art came about as part of a major urban development programme. Again, it is housed in a repurposed industrial building, in this case an imposing disused flour mill on the banks of the River Tyne. The Centre opened in 2002 and hosts a rolling programme of international contemporary art.

In the twentyfirst century, a number of galleries were established which celebrated contemporary art in a different way, by celebrating famous British artists. The Turner Contemporary Gallery is in Margate in Kent, located in the area where Turner regularly stayed and painted. It opened in 2011 for exhibitions of contemporary and historical art and has proved very successful. The sculptress Barbara Hepworth is memorialised at the award-winning Hepworth Gallery in her birthplace, Wakefield in Yorkshire. It contains studio models of her work and temporary exhibitions of contemporary art as well as art from the town's collection. Yorkshire's other notable sculptor Henry Moore was born nearby.

The work of the most recent famous Yorkshire artist, David Hockney, is commemorated at Salts Mill Gallery, Saltaire, in his birthplace, Bradford. Salts Mill was a huge mill for making alpaca cloth, founded by the nineteenth-century industrialist and philanthropist Titus Salt, who built the model workers' village next to it. It has been converted into a shopping centre, restaurant, and a gallery devoted to Hockney's work. Leeds Art Gallery has also opened a gallery devoted to his work.

From 1982 Pallant House Gallery has showcased modern British art from 1900 to the present in an eighteenth-century townhouse in Chichester. Pallant House is an important Queen Anne house which was acquired by Chichester Council and used as council offices until 1979. The house was extensively restored when the Dean of Chichester Cathedral, Walter Hussey, offered his important collection of modern British art to the council on condition it was housed in Pallant House. An extension was added in the 1990s to create space for another large collection donated by Sir Colin St John Wilson (the architect of the British Library). The Gallery holds work by, among many others, John Piper, Graham Sutherland, and Henry Moore, as well as modern Continental artists such as Cezanne, and one of the best collections of British Pop Art anywhere.

These most recent projects for new art galleries broke new ground – by becoming a successful part of city redevelopment projects, or proudly recognising British artists, or establishing outdoor sculpture parks as a new kind of gallery. With modern and contemporary art now widely accessible, it would seem the story of the British public art gallery had come to a happy ending. And so it did – for the briefest of moments. But all too soon, national funding declined, money was tight, and hard decisions were on the agenda.

Once again public art galleries have had to justify their funding in the midst of debate about their purpose and their place in national life. They have been encouraged to seek funding from corporations and private individuals – not easy for galleries outside London. Nevertheless, major developments are still taking place: the Victoria and Albert Museum has established outposts in the Queen Elizabeth Park in East London and in Dundee, Scotland, the National Portrait Gallery is undergoing a major redevelopment, and the National Gallery is designing a new more welcoming entrance area.

Have things come full circle? Well, no. Some smaller regional and specialist galleries may struggle to survive, but the work of most public galleries is built on firm foundations. The Art Fund can help with acquisitions to refresh collections, and the Tate has started a touring programme of Art Rooms exhibiting modern art, to enliven regional galleries and provide a new reason for a visit. The glory days of the late nineteenth century and the turn of the twenty-first century are over, but tourist numbers alone indicated that Britain today is indeed "a favourite abode of the polite arts". But reassessments were in the air…

15. Reassessment

PUBLIC ART GALLERIES have always evolved from one era to the next, reflecting public attitudes to art and to art funding. Up to the 1960s this development can be quite reasonably seen in class terms: the elite had their libraries, parkland, cabinets of curiosities, and art collections. Now everyone had access to public libraries, municipal parks, museums and art galleries. The development of public art galleries was part of a wider movement. And in the late 1940s not only did secondary education became free for everyone, but grants were made available for university education for the less well off. With this, it could be said the democratisation of culture was complete (at least in theory).

But up to that point the art which was displayed nearly always reflected Matthew Arnold's "high culture". That meant the most prized exhibits were those considered to be within the "canon", the list of art and artists which the cultural elite deemed to be of the highest quality. The National Gallery reflected this almost precisely. This does not mean the canon was static, in fact artists and artistic styles could and did move in and out of the canon as tastes changed, though relatively rarely.

(Titian is probably the only artist who has been held in the highest esteem during his lifetime and ever since, while previous chapters have shown how internationally acclaimed Victorian artists could completely fall from grace within a few decades of their deaths. The John siblings are an interesting example: Augustus was very highly regarded in his day (the first half of the 20th century), but his reputation has considerably declined since, while his sister Glynis was little known in her lifetime but is now definitely within the canon of British art. Interestingly, Augustus John himself generously and truthfully said that in the end his sister would be the more highly regarded artist.)

What type of art was included in the canon could change too. New art forms could be incorporated, though often after initial rejection. After the Second World War, for example, American Abstract Expressionism gained official acceptance by the British art establishment. After due consideration by the right people, the definition "canonical art" could simply be expanded to include the new.

That began to change in the 1960s, as some people began to question not just which artists were on the walls, but which artists weren't. And they began to question why the decision makers who ran the galleries as curators and administrators came from a pretty small pool. What's more, the whole concept of the canon began to come into question.

But before looking at these points, there is a more fundamental issue to consider. In 1935 the cultural critic Walter Benjamin wrote the essay "Art in the age of mechanical reproduction". He claimed that originally art had had an "aura", which produced awe and reverence in its audience. This was because art originally had a religious purpose, and each object was individually produced by people who saw it in that light. (This is still true of icons produced for the Christian Eastern Orthodox Churches.) The unique work of art thus had an appeal which was not available to everyday objects like pottery utensils.

Although works of art were often copied for various reasons, and paintings had long been reproduced through prints or etchings, the modern era introduced something new. It became possible to produce cheaply good quality full colour reproductions of images through photography or film. Benjamin argued that this could lead to the one-off work of art losing its allure.[63]

As a Marxist, Benjamin could see this as a positive, as good quality reproduction could be used effectively in political propaganda. The museum director might have something to worry about though. If the unique work of art lost its attraction, who would visit art galleries?

In the event, it seems there was no need for concern. The modern audience is not only surrounded by high quality images nearly all of its waking hours, it is usually carrying a device which allows it to take high quality images of its own whenever it wants. But visitor numbers for public art galleries have held up, and blockbuster exhibitions still attract large crowds. This is no doubt helped by the shorter working hours, paid holidays, and much wider travel enjoyed by most people in Britain since the Second World War. But Andy Warhol's continuing high reputation and the market value of his prints shows that reproduced art can more than hold its own.

And this is without taking into consideration new forms of art which have appeared since the 1960s – art not made but created from assembling found objects, art as performance or as sound, video art, and art which is intended to be ephemeral rather than eternal. Plus the fact that it is now possible to have virtual tours of art galleries and exhibitions which provide the perfect view and close-ups of detail usually impossible to achieve in real life.

Many people both see the exhibition and buy the postcard, wanting both the real-life experience and the reproduced reminder. So it is probably safe to assume the public art gallery will still have an audience for the foreseeable future. Though it may be that the constant visual stimulus available in contemporary life will result in audiences demanding a higher level of entertainment and spectacle than before.

The questioning of the content and context of public art has definitely not been settled however. The first salvo came from feminism. Why were there so few works by female artists displayed in public art galleries? Why were so few female artists considered canonical? Why did female artists with high reputations in their lifetimes so often fall out of favour soon after their deaths? Much work was done to rediscover forgotten female talent and make it known to a wider audience.

Thus a 1971 essay by American art historian Linda Lochlin called "Why have there been no great women artists" was initially greeted by feminists with some dismay. However, Lochlin was not referring to individual merit, but to the historical institutional barriers to success that would-be women artists had to face, including lack of access to suitable training, studio space, and professional support. Not to mention probable lack of support for a professional career from family and society in general. Her essay prompted critical examination of art education and renewed efforts to exhibit neglected women artists, and is considered the beginning of feminist art history.

In Britain, Griselda Pollock and Rozskiska Parker's 1981 book *Old Mistresses: Women, Art and Ideology* was a ground-breaking study of sexism in art practice and the idea that "the artist" was almost exclusively male. At the same time, the absence of recognition of artists of colour in Western European art was noted, as was the absence of work by artists from places not in Europe or North America. The fact that most decision-making staff in art galleries were white males also drew critical attention.

In the decades that followed there was some movement in all these areas. Currently, many people are impatient with the pace of change and want to complete the process by "decolonising" the gallery. This can mean challenging possibly unconscious assumptions about what art is, how art should be judged and presented, and its meaning to society. It can also mean making sure that decisions and judgements are made by a wide range of people, and include those whose life experiences may enable them to make a more pertinent contribution. Similarly, people should be careful not to make assumptions about where to find the best art or artists at any given time. Last, but by no means least, though probably the most difficult proposition, visiting public art galleries should be seen as an attractive proposition by all the public.

"Decolonising" also means examining the origins of museum objects to ensure they have not been stolen or forcibly acquired from their country of origin. In the case of historical collections of European easel painting, this could apply, for example, to works taken by the Nazis or looted by Napoleon.

But in Britain it is more likely to apply to non-European art acquired during the time of the British Empire, and particularly affects the Victoria and Albert Museum because of its huge collection of non-European art from all over the world. The collection transferred to the Museum from the India Office in the nineteenth century has already been mentioned as a case in point. The Museum is in fact currently in discussions with several countries about the possible return of objects of particular significance to their country of origin.

As the process of decolonisation is ongoing and relatively recent, it is not yet possible to know how it will develop, or what its ultimate effect will be. In any case, this book is about history rather than about the future. But controversy is, of course, much better than indifference.

One word of caution, however. This book has shown that the demand for public art galleries came from below (mainly from the middle class, so not that far below, but below none the less). The British public art gallery is not a top-down elite project. The art belongs to the public at large rather than art gallery administrators, and ongoing funding comes from the taxpayer or the Lottery ticket buyer. It is therefore highly desirable that any radical change is carried out in consultation with that audience, otherwise the changes may provoke a backlash and the end result may be that the changes do not stick.

And in any case we have already seen that visitors – from John Ruskin to East End cockneys and suffragettes – have an unfortunate habit of coming to their own conclusions about art…

References

[1] "High Art and Low Politics: A New Perspective on John Wilkes", Jonathan Conlin (2001) *Huntington Library Quarterly* 36(4), 1-19

[2] *The Ephemeral Museum*, Francis Haskell, New Haven & London: Yale University Press, 2000, pp.30-45

[3] *Towards a Modern Art World*, ed. Brian Allen, New Haven & London Yale University Press, 1995, p.8

[4] "Cultural production: Consumption and the place of the artist in eighteenth-century England", John Brewer in *Towards a Modern Art World* ed. Brian Allen, New Haven & London: Yale University Press, 1995

[5] Waterfield G, *Rich Summer of Art*, Dulwich Picture Gallery, 1988, p.8

[6] ibid pp.8-12

[7] ibid p.29

[8] ibid p.18

[9] Afinoguenova, E, "Art education, class and gender in a foreign art gallery: nineteenth century cultural travellers in the Prado Museum in Madrid", *Nineteenth Century Contexts*, Vol 32, No 1, Mar 2010, pp.47-63

[10] Waterfield, G, *Rich Summer of Art*, Dulwich Picture Gallery, 1988, p.12

[11] Bermingham, A. "An Exquisite Practise: The Institution of Drawing as a Polite Art in Britain", from *Towards a Modern Art World*, ed. Brian Allen, New Haven & London: Yale University Press, 1995, pp.28-47

[12] Darley, G, John Soane: *An Accidental Romantic*, New Haven & London: Yale University Press, 1999, p.208

[13] Waterfield G, Clifford T, *Palaces of Art, London*: Dulwich Picture Gallery, 1992, p.100

[14] Conlin, J, "National Gallery: Art for the People", History Today, Vol 56, Issue 11, Nov 2006, p.29

[15] ibid p.42

[16] ibid p.30

[17] ibid p.35

[18] ibid p.31

[19] ibid p.33

[20] Kronk, C, "Mounting Vision: Charles Eastlake and the National Gallery of London", *Art Bulletin*, June 2000, Vol LXXXII, No 2, pp.331-344

[21] MacLeod, S, "Civil Disobedience and Political Agitation: The Art Museum as a Site of Protest in the Early 20th Century", *Museum and Society*, 5(1), Dec 2006

[22] Waterfield, Giles, Clifford, T, *Palaces of Art: Art Galleries in Britain 1790-1990*, Dulwich Picture Gallery / National Gallery of Scotland, 1992, p.109

[23] Barringer T, "A Victorian Entrepreneur's Extraordinary Collecting Project", *Fine Art Connoisseur*, Mar-April 2009

[24] Robertson B, "The South Kensington Museum in context: an alternative history", *Museum and Society*, (1), Mar 2006, pp.63-72

[25] Waterfield, Giles, Clifford, T, *Palaces of Art: Art Galleries in Britain 1790-1990*, Dulwich Picture Gallery/National Gallery of Scotland, 1992

[26] "Murder and Suicide in the National Portrait Gallery", *The Times*, 25 Feb 1909

[27] MacLeod, S, "Civil Disobedience and Political Agitation: The Art Museum as a Site of Protest in the Early 20th Century", *Museum and Society*, Vol 5, No 1, Dec 2006

[28] Szreter, Simon, "Rapid Economic Growth and the Four 'Ds'", *Tropical Medicine and International Health*, Vol 4, No 2, pp.146-152, Feb 1999

[29] Undated article on Edward Edwards in Wight Life at <u>woottonbridgeiow.org.uk</u>

[30] Hill, R, *God's Architect: Pugin and the Building of Romantic Britain*: London, Penguin, 2008

[31] Jackson, Kevin, *The Worlds of John Ruskin*: London, Pallas Athene/Ruskin Foundation, 2011 pp.36-83

[32] Breton, Rob, "Work Perfect: William Morris and the Gospel of Work", *Utopian Studies*, Vol 13, No 1, 2002 pp.45-56, Penn State University Press

[33] Pater, Walter, *The Renaissance*: Oxford, Oxford University Press, 1998, p.153

[34] Arnold, Matthew, *Culture and Anarchy*: London, Smith, Elder & Co, 1869 (Google Books online facsimile), pp. (in order) (viii), 145, 13, 71, 81,96, 109, 265, 51, 167-8, 133, 74, 190-1, 205

[35] Duncan, Carol, *Civilising Rituals: Inside Public Art Museums*: London & New York, Routledge, 1995, pp.7-20

[36] Smith, G, *A Short History of Secularism*: London & New York, I B Tauris, 2008, pp.161-166

[37] Waterfield, Giles, Clifford, T, *Palaces of Art: Art Galleries in Britain 1790-1990*, Dulwich Picture Gallery/National Gallery of Scotland, 1992, p.84

[38] Perry, G, Cunningham B (eds), *Academies, Museums and Canons of Art*: New Haven & London, Yale University Press/Open University, pp.244-6

[39] Haskell, F, *The Ephemeral Exhibition*: New Haven & London, Yale University Press, 2000, pp.82-9

[40] Woodson Boulton, Amy, *Transformative Beauty: Art Museums in Industrial Britain*: Stanford Calif., Stanford University Press, 2012

[41] Waterfield, Giles, Clifford, T, *Palaces of Art: Art Galleries in Britain 1790-1990*, Dulwich Picture Gallery/National Gallery of Scotland,1992, p.89

[42] Ibid. pp.21 and 92

[43] Moore, J. R., "Periclean Preston, Public Art and the Classical Tradition in Late Nineteenth-Century Lancashire", *Northern History*, XL:2, Sept 2003, p.309

[44] Waterfield, Giles, Clifford, T, *Palaces of Art: Art Galleries in Britain 1790-1990*, Dulwich Picture Gallery/National Gallery of Scotland, 1992, p.80

[45] Lecture by Lucilla Burn on her book *The Fitzwilliam Museum: A History*: Phillip Wilson Publications, 1999, available on *YouTube*

[46] Ibid.

[47] Waterfield, G, Smith, N, "Art for the People", *History Today*, Vol 44, Issue 5, p.5

[48] Crowther, L, "Et In Suburbia Ego: A Cultural Geography of Craft in the London Suburbs". *The Journal of Modern Craft* 3.2 (2010): 143+, Academic One File, Web. 2 July 2011

[49] Waterfield, Giles, Clifford, T, *Palaces of Art: Art Galleries in Britain 1790-1990*, Dulwich Picture Gallery/National Gallery of Scotland, 1992, p. 95

[50] Matthews-Jones, L, "Lessons in Seeing: Art, Religion and Class in the East End of London 1881-1889", *Journal of Victorian Culture*, Vol 16, No. 3, Dec 2011, 385-403

[51] Barringer, T, "Victorian Culture and the Museum: Before and After the White Cube", *The Journal of Victorian Culture*, 11.1, 2006, p.137

[52] Ruskin, J, "The Nature of Gothic", *On Art and Life*, London: Penguin Books, 2004, p.24

[53] Harrison M, "Art and social regeneration", *Manchester Region History Review*, Vol 7, 1993, pp. 63-72

[54] Hamilton J, *A Strange Business: Making Art and Money in 19th Century Britain*: London, Atlantic Books, 2015, pp.173-230

[55] Sacko-MacLeod, D, "Art Collecting and Victorian Middle-Class Taste" *Art History* Vol 1, No 3, Sept 1987 ISSN 0141-6790 pp.328-349

[56] Barringer T, "A Victorian Entrepreneur's Extraordinary Collecting Project" *Fine Art Connoisseur* Mar-April 2009

[57] Sacko-MacLeod D, Op. Cit. pp.328-349

[58] Woodson-Boulton A, "The Art of Compromise: The Founding of the National Gallery of British Art 1890-92" *Museum & Society* Nov 2003 1(3), 147-169, 2003, ISSN1479-8360

[59] Duncan, C, *Civilizing Rituals: Inside Public Art Museums*: London and New York, Routledge, 1995 pp.72-101

[60] Roth, M, "Grand Designs", *Art Quarterly*, Summer 2012

[61] University of Glasgow website carp.arts.gla.ac.uk/essay.1

[62] *smithsonian.com* "The Artist Who Hated Picasso"

[63] Benjamin, W, *Illuminations*, London: Pimlico, 1999, pp.211-244

Bibliography

Allen, Brian (ed), *Towards a Modern Art World*, Yale University Press: New Haven & London, 1995

Arnold, Matthew, *Culture and Anarchy: An Essay in Social and Cultural Criticism*, Smith, Elder & Co, 1869 (Google Books online facsimile)

Benjamin, Walter "The Work of Art in the Age of Mechanical Reproduction", *Illuminations*, Pimlico: London, 1999

Burn, Lucinda, *The Fitzwilliam Museum: A History*, Phillip Wilson Publications, 1999

Carlyle, Thomas, *On Heroes, Hero-Worship and The Heroic in History*, independently published, 2020

Darley, Gillian, John Soane: *An Accidental Romantic*, Yale University Press: New Haven & London, 1999

Duncan, Carol, *Civilising Rituals: Inside Public Art Museums*, Routledge: Abingdon, Oxon, 1995

Hamilton, James, *A Strange Business: Making Art and Money in Nineteenth-Century Britain*, Atlantic Books: London, 2014

Hamilton, Ian, *A Gift Imprisoned: the Poetic Life of Matthew Arnold*, Bloomsbury: London, 1999

Haskell, Francis, *The Ephemeral Museum*, Yale University Press: New Haven & London, 2000

Hill, R, *God's Architect: Pugin and the Building of Romantic Britain*, Penguin: London, 2008

Jackson, Kevin, *The Worlds of John Ruskin,* Pallas Athene & The Ruskin Foundation: London, 2010

Morris, William, *Useful Work and Useless Toil*: Penguin Great Ideas: London, 2008

Nevola, Francesco, *Soane's Favourite Subject: The Story of Dulwich Picture Gallery*, Dulwich Picture Gallery: London, 2000

Pater, Walter, *The Renaissance*, Oxford World Classics, Oxford University Press: Oxford, 1998

Perry, Gill (ed), *Academies, Museums and Canons of Art*, Yale University Press: New Haven & London, 1999 (in association with The Open University Press)

Ruskin, John, "The Nature of Gothic", *On Art and Life*, Penguin Books: London, 2004

Ruskin, John, *Unto This Last*, CreateSpace Independent Publishing Platform, 2017

Smith, G, *A Short History of Secularism*, I B Taurus: London & New York, 2008

Waterfield, Giles, *A Rich Summer of Art: A Regency Picture Collection Seen Through Victorian Eyes*, Dulwich Picture Gallery: London, 1988

Waterfield, Giles, *Soane and After*, Dulwich Picture Gallery: London, 1987

Waterfield, Giles & Clifford, Timothy, *Palaces of Art: Art Galleries in Britain 1790-1990*, Dulwich Picture Gallery/National Gallery of Scotland, 1992

Waterfield, Giles, *Art Treasures of England: The Regional Collections*, Merrell Holberton Publishers: London, 1998

Woodson Boulton, Amy, *Transformative Beauty: Art Museums in Industrial Britain*, Stanford University Press: Stanford, Calif., 2012

Index

Aesthetics/aestheticism — 13, 18, 57, 73, 75, 77-78, 82, 87, 118, 120, 125, 128
Aitkin, Charles — 148
Alexander, William Henry — 60
Ancoats (Manchester) — 121-123
Anderson, Robert — 62
Angerstein, John; Julian — 33-34, 37
Arbroath, Declaration of — 8-9
Architectural Museum — 51
Arnold, Matthew — 73, 78-81, 95, 118, 15
Art Fund — 41, 168
Art Nouveau — 134, 161
Art Unions Act 1846 — 102
Arts & Crafts — 50, 73, 77, 111, 117, 139
Ashmoleon; Ashmole — 13-15, 65, 110-111, 140, 152
Assessed Rates Act 1869 — 68
Audubon, John James — 87
Bailey, Abraham — 61
Baltic Centre of Contemporary Arts — 164
Banksy — 107
Barbara Hepworth Gallery — 167
Barber Institute of Fine Art — 141, 152
Barnett, Samuel — 118-119, 121, 138
Beardsley, Aubrey — 78
Beaumont, Sir George — 34, 89
Bellini, Gentile — 42
Bentham, Jeremy — 81-82
Berlin Museum of Decorative Arts — 28
Bernard Stevenson, C. — 109
Bethnal Green Museum — 50, 52, 60, 119, 136
Bicknell, Elhanan — 126
Birmingham — 8, 42, 64, 67, 75, 92-94, 101, 141, 152, 164
Blake, William — 48
Blundell, Henry — 84
Bodleian Library — 14, 120
Bomberg, David — 119, 149
Boucher, François — 6, 134, 148
Bourgois, Francis — 20, 23-25, 29-30
Bowes Museum — 132-134, 136, 141-142, 149
Bowes, John — 133-134, 136
Brassey Institute — 103
Bridgewater, Duke of — 12
Brighton Free Museum — 109
Brighton Improvement Act 1850 — 108
Brighton Royal Pavilion — 108
Bristol — 28, 106-107, 154
British Institution — 18, 25, 34
British Museum — 5, 9, 25, 28, 41, 59-60, 69, 86, 109, 137
Brooklyn Museum — 121
Brotherton, Joseph — 68
Brown, William — 88-90
Buchanan, William — 18

Buckingham Palace — 5, 54
Buckingham, James — 68
Burdett Coutts, Baroness — 117
Burke, Edmund — 79
Burne-Jones, Edward — 50, 117, 128-129, 138-139
Burrell, William — 97, 160-162
Cambridge School of Art — 112
Camden Arts Centre — 166
Canaletto, Giovanni — 8, 12, 135
Capitoline Gallery (Rome) — 7, 19
Carlisle, Lord of — 12, 117
Carlyle, Thomas — 26, 39, 42, 57-58, 61-62, 66, 73, 75-77, 82, 92
Catherine the Great — 9
Cézanne, Paul — 159, 167
Chamberlain, Joseph — 68, 93, 152
Chantrey, Francis — 126, 129-131
Chardin, Jean-Baptiste-Siméon — 14
Charles I — 9, 11, 13, 19
Charles II — 11, 15
Cheltenham Art Gallery — *See 'Wilson, The'*
Chester — 104
Chichester — 141, 167
City of London (Guildhall Gallery) — 66, 110, 149
Clark, Kenneth — 152-153, 159, 178
Cockerell, Charles Robert — 107, 110
Cole, Henry — 27, 29, 45-58, 51-54, 82, 110, 147, 150
Constable, John — 26, 34, 94, 128
Cotton Collection; Cottonian — 5, 104
Courtauld Gallery — 141, 160
Courtauld, Samuel — 157, 159-160
Crane, Walter — 117
Cromwell, Oliver — 9, 19, 54
Cust, Lionel — 60
Davies, Gwendoline; Margaret — 159
Derby, Earl of — 87
Derby Museum — 88-89, 102-103
Desenfans, Margaret — 23-24
Desenfans, Noel Joseph — 20, 23-25, 29
Devon & Exeter — 108
Dickenson, John — 102
Diderot, Denis — 6
Disraeli, Benjamin — 56
Dixon, Thomas — 102
Dulwich Picture Gallery — 20, 22-29, 35, 37, 45, 65, 106, 110, 116, 134, 141-142, 145, 148, 153-154, 165
Duveen, Joseph — 147, 158
Dyce, William — 37, 46
Eastlake, Charles — 38-40, 112
Edwards, Edward — 69
Egalitarianism — 76
Ellesmere, Lord — 58
Ellis, George Agar — 33, 35
Estorick Collection — 165
Estorick, Eric — 165
Eton College — 28
Etty, William — 26
Evangelical movement — 73, 80-81, 150

Evans, Arthur   110-111
Ewart, William   68
Exeter   107-108
Fauvists   160
Female School of Art   54
Ferrières, Charles Baron de   105
Fildes, Luke   54, 96
Findlay, John   61
Fitzhenry, J.H.   51
Fitzwilliam Museum   15, 16, 65, 107, 111-112, 141, 152
Fleming Gallery   166
Foundling Hospital   9-10
Fowke, Francis   47-50, 99
Frick, Henry Clay   137, 142
Frith, William Powell   128
Fuseli, Henry   34
Genre   14, 20, 37, 119, 125-127, 129
Gertler, Mark   119, 149
Gherandini Collection   51
Gigli-Campana Collection   51
Giotto   75
Giovanni   42
Glasgow   14, 65, 97-98, 111, 141, 152, 154, 160-162, 166
Glasgow Boys   97, 160, 166
Gothic   51, 62, 73-77, 95, 107, 111
Gower, Lord   12
Grafton Gallery   157
Graham, William   128
Grand Tour   12
Great Exhibition 1851   45-47, 90, 108, 126
Great Man Theory   58, 62, 75
Grosvenor Museum   104
Grosvenor, Lord   12, 104
Guildhall Art Gallery   42, 110, 149, 154
Gurney, John Henry   106
Hampton Court   5, 42
Hapsburg collection   19
Harley Collection   5
Harris Museum and Art Gallery (Preston)   95
Hastings Museum   103
Hayter, George   59
Hayward Gallery   164-165
Hayward, John   108
Hazlett, William   37
Hedley, Ralph   102
Henry VIII   9
Henshaw, Bertha   122
Hepworth Gallery   168
Hermitage Collection   9
Hertford House   136, 137
High Culture   73, 78-79, 118, 150, 169
Hill, Octavia   117
History painting   17, 127
Hockney, David   141, 159, 167
Hogarth, William   10, 14, 16, 18, 34, 109, 129
Holloway College   128, 140-141
Holloway, Thomas   128

Hollwell Car, William	41
Holman Hunt, William	26
Hope, Thomas	12
Horsfall, T.C.	119-120
Hugh Lane Gallery	157
Hull Art Gallery	42
Hume, Joseph	36
Hunt, Annie	61
Hunter, William	14-15, 65, 111, 141
Hunterian Museum (Glasgow)	14-15, 65, 111, 141
Ikon Gallery (Birmingham)	164
Impressionists	160
Industrialisation	66, 77, 101
Inglis, Robert	36
Institute of Contemporary Art	162
Ionides, Alexander	53, 117
Ionides, Constantine	53, 137
Jackson, Agnes	135
Jackson, Richard	135-137 *see also Richard Wallace*
James, M.R.	112
Jekyll, Gertrude	54
John, Augustus; Glynis	169
Kelvingrove	97, 154, 162
Kelvinside	151
Kensington Schools	54
Kingsley, Charles	37
Lady Lever Gallery (Liverpool)	141, 151-152
Laing, Alexander	109
Laing Art Gallery (Newcastle)	109
Lambeth School of Art	110
Landseer, Edwin	48, 94
Lane, Hugh	99, 147, 157-159 *see also Hugh Lane Gallery*
Lawrence, Thomas	10, 34, 110
Leeds Art Gallery	8, 69, 91, 95, 105, 110, 167
Leicester, John	125
Leighton, Lord	116-117, 121, 129-130, 138-140
Lessing, Julian	28
Liverpool	28, 67-68, 84-89, 92, 94, 101, 109-110, 128, 130, 141, 144, 151-152, 164-165
Lloyd Webber, Lord	141
Lorraine, Claude	5, 34, 40, 49
Louvre	11, 18-19, 36, 38
Lubbock, John	117
Macauley, Thomas Babington	58
Mackintosh, Charles Rennie	160
Magna Carta	8
Manchester	42, 85, 89-92, 94-96, 110, 121-122, 126
Manchester Art Treasures Exhibition	59, 90-91, 95, 126
Marlborough House	38, 46, 48-49, 51, 127
Martin, John	109
Mellon, Andrew	142
Metropolitan (New York)	53, 138
Michelangelo	34
Millais, John Everett	42, 48, 50, 61, 131, 140
Millennium Gallery (Sheffield)	120
Milner, James	61
Modern One (Edinburgh)	166

Mond, Ludwig	41
Moody, Frank	49
Moore, Albert	78
Morris, William	50, 73, 76-77, 83, 93-94, 121
Movements (Art in General)	162, 165
Municipal Corporations Act 1835	66
Municipal Franchise Act 1869	68
Municipal Gallery of Modern Art (Dublin)	*See Hugh Lane Gallery*
Museum of Manufactures	*See Museum of Ornamental Arts*
Museum of Ornamental Arts	46
Napoleon	11, 19, 127, 135-136, 172
Narrative Art	78
National Art Training School	46, 54
National Gallery	1, 10-12, 15, 19, 26-32, 34-38, 40-42, 47-50, 52-53, 60-61, 65, 78-79, 89-90, 98-99, 112, 115, 127, 129-131, 140, 142, 145-147, 150-154, 157-160, 166-167, 169
National Portrait Gallery	41, 42, 50, 56-58, 60-62, 65, 73, 91, 119, 138, 147-148, 154-155, 167
New Walk Museum and Art Gallery (Leicester)	42, 104-105
Nicolson, Ben	164-165
Picton, James	87-88
Poor Law	74, 89
Newcastle-on-Tyne	105, 109
Norfolk and Norwich Museum	107
Northcote, Stafford	108
Norwich Castle Museum and Art Gallery	105
Nottingham Museum	104
Orleans, Duke of	11-12, 15, 141
Orrock, James	151
Pallant House	141, 167
Parker, Rozskisker	171
Passmore Edwards, John	116
Pater, Walter	77
Peel, Robert	41
Penrose, Roland	162-163
Perse School (Fitzwilliam)	111
Petrie Flinders	121
Piombo, Sebastiano del	11
Pissarro, Camille	27, 161
Plymouth Art Gallery	103-104
Pollock, Griselda	171
Poussin, Nicolas	5
Prado Museum (Madrid)	19, 29
Prince Albert	40, 46-47, 50, 52, 98
Prince of Wales (George V)	40, 46, 108, 135
Protestantism	75
Public Health Act	67
Public Libraries Act 1850	69
Pugin, Augustus	73-76
Queen Victoria	41, 46, 54, 58, 106, 108
Queen's Park Gallery	121
Queensbury (Marquis of)	135-136
Rae, George	128
Raphael	34
Read, Herbert	162

Reform Act 1833 67
Reid, Alexander 161
Rembrandt 5, 14
Reynolds, Joshua 10, 16, 18, 38-39, 127, 135
Richardson, Mary 41
Rijksmuseum (Amsterdam) 105
Robinson, J.C. 51, 117
Rogers, Charles 104
Romantic Movement 24, 39
Roscoe, William 86-87
Rossetti, Dante Gabriel 52, 102, 128
Rossiter, William 115-118
Royal Academy 10, 25-26, 29, 34-35, 37, 38, 42, 59, 96, 102, 116-117, 126-127, 130, 137, 149, 163

Royal College of Art 52, 54, 151
Royal Libraries 5
Royal Society 10, 13, 117
Ruskin, John 27, 29, 37, 70, 72-77, 80, 82-83, 87, 91-92, 94, 102, 108-110, 115, 118-123, 125, 138, 148, 172

Salt, Titus 90, 167
Salting, George 41, 51
Salts Mill Gallery (Saltaire) 167
Scharf, George 59-60, 91, 147
School of Design 49-52, 102
Scott, George Gilbert 62, 111, 165
[Royal] Scottish Academy 98
Scottish Colourists 97, 160
Scottish Museum of Modern Art 166
Scottish National Gallery 98, 154, 166
Scottish Portrait Gallery 61
Second Reform Act 1867 68
Secularism 6, 80-81, 146
Sheepshanks Gallery 48-49, 105, 127
Sheepshanks, John 48, 127
Sheffield 8, 67-68, 94, 120
Slade Professorship 112
Smith, Adam 17, 62, 76
Soane, John 5, 20, 24-25, 29, 89, 106, 111, 141, 149, 165
Society of Artists 10, 17
Somerset House 37, 160
Soulages Collection 51
South Kensington Museum 27, 29, 38, 40, 45-54, 59-60, 65, 82, 90, 93, 96, 110, 117, 119, 127-128, 130, 151

South London Gallery 114
St John Wilson, Colin 167
Stafford, Marquis of 12
Stanhope, Earl 58
Strong, Sir Roy 155
Stuart Mill, John 57, 76, 80, 82
Stubbs, George 14, 163
Summerly, Felix *See 'Cole, Henry'*
Sunday Observance Act 1781 80
Sunderland Art Gallery 101-102, 109
Tate, The 40-41, 49, 127, 129, 131, 138-139, 147-148, 154, 158-160, 163-165

Tate Britain 124, 131, 165
Tate Liverpool 144, 164-166

Tate Modern   131, 156
Tate St Ives   164
Tate, Henry   130-131, 142
Temple, Alfred   110
Terry, Ellen   139
Thompson, Andrew   33
Thompson, Mark   102
Townley, Charles   84
Tradescant, John   13-14
Truchsess, Joseph   18
Trust Deed 1891   116
Turner, J.W.   25-27, 40, 48-49, 74, 94, 99, 110, 126, 128, 147-148,
                                                   159, 166

Turner Contemporary Gallery   166
Tytler, Mary   139
Uffizi Gallery (Florence)   19
Unwins, Thomas   36
US National Gallery (Washington)   147
Utility/Utilitarianism   53, 73, 79, 81-83, 150
Van Gogh, Vincent   26, 161
Vatican Collection   7, 19
Velásquez, Diego   41
Vernon Collection   38, 40, 48-49, 127
Victoria & Albert Museum   27, 38, 41, 44-45, 47, 54-55, 77, 105, 137, 146-147,
                                                   149-151, 167, 172

Waagen, Gustav von   26-27, 37, 39, 90-91, 125
Walker Art Gallery (Liverpool)   84
Wallace Collection   41, 54, 77, 119, 134-137, 142, 148, 152
Walpole, Horace   5, 9
Walpole, Robert   5, 9
Waterfield, Giles   i, 29, 45
Watts, G.F.   53, 129, 131, 137-141
Webb, Aston   54
Webb, John   51
Webb. Phillip   50
West, Benjamin   10
Whistler, Rex   ·53, 78, 131, 148
Whitechapel Gallery   119, 121-122, 138, 149
Wilde, Oscar   78
Wilkes, John   4-10, 17, 19-20, 33, 41, 42, 47, 57, 65, 85
Wilkie, David   26, 34
Willett, Henry   109
Wills, William Henry; Frederick; George   107
Wilson, The (Cheltenham)   105
Winckelmann, Johann   6-7
Wright, Joseph   102-103

About the Author

ISABEL WILKINSON was born in Edinburgh, lived most of her adult life in London, and now lives in East Anglia. She has studied both Social Sciences and Art History, which has given her a keen interest in cultural history. In her spare time, she visits as many public art galleries as she can, which has the added benefit of introducing her to unfamiliar parts of her home country.